GUERNSEY
UNDER
GERMAN RULE

GUERNSEY
UNDER
GERMAN RULE

by Ralph Durand

Foreword by
Sir Richard Collas, Bailiff of Guernsey

Introduction by Stephen Foote,
Vice-Chairman of the Guernsey Society

Guernsey Society
2018

First published by the Guernsey Society, 1946.
This second edition published by the Guernsey Society, 2018.

www.guernsey-society.org.uk

Main text © Ralph Anthony Durand 1945

Foreword © Sir Richard Collas 2018
Introduction © Stephen Foote 2018

ISBN 978-0-9928860-4-2 (paperback)
ISBN 978-0-9928860-5-9 (hardback)
ISBN 978-0-9928860-6-6 (ebook)

Printed by Short Run Press, Exeter.

All rights reserved. No part of this book may be reproduced or transmitted in any form without the written permission of the publishers.

CONTENTS

	Foreword	vii
	Introduction	ix
	Dedication	1
	Note (to the First Edition)	2
I	The Prelude to the German Occupation	3
	War comes near. The Island disarmed. Children evacuated.	
II	Panic	13
	Emergency measures. Evacuation of half of the population.	
III	The Last Week of Freedom	27
	German air raid.	
IV	Germans Land in the Island	36
	An apparently benevolent despotism.	
V	"Innumerable and Pressing Problems"	43
	The Controlling Committee gets to work.	
VI	Siege Conditions, 1940	49
	Some assets.	
VII	Siege Conditions, 1940	59
	Expedients and Economies	
VIII	Siege Conditions, 1940	68
	No Real Hardship Yet	
IX	Narrative, 1940	75
	A British reconnaissance raid. Deportation of Islanders for harbouring British agents. H.M. Procureur condemns an escape.	
X	Narrative, 1940	94
	Islanders imprisoned for "high treason". Radios confiscated. An underground news service. Release of prisoners and return of radios.	
XI	Narrative 1941	110
	Germans hoaxed. The battle of the 'V's. German humour at its worst.	

XII	Narrative 1942	135

German policy inconsistent and short-sighted. Radios again confiscated. Deportations to Germany. German planes shot down by German gunners.

XIII	Siege Conditions 1941-1943	158

Novel kinds of food.

XIV	Siege Conditions 1941-1943 (continued)	179

Hunger periods. Domestic difficulties.

XV	Where the Fetters Chafed	189

Anxiety about kith and kin. No appeal against injustice. Insecurity of tenure – and of property. The Royal Court degraded.

XVI	Alderney, Herm, and Sark	201

"The honour of the German army". Historic raid on Sark.

XVII	Our Marionette Press	213

Futile German propaganda.

XVIII	Problems Solved – or Shelved	228

The Reichskreditkassen swindle.

XIX	The Germans	241

Government by cajolery and threats. Examples of German kindness, courtesy, uncouthness and swinish behaviour.

XX	We Ourselves	266

Not unanimous in attitude towards Germans. German attempts to fraternise met with "passive resistance". Sycophants and informers.

XXI	Narrative, 1943-1944	280

More escapes. Heavy air-raids. Many robberies. Increasing hunger. Dwindling resources. Help from the Red Cross.

XXII	Narrative, 1945	300

Acute fuel shortage. Gas and electricity fail. Germans take our food. Red Cross supplies inadequate. A breadless period. Stock of potatoes and roots exhausted. But the end in sight.

XXIII	An Attempt at a Right Judgement of our Enemies	317

We waged war not only for our own sake but also for every decent German.

	Index	323

FOREWORD

The story of the German Occupation of the Channel Islands from the summer of 1940 through to May 1945 continues to fascinate. Islanders and others living elsewhere throughout the world are intrigued to know more about our unique history. The number of people who lived through, and can remember, the events of the time is forever diminishing. Those of us who wish to learn about and understand what occurred and the impact it had on the islands and their inhabitants have to resort to reading about the experiences.

Fortunately new books continue to be published seeking to satisfy what seems to be an insatiable appetite to find out more. Ralph Durand's work which was published in May 1946 is a significant part of the body of literature describing the wartime events of this small piece of British soil that was occupied for nearly five long years.

Many first hand memoirs have been written, some by third parties based on diaries kept by islanders. Most have been written many years after the War when the memories they are describing have, inevitably, been shaped by the passage of time. Others have been written by historians who have had access to official documents and records and who have written with analytical objectivity and dispassion.

Ralph Durand wrote this book in response to a request that my predecessor, the Bailiff of the day Victor Carey (later Sir Victor), made in the early days of the occupation. Sadly, Durand died within months of the end of the occupation as a result of the effects of malnutrition. Thus he never saw the book published. Reading the book in the knowledge that the deprivations he described in vivid detail led to his own death adds to the poignancy of the words on the page. His description of his first-hand experiences written as he saw, and heard, them makes for compelling reading. The reader has the sensation of experiencing those events through the eyes and ears of someone who lived through and wrote about them at the very time when they took place.

The Guernsey Society took on the responsibility of producing the First Edition in 1946. Only 2,000 copies were printed and no one can know how many copies survive. My father had one of those original copies which I can remember reading with fascination several times when I was a teenager. My recollection is that it was printed on poor quality paper, not dissimilar to newsprint. I believe that our copy has not survived and I suspect that many other copies have been lost.

I therefore welcome this reprint organised, once again, by the Guernsey Society to whom I extend my thanks and appreciation. It continues to make for fascinating reading and will be a welcome addition to any collection of Second World War books that does not already include one of the increasingly rare first editions.

Sir Richard Collas
Royal Court, Guernsey
January 2018

INTRODUCTION

The January 1946 edition of the *Bulletin of the Guernsey Society* contained the following notice:

> The Society is publishing a book by Mr. Ralph Durand entitled *Guernsey Under German Rule*. The Hon. Secretary, who has read the manuscript, strongly recommends it to the notice of members. The price in paper covers will be 6s. 6d. post free and it can be ordered either direct from Mr. Durand, Candie House, Guernsey, or from the Hon. Secretary, or from a bookseller. It is being printed by Messrs. C. W. Clark & Co. Ltd., 24, Clement's Road, Ilford. The book was written in response to a request made by the Bailiff in the early days of the German occupation. Mr. Durand describes many aspects of the occupation in a most interesting way, and, though not free of criticism, he seems to have maintained a very fair balance in his judgement of events. The book, in conforming to wartime standards of printing and paper, has its 160 pages well filled.

Ralph Durand, librarian of the Priaulx Library during the occupation, was uniquely well-placed to take on this task. In addition to his responsibility for the island's local studies library, he was also a successful author having published a number of novels, as well as numerous short stories, magazine articles and works of non-fiction.

Although not a Guernseyman by birth, he was a true Guernseyman in almost every other respect – both of his parents Reverend Havilland Durand and Mary née Hawtrey were descended from members of Guernsey's aristocracy and could trace their families back in the island for several generations.

The Durands were a Huguenot family from Montpellier – Ralph's great-grandfather, Reverend Daniel Francis Durand, came to the island in 1767 and was appointed Dean of Guernsey

Ralph and Violet Durand in the garden of the Priaulx Library

in 1796 – a position which he held until his death in 1832. He was also a leading member of the syndicate which financed the construction of the Assembly Rooms – which made him a member of the renowned 'Sixties' – the nickname given to the upper echelon of Guernsey's social hierarchy.

On his mother's side, Ralph's great-grandfather, the Reverend John Hawtrey, came to Guernsey as rector of St James the Less in 1839 – a position which he held until 1850. Whilst in the island, John's eldest son Montague met and married Louisa Dobrée, a niece of Admiral Lord de Sausmarez, meaning Ralph

INTRODUCTION

was descended from the island's elite on both sides of his family.

Ralph Anthony Durand was born in 1876 in Earley near Reading in Berkshire, where his father, Havilland, was rector. When he was just eight years old, his father died suddenly, leaving his mother Mary a widow with seven children to support. Although his father had left the family well provided for, they subsequently lost all their property in a bank failure. Fortunately, their family and friends came to their rescue, raising £2,000 to establish a fund to support them.

Their Dobrée relatives also took steps to ensure that the children received a good education and that Mary and the younger children had somewhere to live. Bonamy Dobrée was a governor of Christ's Hospital – a boarding school in the City of London – and he secured places there for Ralph and his younger brother Charles. His mother moved to Guernsey with the younger children, staying initially at Beauregard House in Hauteville – a Dobrée family property – and later settling more permanently into Moulin Huet House in St Martin's.

Ralph spent seven years at Christ's Hospital. As he was entering his final year, his family tried to steer him towards a career in the Church. Not only did he come from a long line of clergy on both sides of his family, but according to an old family legend, his ancestor Rev. François Guillaume Durand had made a 'pact with the Almighty' when he fled persecution in France in the 1690s. In exchange for the Lord's protection, the Calvinist pastor promised that every male Durand would become a Protestant clergyman – those who did not would be unable to produce male heirs.

But Ralph was determined to become a writer – he rejected the security of the Church – and yearned for adventure. When he learned that an aunt in Australia had offered to find work for her nephew on a cattle station, he leapt at the chance. So at the age of sixteen, just a few months after leaving school, he left London for Australia. After what he described as a 'royally gorgeous' crossing, he arrived in Sydney in late 1892 having spent all his money on the journey. However, his aunt concluded that the bespectacled 'shy clumsy dreamer' (his words) was totally unsuited to life on a cattle station, and found him a job in a bank instead. After much persuasion, she eventually relented and persuaded a cattle station owner to give him a six-month trial – which only served to confirm his aunt's initial impressions, as he was given the sack at the end of the six-month period. He bought into a tin-mining venture, only to get cheated out of his share by his partner, who abandoned him in the outback. Ralph walked seventy miles in three days without food before he reached civilisation.

He went on to spend five years in Australia where he accumulated much life experience which he would later draw on in his novels, working as a sheep shearer, a sugar plantation coolie, cook to a party of cattle drovers and labourer to a feckless Irish farmer. His life in the open air with hard physical work and long hours was hard, but he was happy, and in the spare time that he did have, he started writing poetry, short stories and articles. He later found work as a tutor to two boys, which allowed him to devote more time to his writing and eventually got an article published in the *Sydney Bulletin*.

In 1897, Ralph came into an inheritance of £200 – and rather than stay in Australia, he decided to seek new experiences on another continent. So he made his way to Salisbury (now Harare, Zimbabwe) in Africa, where his brother Francis was working with the Colonial civil service. But he arrived at a bad time, shortly after a native rebellion, the cost of living was soaring and his brother had just left the city, heading north. He eventually caught up with him near Lake Nyasa (now Malawi), and they decided to start a business trading cattle between Nyasaland and Salisbury – a distance of 500 miles. The potential returns were significant – cattle could be sold in Salisbury for ten times as much as they could buy them in Nyasaland – but the risks were also great. If they could protect the herd from big game and tropical diseases, they stood to make a fortune. After some success, Ralph was forced to part company with the business following a particularly severe attack of fever. After his recovery and a period working on a sugar plantation, he travelled to South Africa, arriving just as the Boer War broke out.

INTRODUCTION

Never one to shy away from a challenge (or potential source of inspiration for his writing), he enlisted in Thorneycroft's Mounted Infantry – an irregular company of volunteers raised by Colonel Alexander Thorneycroft of the Scots Fusiliers. In the first four months of 1899, they took part in two bloody and unsuccessful attempts to relieve the siege of Ladysmith, during which half of their men were either killed or wounded – the Battles of Spion Kop and Vaal Krantz. However, from Durand's account, it seems he missed out on these battles, complaining of the boredom of endless patrols searching in vain for Boers. So when he fell from his horse and sustained a minor injury, he leapt at the opportunity to obtain a discharge.

The following year, through another of his mother's cousins, Rev Henry Carey Dobrée, he found a teaching job at Michaelhouse School, a new school formed on public school lines in the Kwa-Zulu Natal province of South Africa. He threw all his energy into this job, in addition to his teaching duties, he started a debating society, contributed articles (including one on Christ's Hospital) to the school magazine, and performed at school concerts. He seemed to have been well-liked by the pupils, who nicknamed him 'Dogface', but without a university degree, it was made clear to him that he would be unable to remain on the permanent staff. So after a year at the school, he left and made his way back to England, after an absence of ten years, to concentrate seriously on becoming a writer. He commented 'I had acquired a far wider knowledge of this great, intensely interesting world than most authors have for their stock in trade'.

Soon after his return from his travels, he met his future wife, Violet Picton-Warlow. Violet came from a large family of minor Welsh aristocracy and had been born in India in 1869 where her father was a colonel in the Indian army.

Colonel John Picton-Warlow had changed his name to Picton-Turbervill as a condition of inheriting the Ewenny Priory estate just outside Bridgend in Glamorganshire after his elder brother's untimely death in 1892. The household was a lively one. Violet's next youngest sister, Edith, was to become one of the first female

MPs. In her autobiography, she describes the transformation that her father's inheritance brought to the family. They were able to move into the mansion that had been in the Turbervill family since medieval times, and enjoyed a significant increase in family income. They played tennis and archery and enjoyed entertaining with all eleven children encouraged to invite their friends to stay.

It seems likely that Ralph and Violet met in Guernsey. By the time Ralph returned from Africa in 1902, his mother was living in Moulin Huet House in St Martin's, and three of Violet's younger brothers were living or had lived in the island. Ivor and Wilfrid were at Elizabeth College, and Ivor's twin Arthur was working as a fruit grower.

Ralph and Violet were married at Ewenny Priory in April 1904 – at what was the society wedding of the year in Glamorganshire. The ceremony was led by Violet's brother, Reverend Frank Picton-Warlow and her sister Beatrice played the organ. The local newspapers reported that the wedding was followed by a reception at the priory, a banquet at a nearby hotel, and a fireworks display.

With his decade of experiences in Australia and Africa, Ralph embarked upon his writing career. He got a job teaching at a small private school to pay the bills, and started submitting stories and soon became a published author. In 1909, his first full-length book, *Oxford: Its Buildings and Gardens* was published, and in 1911 his first novel, *John Temple* appeared, which was described as 'a good gift-book for a boy at Christmas-time' by the *Evening Standard*.

In 1914, two more works appeared – *A Handbook to the Poetry of Rudyard Kipling* and another novel, *Spacious Days* – just as war broke out. By the end of that year, two of his brothers had been killed: Francis at the Battle of Givenchy in France, and Havilland at Gallipoli. To make matters worse, Violet's younger brother Wilfrid, serving with the Royal Flying Corps, had gone missing over the English Channel, and two other brothers had been taken prisoners-of-war. By 1914, Ralph was thirty-eight years old – and could have easily have avoided conscription.

INTRODUCTION

But – like many of his friends and family – caught up in the tide of patriotic fervour sweeping across the country, he voluntarily enlisted with the West Kent Yeomanry, who would only accept him as squadron cook due to his age. He applied for a commission, and in February 1915 was accepted into the 22nd (Kensington) Battalion of the Royal Fusiliers as Second Lieutenant. His battalion spent most of 1915 in training, and the first contingent was sent to France in November. Ralph had to wait until May 1916 to be sent to the front – by which time, the battalion was preparing for the Battle of the Somme. After six muddy, bloody months of trench warfare in the Somme Valley, 2nd Lieut Durand, as Battalion Cook, was attempting to secure sufficient pork and beer from a local farmer for the battalion's Christmas lunch, when he suffered a severe attack of 'gallstone colic' and was sent back to England.

After two months in hospital, his battalion refused to have him back, and he returned to Guernsey, transferring to the newly-formed Royal Guernsey Light Infantry. During this period, Violet was working as a Recruiting Controller for the southern region of the Women's Army Auxiliary Corps, travelling the southern counties signing up women to contribute to the war effort, and, despite his best efforts, Ralph was unable to get permission to travel to see her. When the RGLI were sent to England to complete their training, Ralph travelled with them. In September 1917, he finally made it back to the front line – but within a month had another attack of gallstones, and was sent directly back to a London hospital. A Medical Board pronounced him as fit only for desk duties at home. He was found a desk job with the newly-established MI5 and within a few months was sent to Italy to help establish an intelligence unit within the Military Misson there. Returning to London in early 1919, he had another gallstone attack, and eventually they operated to remove his gall bladder, leaving a seven-inch scar down his abdomen.

He was demobilised in September 1919, and could at last resume his writing career. Over the next decade, he was able to firmly establish himself as an author when his second novel, *The*

Mind Healer, which was written in hospital in Cornwall while he was recovering from surgery, won second prize in a competition by the publisher Collins.

In 1924, Violet inherited a large sum on the death of her father, enabling them to move house to a fashionable square in Pimlico. Two more novels followed in 1928, *Set a Thief* and *Servants of the King*. The African Society, of which Ralph was a member, concluded 'on the whole it smacks truly of Africa ... We hope Mr Durand will give us more novels like this one'.

In 1929, an opportunity arose in Guernsey for a librarian for the Priaulx Library. Ralph applied and was successful, so he and Violet settled in the island. Once there, he continued writing but also threw himself into island life. In 1931 he published *Steep Ascent*, a novel based on his experience in the Australian outback as well as his WW1 experience on the Somme. He also gave talks on his experiences in Africa and published *Elephant Swamp* an adventure story set in Central Africa. He joined La Société Guernesiaise and, in 1933, published *Guernsey Past and Present* – a short history of the island. This same year, he was elected member of the Council of La Société, and the following year he became Honorary Secretary of the Editorial Committee. He contributed papers to the Société's *Transactions* on Militia Orders, Sir Isaac Brock, Major-General John Gaspard Le Marchant and Lukis & Island Museum (of which he had been appointed curator in 1938).

By 1933, it had also become clear that the Durand 'family curse' had come true, and that Ralph and Violet would not have any children of their own. They adopted ten-year-old Rosemary Edmondes, the grand-daughter of Violet's elder brother Charles, who was severely disabled, and she came to live with them at Candie House.

When war broke out again in 1940, no-one expected it would have much impact on island life, other than the occasional nuisance air raid, as Ralph describes in the first chapter. By the time it became clear that the islands were going to be occupied, there were no further opportunities to evacuate. The Bailiff, Victor Carey, contacted Ralph and asked him to keep an account

INTRODUCTION

of events for posterity, and arranged for him to have exclusive access to the private minutes of the Controlling Committee.

The Bailiff's request was not like any previous writing challenge the author had attempted. It could not have any flights of imagination that a novel would have, nor could it be as personal as a memoir, and unlike many other official histories, it would not have the benefit of hindsight or distance from the events being described. Throughout the occupation, the German authorities strove to suppress BBC news, and ensure their own propaganda dominated the local newspapers. So Ralph trod a fine line between keeping an accurate record and avoiding the consequences should it be discovered by the Germans.

This could explain why, even when relating personal events, he does so in the third person. Two particular examples of this are the tale of how Durand was able to pass off a couple of cheap H.G. Wells paperbacks to Nazi censors demanding the surrender of all anti-German books (Chapter XIX, p. 259) and his account of a meeting with a German officer looking to unburden himself of the horrors the Nazis had unleashed on the world (Chapter XIX, p. 264). In both instances, he is careful not to identify himself, nor to incriminate the Germans involved.

Whilst he does ensure a balanced coverage of the main events – there are a couple of strong themes which run throughout his account which illustrate the challenges that received the most attention from the occupied islanders.

The most significant preoccupation is the challenge of obtaining the basic essentials – sufficient food and fuel. The island was not only heavily reliant on imports from England, but the island's pre-war economy was also reliant on the export of tomatoes and flowers to the mainland – so with trade in both directions cut off, the island was dependent on imports from France. Following D-Day, when the liberation of Normandy had effectively cut off the import of food and essential commodities from France, even bread had become a luxury.

Durand was no stranger to deprivation – he had almost starved when deserted in the Australian outback by his mining partner and during WW1 had been responsible for the battalion canteen. But, in the light of the fact that towards the end of the book he was dying of malnutrition, the most poignant anecdote, told in the third person but undoubtedly based on painful personal experience, was the description of his feast after the arrival of the Red Cross ship SS *Vega* in March 1945, bringing flour. The Red Cross ship was eventually permitted to bring emergency supplies in December 1944, but was not able to bring flour until her third visit two months later:

> On March 6th the *Vega* came again. This time, to our great delight, she brought 155 tons of flour besides parcels and two days later we received a ration of 2 pounds of bread. It came just in time for in that week we ate the last of our potatoes. Once again it was possible to spread butter and jam on something more suitable than boiled potato. The temptation to indulge imprudently was too great for one person at least. With his afternoon tea that day he ate two thick slices of bread and butter, two thick slices of bread and jam and a captain's biscuit lavishly spread with butter. Such indulgence seriously depleted his stock of butter and jam and, as if Fate wished to punish him for his greed, the last meal that he ate before parcels were again distributed consisted of the tough outside leaves of broccoli, minced, stewed and enriched with so-called 'calves' foot jelly' made by boiling down hides. But the orgy was worth the cost. Normally he rose from a meal feeling that he would gladly sit down at once to another, but the lavish meal that he ate so improvidently gave him a blessed sense of repletion such as he had not had for many months. (Chapter XXII, p. 313)

Ralph may have been stoic in the face of his own hardships, but when the threat of deportation arose in late 1942, it threatened his whole family. In September 1942, in retaliation for the deportation of Germans from Iraq, Hitler ordered 2,000

INTRODUCTION

British-born islanders to be deported to internment camps in Germany. The fact that Durand was born in England, and had been an officer during WW1, qualified him twice over for deportation. However, he was able to successfully plead for an exemption on the basis that he was the sole carer for his wife, who he described as 'an invalid' and their adopted daughter, Rosemary, who he described as 'an 18-year-old helpless cripple'. His appeal, supported by medical assessment, was sufficient to persuade the authorities to remove him from the list (as he alludes to in Chapter VII p. 154). It is also worth noting that Rosemary's birthday was in May, so it is likely that the black market birthday 'festal dinner' in 1943 referred to in Chapter XIV (p. 184) is another veiled reference to the family's personal experiences.

The other major theme which runs throughout this book is Durand's obvious outrage at German attempts to subvert the local newspapers with their own propaganda. Not only does he dedicate a whole chapter to the subject (Chapter XVII 'Our Marionette Press'), but there are also numerous other references throughout his book. This interference became particularly demoralising to islanders after the confiscation of wireless sets in 1942 meant that the islanders were less able to distinguish the real news from German 'fake news' with the aid of BBC's account of events.

Ralph was familiar with propaganda – this is precisely what he would have been involved in whilst with MI5 in Italy towards the end of World War 1. But to be on the receiving end of it, appears to have particularly irritated him. It is no surprise therefore that he was an active participant in the Guernsey Underground News Service (GUNS) which operated between May 1942 and February 1944, circulating summaries of the BBC news to islanders after the wireless ban. Whilst it was coordinated by a small group of five who listened to the news and typed up the news sheets, it relied on a much larger network to disseminate them. Ralph would conceal one of these news sheets each day in a nominated book in the library – where, those in the know, could come and read the latest GUNS news sheets. Despite the dangers, he saw it as another of his adventures:

> A daily excitement after our radios had been confiscated was the collection and dissemination, at the risk of a term of imprisonment, of war news broadcast by the BBC. No one of the hundreds who engaged in it could complain that his life was dull and insipid. (Chapter XX, p. 268)

In February 1944 GUNS was betrayed and the five 'ringleaders' were sentenced to imprisonment in Germany. By the end of 1944, news reached Guernsey that the leader of GUNS, Charles Machon, had died in Germany. One of the others, Joe Gillingham, did not return home either and was presumed dead in 1947 (his final resting place was only discovered in 2016). The three remaining prisoners, Frank Falla, Ernest Legg and Cecil Duquemin, all survived their imprisonment but were to suffer from the effects for the rest of their lives. It therefore seems particularly appropriate that Ralph Durand chose to dedicate this book to them.

Even after the liberation of the islands on 9 May 1945, the prolonged food shortages had left many islanders seriously weakened and suffering from the effects of malnutrition, and Ralph was no exception. He nevertheless set about preparing his account for publication. But even this was not plain sailing – the island's printers had insufficient staff to keep up with urgent demands from the States, let alone find time and resources to prepare his book for the presses. On 23 October, he wrote to the States Supervisor, trying to negotiate whether some of their less urgent work could be deferred in favour of his book. He received a curt response – insisting that all of their work was 'of the most urgent nature'. Less than two months later, Ralph Durand died, aged 69 years. The official cause of his death was 'acute bronchitis, asthma, and cardiac failure' but the underlying cause was the effects of malnutrition. He was buried in the Maingay vault, the family of his paternal grandmother, in Candie Cemetery, just a few yards from the library that had been his home for the last

INTRODUCTION

sixteen years.

As a result of the challenges of getting the book printed in Guernsey, Ralph had made contact with Air Commodore Henry Le Marchant Brock, one of the founder members of the Guernsey Society, which had been formed in London in 1943. After Ralph's death, Brock took personal charge of the undertaking and saw the book through its final stages of publication. He found a printer in Essex prepared to take it on. Even though printers in England were not as constrained as those in the Channel Islands, there was still a shortage of labour and raw materials. The book finally emerged in May 1946 – 182 pages of small densely-packed type on austere fragile paper, with a soft plain red cover. The fact that this current edition is more than twice as thick and runs to just over 300 pages illustrates the extent of the restrictions compared to modern standards. Society records show that 2,000 copies were printed. Although the Society did consider a reprint in the 1960s, this never materialised.

The book was well-received – not just by a curious British public but also by those who had lived through the occupation. Amongst these were Sir Ambrose Sherwill, President of the Controlling Committee during 1940 and successor to Sir Victor Carey as Bailiff of Guernsey after the war. In his papers in the Island Archives, there is an undated memo which records his thoughts:

> I greatly regret that Ralph Durand's *Guernsey Under German Rule* published by the Guernsey Society is long since out of print. It is less readable than *Islands in Danger*, but, in its content, is in my opinion, much superior to it. It contains masses of information available generally in no other publication... In particular, I commend to the attention of all serious readers his final Chapter (XXIII: An Attempt at a Right Judgement of our Enemies). [Sherwill papers, AQ867/150, Island Archives]

More recently, Richard Heaume, Director of the German

xxi

Occupation Museum in Guernsey has offered his own perspective:

> I first read the book prior to opening the German Occupation Museum in the mid 1960s and it was invaluable in terms of the wealth of detail regarding the siege conditions which prevailed at the time and which would have been recorded at great risk to himself and his wife.
>
> Ralph collected material at a time when hearsay and rumours were rife and serious historians will note incidents recorded by Ralph, which we, with the luxury of hindsight, have been able to correct.
>
> I can, however, recommend this re-publication by the Guernsey Society, as a 'Must Read' for all Islanders and Students of Occupation History.

Despite his long and successful career as a writer, this book is probably the one for which Ralph Durand is best remembered. Copies are increasingly difficult to find, and so the Council of the Guernsey Society considered republishing it a fitting way to mark the Society's 75th anniversary year. Written by a Guernseyman, an author and a man with so much life experience – but most importantly someone who had lived through the experiences he relates – Ralph Durand's account is likely to remain one of the most authoritative accounts of this traumatic period in our island's history.

Stephen Foote
January 2018

INTRODUCTION
Further Reading

If you would like to find out more about the life and work of Ralph Durand, please refer to the following articles, which have helped in the writing of this introduction:-

- Ralph Durand, 'The Career of a Rolling Stone', *Pall Mall Magazine*, April 1929.
- Dinah Bott's articles on the Priaulx Library website: 'Ralph Durand' and 'The Works of Ralph Durand', www.priaulxlibrary.co.uk.
- Stephen Foote, 'Cook, Novelist, Soldier, Spy: The WW1 Career of Ralph Durand', *The Review of the Guernsey Society*, Winter 2014.
- Edith Picton-Turbervill, *Life is Good: An Autobiography* (London, 1939).
- Durand family papers (AQ 0440-41), Island Archives.

For more details of the Guernsey Underground News Service, see:-

- Frank Falla, *The Silent War* (1967).
- The Frank Falla Archive, www.frankfallaarchive.org.

Acknowledgements

I would like to thank the following people who have contributed to the production of this second edition.

Sue Laker and the staff of the Priaulx Library.
Darryl Ogier and Nathan Coyde of the Island Archives.
Clifford Jones of Christ's Hospital School Archives.
Jane Weare for information on her grandfather, Rev Henry Carey Dobrée and Michaelhouse School.
Nicholas Drake, Ralph Durand's great-nephew, for additional material on the Durand family.
Susan Ilie, Keith Le Page and Michael Paul – my colleagues on the Council of the Guernsey Society for their encouragement and assistance.
Edward Bettison for the cover design.
Steve Powell for the cover photograph.
Richard Heaume MBE, Director of the German Occupation Museum for his reassessment of the book.
Sir Richard Collas, Bailiff of Guernsey, for the Foreword.

DEDICATED

TO THE

GUERNSEY UNDERGROUND NEWS SERVICE

And all the stout-hearted men and women of Guernsey who, when our German oppressors demanded the surrender of our radios, ignored the order and at the risk of imprisonment and exile, listened to the official British war reports and passed them on to their fellow islanders. To these and their allies – the cinema manager who lent earphones for use with the home-made wireless sets, and the members of the Guernsey Wireless Retailers Association who kept secretly-owned radios in working order, we owe a debt of gratitude that is incalculable. But for them we should have been without authentic views of how the war was going for nearly three years. The anxiety and gloom that this would have caused, added to our other troubles, would have made us miserable indeed.

NOTE
(to the First Edition)

The Council of the Guernsey Society deeply regret that Ralph Durand died before it was possible for him to read the proofs of his book. Malnutrition during the German occupation had seriously weakened him and it was only with a great effort that he was able to complete the last chapters and revise the whole manuscript before sending it to the printers in November. He died on December 22nd, 1945.

The book has been seen through the Press by the Society's Honorary Secretary, who had read the manuscript in Guernsey in September and discussed it with the author. In reading the proofs, he has thought it better not to attempt to make many alterations, but to confine these to the change of a word here and there, where the meaning of a sentence was obscure, and the insertion of a few punctuation marks, which were rather scarce in the manuscript. No doubt the author would have made other alterations if he had been able to correct the proofs. He had already cut out a great deal from his original manuscript.

The Council are very glad to have had the opportunity of publishing the book, which they believe to be of considerable historical value.

Air Commodore Henry Le Marchant Brock
Honorary Secretary, The Guernsey Society
March 1946

CHAPTER I

THE PRELUDE TO THE GERMAN OCCUPATION

Throughout the whole period of their occupation of Guernsey the Germans worked incessantly to render the island impregnable to any attempts at recapture that the British might make. They imported a large number of heavy guns, massive 48-wheeled trollies to carry them to the positions chosen for them, and hundreds of workmen – both German mechanics and labourers from occupied territories – to construct concrete emplacements for them. They quarried tunnels deep into hillsides to serve as bomb-proof ammunition stores, and knocked down any houses that interfered with their guns' field of fire. They buried land mines all round the coast. They dug trenches and machine-gun posts in private gardens. They surrounded the houses in which they quartered themselves with barbed wire entanglements and they placed garrisons on even such insignificant islets as Brecqhou and Burhou.

By comparison the measures taken by the States of Guernsey, before it was demilitarised, to defend the Island, seemed ludicrous. In August 1939, while there was still hope that war might be averted, they ordered four guns – two 4.7 guns for coast defence and two Light Anti-Aircraft guns – but cancelled the order after the war had actually broken out. The last of the four guns could not have been delivered until eighteen months had elapsed, by which time, it seemed probable, the Royal Regiment of Artillery would be too busy to be able to spare instructors to train Guernseymen in their use. It was decided instead to concentrate only on providing adequate protection against low-flying aircraft by means of Lewis guns.

Obviously the States' military advisers considered that our danger of attack from the sea was remote and all that we really had to fear was mere nuisance raids from aircraft. For attacks of that kind we needed fire-fighters and stretcher bearers more than soldiers, and the men of the Royal Guernsey Militia –

conscripted by immemorial custom for the defence of the island – were released so that they might volunteer for more active service overseas. Their place was taken by a Defence Force – still, however, to be called the Royal Guernsey Militia – consisting of five officers and one hundred men, all over military age or otherwise unfit for active service, who lived in their own homes and were allowed to undertake part-time civilian work on days when they were not on duty as sentries guarding the oil depot, the telegraph cable and other vulnerable points.

All other defence measures adopted by the States during the first eight months of the war were of the nature of air raid precautions. All gatherings for sport or other purposes – except religious services – were prohibited. Cinema theatres were closed. A number of paid watchers were appointed. Sirens were installed at nine vantage points to give warning of the approach of raiders. Black-out regulations were enforced. Gas masks were imported and distributed free of cost to everyone. First Aid Posts – four of which were fitted with special arrangements for the decontamination of gas cases – were established in different parts of the island, at a price that many taxpayers considered was not warranted by the extent of the danger. The Castel Hospital and the Children's Hospital were evacuated so that they could be made ready for instant use as emergency hospitals. A beginning was made in the construction of air raid shelters. Elizabeth College boys dug trenches the object of which was somewhat obscure unless they were intended to afford cover for anyone caught between the school gate and the school doors, and people were officially urged to carry with them wherever they went luggage labels inscribed with their names and addresses.

The first feverish excitement died down very quickly. Very soon cinema theatres were allowed to reopen. Sports gatherings were resumed. Gas masks drifted to the backs of cupboards. On the grounds that 'black-out regulations must be revised if trade is to be revived' shopkeepers agitated for permission to illuminate their windows again. In fact the belief that actual conflict was as little likely to reach our shores as if our island were one of the Western Hebrides became so general that the Chamber of

THE PRELUDE TO THE GERMAN OCCUPATION

Commerce suggested that Guernsey should be advertised as a place of safety to which inhabitants of danger zones in England might well be advised to migrate.

This sense of security lasted till well into the spring of 1940. Then news of the surprise invasion of Holland, Belgium and Luxembourg, and especially of the use of air-borne troops dropped by parachute, gave a severe shock to our complacency and prompted the local authorities to adopt more vigorous defence measures. Details from an English Training Battalion quartered in the Island were employed to guard places of special importance such as the Telephone Exchange, where a machine-gun post was established, and the harbour, where a Lewis gun was mounted on a tripod as an anti-aircraft weapon. Enemy aliens were interned. Other aliens were ordered to keep within doors between 10pm and 6am. A force of more than a hundred men above or below military age was enrolled under Major-General Williams to deal with air-borne enemy troops, and maroons were placed at various points to give warning of their approach. Incidentally, for the greater confusion of parachutists who might come provided with maps of the Island, all signposts in the country were removed.

From the last week of May onwards Guernsey's export trade was sometimes dislocated by the non-arrival of cargo ships. On one day alone no less than 50,000 packages had to be left on the White Rock because cargo space could not be found for them. This was a serious matter because it was in early summer that the bulk of Guernsey's principal export trade – tomatoes, early potatoes and flowers – was done. To relieve the situation the States granted a credit of £2,000 towards the cost of chartering more cargo boats; the digging of early potatoes for export was prohibited; exporters of flowers were advised not to pick them till the transport situation improved and the States Supervisor was given dictatorial powers to regulate tomato shipments.

It was obvious to anyone with sufficient foresight that if the dislocation of traffic continued and became worse not only exporters but everyone in the Island would suffer, because it would be difficult to import sufficient stocks of food and such essential commodities as coal and petrol. For this reason people of leisure who had no particular ties to bind them to the Island, especially those who had children dependent on them, began to leave it in search of greater security in the parts of Britain that had become known as 'reception areas.'

On May 26th two French fishing-smacks came into St Peter Port densely crowded with men, women and children refugees from Havre. On June 13th three more arrived containing sixty-nine refugees including elderly men, women and children in arms. These were in a pitiable condition of semi-starvation, as owing to persistent calm weather it had taken them no less than three weeks to come under sail from Boulogne. They had at first intended to go no further than Cherbourg but when they neared that port it was being heavily bombed, so they altered course for Alderney which they had reached on the previous day, and where they had been given money, food and – what they needed most – water. In Guernsey also they were hospitably received, especially by members of the French colony. Clothing and money was hastily collected for them and after spending a night in the comfort of hotels near the harbour they sailed for Brittany. On the same day a boatload of twenty-five people was hospitably sped on its way by the people of Sark. On June 19th a hundred and twenty refugees arrived from Cherbourg, mostly Naval ratings, soldiers and dockworkers. They came in six small harbour craft, which they abandoned here, and went by steamer to England to join General de Gaulle's Free French forces.

Up till now, probably, some Guernsey people had taken more interest in local football matches than in the progress of the war, but the pitiable condition of some of these refugees made even the most apathetic and the most illiterate realise that the war and its horrors were coming very near to us and there spread throughout the island a vague feeling of uneasiness that was felt most acutely by those who understood it least. To those in authority it was obvious that the fall of Cherbourg, which brought this island within forty-five miles of German occupied aerodromes, had materially increased our danger from air raids. But few people as yet, even among those best qualified to form

THE PRELUDE TO THE GERMAN OCCUPATION

an opinion, feared anything worse than occasional air raids. It was true that the authorities had taken steps – ridiculously inadequate steps they now seem in view of what happened later – to deal with attempts at invasion by air-borne troops, but these precautions the average man regarded in the same way that one regards a fire insurance policy – a provision against a possible but by no means probable event. This optimism was based on the well-grounded belief that under modern war conditions the island was of no military value. The average man failed to realise the great importance that the Germans would attach to the prestige derivable from the possession – however ingloriously won – of one insignificant fragment of the British Empire, and he had no means of knowing to what extent Britain's power to defend the island had been weakened by the enemy's invasion of Normandy.

His optimism might have been shaken if he had been able to attend a secret session of the Royal Court on Tuesday, June 18th. The British Cabinet was then in session debating whether to defend the Channel Islands or to disarm them, and from an early hour an official of the Home Office at the London end of the telephone wire and Mr L. A. Guillemette, the Bailiff's Assistant Secretary, at the Guernsey end of the wire, were busy transmitting discussions between the British Cabinet on the one hand and the Royal Court of Guernsey on the other hand as to the fate of the island. The outcome of the discussion was revealed under pledge of secrecy to a few people in the island who were in key positions but it was not known to anyone else until three weeks later when those of us who listened to a BBC broadcast on July 11th learned that, in a statement made to the House of Commons, the Secretary had said that he had offered to arrange for the total evacuation of the Channel Islands, that the Channel Islands Authorities had said that probably many of the inhabitants would be unwilling to evacuate and that, nevertheless, transport for all who wished to evacuate would be provided.

It was apparently at the same time that our local authorities were informed of the British Government's intention to demilitarise the Island, though official notification did not arrive until later. Whether it was necessary to pledge to secrecy the few who were informed of this intention it is impossible for an outsider to judge, but there can be no question that the general public would have been spared much painful anxiety if an official announcement had been made not only that the Island was to be disarmed but especially that the British Government's object in taking this step was to spare us from the ruthless bombardments that were to be expected if troops and munitions remained here. In any case the secret could not be kept from anyone who happened to be on the White Rock that evening, if he had eyes to see and a brain alert enough to draw conclusions, for harbour officials, dock-workers and the crowds that normally frequented the harbour on fine summer evenings saw lorry after lorry loaded with munitions drive down to the ships' loading berths. Those who knew why these munitions were being returned to England could give no explanation for they were pledged to secrecy, and in consequence a rumour spread that troops stationed in the Island were leaving us and that the Island was to be abandoned to its fate; and that fate – for lack of an official reassurance on the subject – would be, in the fevered imagination of many, a fate such as that from which the refugees of Boulogne and Havre had fled. Thus were sown the seeds of widespread unreasoning fear that was heightened rather than allayed on the following day, June 20th, when *The Star*, distributed gratis at the expense of the States, had the following headlines in bold capitals stretching right across the first page:-

ISLAND EVACUATION
ALL CHILDREN BEING SENT TO THE MAINLAND TO-DAY
MOTHERS MAY ACCOMPANY THOSE UNDER SCHOOL AGE
WHOLE BAILIWICK TO BE DEMILITARISED

Even the order in which these headlines appeared was unfortunate. If the last line had been printed first, the reader to whom the word 'demilitarised' was unfamiliar might have sought a definition from someone better informed and received with it a reassuring explanation that the step was being taken with the intention of saving us from bombardment. In the order in which they appeared the lines too vividly suggested the sinking ship in which women and children take precedence over men.

The headlines were followed by two official announcements over the Bailiff's name, both of which were published again that afternoon in the *Evening Press*. One was to the effect that as the Bailiwick of Guernsey was to be entirely demilitarised, the Royal Court had ordered the immediate demobilisation of the Royal Guernsey Militia and the Guernsey Defence Volunteers; the handing in of arms, uniform and equipment; and the surrender to the Constables of parishes of all firearms in the possession of private individuals. The other announced that arrangements were being made for the evacuation of children whose parents desired it to reception areas in the United Kingdom, gave detailed instructions as to where the children and their escorts were to assemble and practical advice as to the luggage, necessarily limited in amount which should be taken; and stated that adults who wished to be evacuated must register with the Constables of their respective parishes; men of military age in particular were strongly urged to leave the Island.

The conclusion to be drawn from these two announcements was obvious. From the second it appeared that the Island was in grave danger, from the first it was clear that armed forces were not to be used to protect it from that danger. Some may even have supposed that the danger out of which the children were to be taken had arisen as a direct result of the demilitarisation of the Island. In justice to the British Government there should have been published as conspicuously as possible a quotation from the Hague Convention of 1907 which prohibits the bombardment of undefended 'ports, towns, villages, dwellings or buildings.' But no explanation of the disarmament of the Island was given and each man was left to judge for himself the nature of the danger that threatened us. Before these announcements were published, those responsible for the evacuation of the school children had already set to work, in great haste but with admirable forethought, coolness and efficiency. They had not been taken by surprise, for two days before a sub-committee of the Education Council had already made such carefully thought-out preparations for the evacuation of school children – if such a step should be decided on – that they had even printed for distribution to parents a leaflet reminding them that the children must take their gas-masks and ration books, and offering sound advice on the subject of what clothes were most essential and what form of food would be most suitable for a long journey. When therefore on the morning of June 19th, the sub-committee was summoned to the Royal Court and – after being pledged to secrecy – asked to make all preparations for the evacuation of the school children, there was little for them to do except wait for further orders. They did, however, summon all the head teachers in Island to meet at 2 o'clock that afternoon. To these – still under the pledge of secrecy – the situation was explained and they were told that if evacuation was decided upon, they and their assistant teachers would be expected to accompany the children to the reception areas to which they might be sent. After an anxious period of waiting for further instructions, a message came from the Royal Court that all children whose parents wished it were to be evacuated and that the matter need no longer be kept secret.

It was now 4 o'clock in the afternoon. There was much to be done and very little time in which to do it, for a first contingent of two thousand children were to be assembled by 4 o'clock next morning ready to be taken to the White Rock for embarkation on three ships due to arrive before that hour. The head teachers had to disperse to their respective schools, summon the children's parents and ask them to decide at once whether to send their children away to an unknown destination or keep them under the shadow of an undefined danger that might or might not materialise. By 9 o'clock that evening they had to inform the Education Office how many children had been registered for evacuation so that it could organise means of transporting them and their luggage to the harbours. In addition to this, voluntary helpers had to be enlisted as it had been decided that no one adult was to have the immediate care of more than fifteen children. As they dispersed the school teachers' hearts must have quailed somewhat at the thought of how much they had to do in so little time. That the work was done – and done very efficiently – is proved by the result.

To have done all there was to do without a hitch would have been almost miraculous, and the miracle did not happen. By 4 o'clock in the morning no less than nineteen hundred children and their escorts were ready to embark, but the first of the promised ships had not arrived and did not arrive until 10 o'clock, so that the children, who can have had no proper breakfast and little sleep during the previous night, had to wait on the jetty for six weary hours. Then three ships arrived in quick succession. The first two took fifteen hundred and ninety-one children but the third was a collier with no accommodation for passengers better than a choice between the holds and the open decks and the Education Authorities were reluctant to send on her, for a voyage that must inevitably take seven or eight hours, children already overtired with excitement and loss of sleep. They therefore persuaded the Sea Transport Officer to exchange the collier for a vessel, normally used for the transport of produce, which, though now a cargo vessel, had been built for passenger traffic. This vessel sailed at half-past two in the afternoon with the remainder of the waiting children.

There were no more serious hitches though there was sometimes cause for anxiety, as for example when, the tide being very low, it was necessary in the dim half light of the dawn to embark from the lower berth of the quay, which was very slippery, some seven hundred children who were only half awake. And the work required of the Education Office staff continued to be difficult and complicated. So far as was possible it was arranged that children embarked on ships that made the journey at night should be drawn from secondary schools who were of an age to endure discomfort better than infants. It was desirable not to summon children from their homes – in some cases from their beds – sooner than was necessary, but on the other hand it was imperative that the ships when they arrived should not be delayed. Military Staff Officers who have to arrange the transport of troops do not find it a very simple matter but they at any rate have to deal with men who are not asked whether or not they wish to be transported. The Education Office staff were handicapped by the fact that not only was evacuation voluntary but also that the parents of the children to be evacuated were apt to change their minds several times in as many hours according to whether the last irresponsible person with whom they discussed the advisability of evacuation was an optimist or a pessimist. Such indecision was trying for the staff but criticism of the parents would be unjust. It was not easy for them to decide whether to send their children to an unknown destination for an indefinite period of time in charge of school teachers and volunteer helpers who, however kind-hearted and trustworthy, were not bound to them by any ties of blood; or whether to keep them at home under the shadow of vague unspecified dangers which might never materialise. Yet the decision had to be made in a few hours and once the child had gone it could not be recalled. So many parents decided at the last moment not to let their children go that it was possible for the Education Office staff to send away a number of children evacuated from Alderney for whose further evacuation no arrangements had been made.

More than five thousand children were evacuated. The last batch left at 9am on the morning of June 21st. The Education Office staff must have felt relieved when the ship that carried it cast off her hawsers. They had had little opportunity to eat and less to sleep during the previous forty-six hours.

Some eight hundred men of military age who had decided to take advantage of the offer of a free passage to England had left on the previous day by another ship. With them went some men over the regulation age who hoped to be allowed to enlist or to find employment in England of greater national importance than could be found in Guernsey. No women were allowed to go with them but a smaller vessel was requisitioned for men who wished their wives to accompany them. All troops stationed in the Island had gone two days before.

CHAPTER II

PANIC

While the evacuation of children and men of military age was in progress a barricade was erected across the approach to the White Rock to safeguard the ships from being rushed by selfish people in their haste to escape from the Island. The precaution was not unnecessary for among many uneasiness had developed into fear and in some cases into panic. There was some excuse for this. The bewildering rush of recent events was not conducive to calm, level-headed thinking. In times of great excitement public announcements are read hurriedly without the deliberate attention they should have. Even well-educated people may in their haste miss an important word and those who hear of an announcement from someone who has read it hastily are likely entirely to misunderstand it. Hence it happened that the combined effect of the official announcements was to give to many feather-brained people the totally unfounded impression that because the Island was to be demilitarised, its whole population was to be compulsorily evacuated.

As soon as they were published the Constables' offices were besieged by those who wished to be evacuated and, though extra clerks were hastily enlisted and the work of registration continued till well after 10pm, many people had to be sent away after being advised to return early on the following morning. It was probably among these crowds that the seeds of the next day's panic began to germinate.

From early in the morning on Thursday, June 18th, the neighbourhood of St Julian's Weighbridge was thronged with people who had succeeded in registering their names and had arrived at the pier with such luggage as they could carry. They were denied passage through the barrier that had been erected and could obtain no information as to when the evacuation of the general public would begin. In the Town many shops did not open and in others the shopkeepers were so busy preparing to depart themselves that they would not attend to customers.

Retailers' stocks of suitcases, kit-bags, etc, were rapidly exhausted. From 7 o'clock in the morning, three hours before the banks were due to open, queues of clients who wished to withdraw their deposits waited outside their doors. The Savings Bank did not open at all; instead a member of its staff stood outside its doors chanting over and over again the announcement that its clients could withdraw their money from any Savings Bank in England. (One Bank client who was not affected by the panic but wished to ask a simple question, seeing that he could not hope to obtain an answer in person without waiting in a queue for several hours, hit on the happy idea of sending his bank-manager a reply-paid telegram from the Post Office nearby: he received an answer to his question in less than ten minutes!) By 10 o'clock in the morning, the High Street in St Peter Port was so crowded as to be almost impassable and the services of St John's Ambulance Brigade were needed to deal with casualties. Before noon one member of the Brigade had to attend four cases of fainting and two cases of hysteria, one of which was so severe that a doctor was called to drug the patient. A few people made it their business to go from group to group in the streets urging the panic-stricken to think calmly before they abandoned their homes and their livelihoods for fear of a danger that might never materialise. These suddenly received help in an unexpected way. A rumour, entirely baseless but wholly beneficial, ran from one to another in the crowded street, that Russia had declared war on Germany. The hope that Britain was not to be left to fight Germany and Italy unaided was so comforting that many, on hearing it, decided to go home and resume their normal lives.

In the country, the panic was worse than in the town. People who had not read the official announcements heard of them from others; or rather – since news that passes by word of mouth in times of excitement seldom loses anything in the telling – heard fantastically inaccurate versions of them. The belief took firm root in many people's minds that the Island's entire population was to be compelled to leave and this belief seemed to be confirmed by the action of some busybodies who – with good intention no doubt, not unmixed with a desire to seem important – stationed themselves at main cross-roads where they advised all who passed to go home and prepare to leave at a moment's notice. Some farmers killed cattle that in the months to come could ill be spared. Some people, before abandoning their homes, turned their pet animals out of doors to fend for themselves; some with still less humanity left fowls and rabbits shut up without food or water. Some houses were left open, beds unmade and the remains of a hurried morning meal on the table. Other houses were so securely locked that men authorised soon afterwards to collect perishable food from abandoned houses had difficulty in entering. A tobacconist gave away his entire stock before closing his premises and a publican before leaving invited his neighbours to go into his bar and help themselves to the liquor there. Panic is bad enough when the panickers are otherwise sober, but panic inflamed by drunkenness degenerates into sheer madness; the consequence of this ill-timed generosity might have been appalling if a passer-by who saw the crowd in the bar had not had the good sense to telephone the police, who took charge of the premises and removed the stock which, incidentally, was the property of a brewery company as it was still unpaid for.

That Thursday morning, the Royal Court met for the formal business of swearing in the Bailiff, Mr Victor Carey, as Civil Lieutenant-Governor, in place of the recently appointed Military Lieutenant-Governor, Major-General Minshall Ford, who was recalled to England when the troops left the Island. For the relief of the banks, an Ordinance was passed which prohibited any depositor, unless he was an employer of labour with wages to pay, from drawing more than £20, and power was given to men appointed for the purpose to enter abandoned houses in order to save perishable foodstuffs left in them. At the same sitting, His Majesty's Procureur, Mr A.J. Sherwill, referred to the panic, which he described as mass hysteria, and stated that ships were on their way and more would follow, but that it would probably be impossible to evacuate anyone after the children, women and men of military age had gone. He appealed to all people to return home and carry on their normal lives and occupations.

Time inevitably elapsed before his advice, uttered before so small an audience the Royal Court, could reach and penetrate the minds of the general public. It was endorsed by a message published that afternoon in the *Evening Press* from the Bailiff who, after strongly exhorting one and all to remain calm and avoid panic and emphasising that evacuation was voluntary, added: 'Beyond teachers – children of school age and under with mothers or other relations in charge, as well as men of military age, it is impracticable for others to hope to be evacuated. The appeal to all to remain calm was sound advice but the opinion expressed both by the King's Procureur and the Bailiff that no more ships would be available after women, children and men of military age had been evacuated must have whetted the eagerness to be gone of those who, being determined to go if they could, were anxious to get away as soon as ships were available to carry them.

Fully half the population had not needed the Bailiff's exhortation to remain calm, the remainder did not heed it and the panic continued. Thousands of people who wished to be evacuated had registered their names at the Constables' offices but could not get, either there or elsewhere, any official instructions as to what they should do next. The people who had come to the White Rock in the morning hoping to embark and had found that access to the pier was denied them, had been informed, on whose authority no one could tell, that an official announcement as to arrangements for the evacuation of the general public would be made on the Victoria Pier at 7pm that evening. The same unauthorised and wholly misleading information was given to some of the people who registered their names at the Chief Constable's office. No one knows who gave it, but it is probable that it was given by one of the temporarily employed clerks who had heard it from an official source and had passed it on in good faith. In consequence, the crowd that assembled at 7pm that evening covered not only the Victoria Pier but also the Quay and the North Esplanade, to such an extent as to make both impassable to wheeled traffic. The Chief Constables were sent for but, as they had no information to give, the crowd obtained no satisfaction from them.

Another rumour, strengthened by the fact that loud-speakers had been installed in a window of the Guernsey Press Company's office, was to the effect that the King's Procureur would make an announcement from there at 7pm. The rumour had not reached Mr Sherwill himself who at that hour was still at his office deeply engrossed in work thrust upon him by the emergency, but when at 7.30pm he learned that a speech was expected of him he at once went to the Press Office to give the crowd such information as he could. He had little to give at this stage. He announced that, notwithstanding malicious rumour to the contrary, neither the Bailiff nor any of the Jurats had left the Island and that neither they nor he himself had any intention of leaving. He said that though he could make no definite promise in the matter those who wished to be evacuated could go if transport was still available after all the school children and men of military age had gone. Those who stayed, he continued, would have to face difficulties of which shortage of food supplies would be the greatest. In reply to a question he said that he could give no assurance as to the continuance of the export of tomatoes as this would depend on what shipping was available. In reply to another question he said that it would be the Island's duty to give substantial support to the wives of men of military age who left. In answer to a further question he gave the first and almost the only intimation that the Islanders ever received from an official source that the authorities foresaw the possibility of a German occupation of the Island, and modified that intimation by saying that it was not on that account but because of the danger of food shortage that the children were being evacuated; asked whether men of military age were compelled to leave the Island, he replied that they were under no compulsion to do so, but Britain needed them and if they remained they might be subjected to 'slave labour' – though this was unlikely. He could not tell whether the Germans would come. Finally he said that the Island Authorities were in continuous touch by telephone with the British Government and that, that very day, the Home Secretary had said how much he deplored the situation the

Islanders were in and that the link between Guernsey and Britain would be maintained after the war.

This last statement should have convinced anyone who happened to hear it, and could, in those hours of feverish excitement, grasp its full import, that the British Government thought it probable that the Germans would occupy the Island. Without the aid of statistics, obviously impossible to compile, it is impossible to say how many Islanders shared this view but it is probable that most, relying on the well-grounded belief that the Island would be of no military value to Germany, thought that the worst we had to fear was shortage of food caused by dislocation of cross-channel traffic. The point is important because nine months after the occupation Jurat Leale, condemning behaviour calculated to annoy the Germans, said that we who stayed after we had had the chance to go knew full well that the Germans might occupy the Island and that 'our staying meant that we accepted that position and were prepared in the event of occupation to act as good citizens.'

By 9am on Friday, June 21st, the evacuation of children and men of military age was completed. In spite of doubts expressed the day before by the King's Procureur and the Bailiff, ships continued to arrive and the evacuation of the general public began.

That afternoon the States, hastily summoned, met to approve a number of important decisions taken without their authority during the previous forty-eight hours and to listen to a proposal made by Jurat the Rev. John Leale that an Emergency Committee of the States consisting of at least three members should be appointed. As a preface to his proposal he spoke of the shortness of notice given by the British Government that the Island was to be demilitarised and emphasised that the Government was solely responsible for that momentous step; in spite of the shortness of notice no less than ten thousand people had up till that hour, been evacuated. He appealed to employers not to make a difficult situation worse by discharging workmen, and to retailers of essential foodstuffs not to insist on cash payments; 'if you want a riot,' he said, 'that is the way to make one.' He then spoke of the possibility that the Germans might occupy the Island and issued a grave warning of the futility and danger of resistance. If they came, he said, we should all have to work desperately hard to survive; there would be a lack of petrol for transport and possibly little or no artificial light; the bulk of our tomato crop would have to be destroyed and other vegetables grown in their place: but he was able to give the comforting assurance, on the authority of local doctors whom he had consulted that morning that health could be maintained on a diet of milk and vegetables. In justification of steps taken without the authority of the States he gave an example of one unauthorised decision. Two days previously he had been in the Procureur's office while the latter had been talking over the telephone to an official of the Home Office and that official had said that if the Government provided shipping for evacuation it must be at the Island's expense; an immediate reply was required but to have consulted the States on the question would have involved a delay of three days; that was a sample of the sort of problem that during the past few hours had had to be settled on the spot. Jurat Leale then spoke of his proposal that an Emergency Committee with very large executive powers should be appointed. Our system of administration by many small committees may serve in peace time he said, but it broke down when we had the alternative of starvation or survival before us. The small Executive Committee that he suggested might be unconstitutional, but with the issues of life and death at stake we must over-ride such considerations and he proposed that His Majesty's Proceureur, Mr Sherwill, be appointed President of the proposed committee with power to chose his colleagues.

The only adverse criticism of the proposal came from Deputy C.H. Cross who asked if we were to have a dictator, but he did not press his objection. In support of the proposal Deputy Stamford Raffles suggested that employers should be forbidden to dismiss their workmen and that farmers who shot their cattle should be punished. Finally Jurat Leale advocated the imprisonment of rumour mongers[1]. His proposal was unanimously adopted; the

1   Among other dangerous rumours that were circulated was one to the

gentlemen chosen by Mr Sherwill to serve on the Emergency Controlling Committee were Jurat A. Drake (Horticulture), Mr R.O. Falla (Agriculture), Mr R.H. Johns (Unemployment, Re-employment and Public Assistance), Jurat Sir Abraham Lainé, K.C.I.E. (Essential Commodities), Jurat the Rev. John Leale (Economics), Deputy Stamford Raffles (Information), and Dr A.N. Symons (Medical and Nursing Services).

The panic passed its peak and began to die down as soon as the school children had gone and ships became available for the evacuation of the general public. Many of those who left, however, showed signs of feverish haste to get away. Some people spent the previous night at the appointed places of assembly for the distribution of embarkation tickets lest they should fail to receive them.

A lady who, had she been less flustered, might have called at her bank on her way to the White Rock, offered a magnificent tip of some £50 worth of Guernsey notes, which she supposed would not be negotiable in England, to a member of St John's Ambulance Brigade, whose ambulance brought her to the boat. That man neglected another opportunity to enrich himself that day for he met relatives who found on their arrival at the Jetty that they had left their available cash in their abandoned home. Fortunately for them his next journey was to the vicinity of their house and he was able to find the money and restore it to them before their ship sailed. The foreman of a large greenhouse property is known to have gone away with only fourpence halfpenny in his pocket. Some people embarked without any luggage and many were wearing light summer clothing suitable to the warm weather of the season, instead of thick winter clothing which prudent foresight would have dictated. As each ship stayed only long enough to embark as many people as it would hold, and because the holds were needed for the accommodation of human freight, it was impossible for them to take on board luggage too heavy to be carried by its owners, and still more impossible to take cars on board. Those people who arrived at the White Rock in their own cars, therefore, either

effect the States intended to discontinue payment of interest on State loans.

sold them – a high-powered car of expensive make, nearly new, was sold for £1 – or gave them away, or simply abandoned them. Many peramublators even were abandoned, until an Ambulance Sister was detailed for duty at the White Rock to assist in the embarkation of mothers hampered with small children. Not being infected by the prevailing panic, she was clearer headed than those whom she was sent to help, and she not only pointed out to harassed parents that perambulators can easily be carried down a gangway and deposited on deck but also invited any mother with a baby in arms who had left her perambulator at home to take anyone she chose from those that had already been abandoned.

Throughout the evacuation period the members of St John's Ambulance Brigade had little chance to rest. Their principal duty was to transport invalids from their homes to the ships where, if the tide was low, they had difficulty in carrying the stretchers down the steeply sloping gangways. In a few cases they were called upon to transport to hospital bedridden patients whose proper guardians had abandoned them. One of their special tasks was to evacuate to the Victoria Hospital the patients of a private nursing-home, the matron of which had deserted her post and fled to England. One of the patients gave them exceptional difficulty. A very dignified but unfortunately very deaf old lady took a long time to understand what the stretcher bearers had come for, and even then flatly refused to go to a hospital where, instead of having a room to herself, she would have to be in a public ward. She said that she had been a paying patient at the nursing home for a number of years and intended to remain there. It seemed quite impossible to make her understand that as no one remained in the nursing home to look after her she would starve if she stayed there, so a certain amount of force had to be used; this was not easy as she weighed over fifteen stone.

The work of the Brigade would have been lighter if many of the people who applied to it for transport had not changed their minds when the ambulance reached them and changed them again after it had gone away empty. This vacillation resulted in an ambulance car visiting one particular house no less than seven times. It is on record that the members of the Headquarters staff averaged fourteen hours of sleep apiece during the whole seventy-two hours of the evacuation period and the other members of the Brigade fared little better.

On Saturday, June 22nd, the newly-appointed Information Officer, Mr Stamford Raffles, had four posters printed and distributed throughout the Island. One of these announced that that day was the last on which people could travel to England without payment and urged farmers and others engaged on essential services to remain in the Island as a patriotic duty. Another poster stated simply 'The rumour that general evacuation has been ordered is a lie'. The other two were intended as sedatives and were perhaps all the more efficacious because they were couched in informal language: 'Keep your heads! Don't be yellow! Business as usual!' said one, and the other: 'Why go mad? Compulsory evacuation is a lie. There's no place like home! Cheer up!'

As a result of these posters and a speech on the same lines made by Jurat the Rev. John Leale during the morning to a crowd waiting at St Julian's Weighbridge for a chance to embark, many who had been vacillating returned home. The last fully loaded steamer left soon after noon, perambulators, suitcases and bundles stacked along her bulwarks and her hatches crowded with passengers. Other steamers came later and left only partially loaded. One even returned empty.

Probably those on board the evacuating ships felt a sense of deep relief when their moorings were cast off and they began to move away from the Jetty. But their troubles were not over. They were taken to Weymouth, a small port already so congested with ships that had brought refugees from Bordeaux that some vessels had to lie outside the harbour for twenty-four hours or more before they could land their passengers. The delay caused unavoidable hardship to those who had not had the foresight to provide themselves with ample supplies of food for the journey, for it was impossible for the stewards of the ships, especially of those ships that normally did not carry passengers, to feed so many. After landing they had to stand for hours in queues in the embarkation sheds awaiting examination by Medical and Immigration Officers. Even when they were free to leave the vicinity of the harbour many had to spend the night in beach shelter, or in the open air because every room in the town was already occupied. Bad as that was, their discomfort would undoubtedly have been worse if it had not been that the Weymouth people, both public officials and private individuals showed them the utmost possible kindness and that three members of the States Civil Service, Mr Robert, Mr Harwood and Mr Veal, had been sent to Weymouth to do all that was possible to lessen their difficulties.

A vivid picture of the temporary hardships endured by the refugees is afforded by an official report made by a member of St John's Ambulance Brigade, Acting Cadet Officer Mrs M. E. Marquand. From 6am till noon on the first day of the evacuation this lady had been on duty at the White Rock helping mothers harassed with children in arms. She had just returned home for a brief rest when she was asked by telephone if she was willing to proceed immediately to England on a steamer whose captain insisted on having a competent nurse on board because he had two hundred women and children on board, some of whom would have to go to hospital on arrival on the mainland, and he had heard that two women on other ships had given birth to children on the voyage.

Mrs Marquand was on board the boat within twenty minutes but it did not leave until late in the evening, during which time she had no easy task in making women and young children as comfortable as the very difficult circumstances would allow. The crew gave up their own sleeping accommodation to those whom Mrs Marquand considered most needed it, and, for the others, covered the iron decks with wooden planks. Some slept on these – fortunately the night was fine and moonlit – some in cattle stalls and some in the hold. 'I was kept on the go', said Mrs Marquand in her report. 'No sooner had I settled down than one of the crew fetched me to a woman in hysterics. Then something would go wrong with another. Children fell down and cut or bruised themselves and there were a few faints.'

The ship reached Weymouth at 7.45am and dropped anchor outside the harbour, where she lay for thirty nerve-racking hours. None of her passengers had foreseen this delay. All the food that they had brought for the journey was finished and all were desperately hungry. The ship could supply none, for it's the custom on small cargo boats that make short voyages for the crew to provide their own food instead of being fed by the ship's owners. The crew 'were goodness itself', going hungry themselves and giving what food they had to the women and children, but a dozen men's food does not go far among two hundred and fifty people. The captain sent a message to the shore asking for food but it was midnight – sixteen hours after the ship had reached Weymouth roads – before a supply of milk, bread, tea, biscuits, jam and margarine was sent on board. Part of this was set aside for the morning and the weary passengers were awakened to eat the rest. The food that had been set aside was consumed in the morning – except a little milk reserved for the babies – and the day dragged on till 2pm when the steamer weighed anchor and came alongside the quay.

By 3pm all had disembarked and were received by Red Cross Sisters, Ambulance Sisters, St John's Ambulance Brigade men, soldiers, sailors and Boy Scouts, who conducted them, after they had passed the Medical and Immigration Officers, to various reception centres.

Mrs Marquand's task was done, but she had to find means of getting home. On returning to Weymouth harbour, after seeing a crippled boy safely delivered at a Red Cross Station, she learned that it was not known whether any of the ships that had come from Guernsey would return there and that, even if one did, it was unlikely that the captain would take the responsibility of carrying her. Anxious not to miss any chance she stayed all day at the harbour – where at one time she helped to disembark some stretcher-cases brought from Alderney – and all the following night, except for three visits to the town made in the hope of being able to telephone to her husband in Guernsey. In the morning she had the good fortune to find that the *Courier* was returning to Guernsey and would carry her.

Life was strenuous for others as well as the St John's Ambulance Brigade during the evacuation period. The Bailiff's Assistant Secretary, Mr L.A. Guillemette, was able to get no more than about three hours sleep each night between Tuesday morning and Saturday evening and a severe strain was placed on other States officials. Bus drivers, taxicab drivers and telegraphists had little leisure. Telephonists, working from early morning till far into the night, besides tending to an abnormal number of calls, had to answer many foolish and hysterical questions; and the Railway Companies' officials snatched their meals when they could and slept, when they had the chance, with their heads on their office desks.

Out of the population of forty-three thousand, twenty-three thousand left the Island. Some of these – farmers, men in key positions and men engaged in public services – the Island could ill afford to lose. More were pensioners and rentiers, 'idle mouths' who by leaving the Island lessened the difficulties of the food problem. Broadly speaking most of those whose duty it was to stay in the Island loyally stayed, and those who could help it best by leaving left. One very valuable result of the evacuation was that it rid the Island of many panic-mongers and 'jitterbugs', whose presence would have a been dangerous nuisance in the real crises that befell us soon afterwards.

It is probable that when the whole situation is reviewed both the British Government and the Island Authorities will be blamed for their treatment of the evacuation problem. It may be said that this or that contingency should have been forseen; that this or that arrangement for the welfare of those who left and those that stayed behind should have been made. It is probable that controversy will arise as to what precisely was agreed during the conversations by telephone that were held between the British Government and the Island Government during the momentous week that ended on June 23rd. Such critics must make allowances for the haste in which everything was done. So great was the haste that, although the disarming of the Island was begun on June 18th and completed on the following day, formal notice of the British Government's intention to take this step was not signed by Sir John Anderson, the Secretary-of-State for Home Affairs, until Sunday, June 24th, five days after the last soldier had left. It took the form of a letter accompanying the following gracious message from His Majesty the King:-

> For strategic reasons it has been found necessary to withdraw the armed forces from the Channel Islands.
> I deeply regret this necessity and I wish to assure My people in the Islands that in taking this decision My Government have not been unmindful of their position. It is in their interest that this step should be taken in present circumstances.
> The long association of the Islands with the Crown and the loyal services which the Islands have rendered to My Ancestors and Myself are guarantees that the link between us will remain unbroken, and I know that My people in the Islands will look forward with the same confidence as I do to the day when the resolute fortitude with which we face our present difficulties will reap the reward of victory.

For some unexplained reason this letter was never published.

CHAPTER III

THE LAST WEEK OF FREEDOM

The sudden loss of more than half the Island's population created a number of problems that needed urgent attention. Many businesses came almost to a standstill through loss of staff and many people were thrown out of work by the departure of their employers. Bakers did not know for how many customers to provide bread. Milk distribution was disorganised. Very few of those who had gone had paid their bills before they left, and as it was near the end both of the month and of the quarter the amount owing to tradespeople was considerable. The dislocation of industry had created a Gilbertian situation; many purchasers accustomed to pay cash were justified by the emergency in asking for credit, and most vendors were just as much justified in demanding cash payments; and a considerable proportion of men in the Island were out of work, while there was a great deal of work that urgently needed doing.

Advertisements in the local newspapers of June 24th showed the efforts that were being made to overcome difficulties. *La Gazette Officielle* announced that growers need not obey the Tomato Growing Ordinance if labour shortage made grading too difficult, but warned them that, owing to the probable shortage of cargo boats, inferior tomatoes must not be exported. Many firms advertised appeals such as 'Be patient and with what staff we have we will do our best', and the Guernsey Special Aid Society, that had begun as an organisation for the sending of parcels to men on active service and had expanded into a canteen for soldiers, advertised that it would supply meals to, and darn the socks of, men whose wives had evacuated.

On the same day the Emergency Controlling Committee appointed custodians of abandoned agricultural and horticultural land, whose duty it was to utilise the land and the crops on it and to bank all profits derived from them on behalf of their absentee owners. Meanwhile Special Constables detailed for the duty searched abandoned houses for poultry and perishable food, which they appropriated on behalf of the States, and arranged for the painless destruction of masterless dogs and cats, which were either starving or living by raiding poultry runs and rabbit hutches. Many cage-birds – canaries, love-birds, golden pheasants and rush-weavers – had been liberated by their owners. These would naturally have starved but for Miss Kay Mouat of the Foulon, who established a receiving depot for such as were captured and brought to her to keep until she could find homes for them. One result of the panic was that Doctor Symons, the member of the Emergency Controlling Committee appointed to deal with public health, had to appeal for the help of V.A.D.'s and others who had experience in nursing, because twenty invalids, whose natural guardians had deserted them, had been taken to local hospitals, which were the less able to cope with this additional burden because seven members of their normal staffs had fled to England. The Town Hospital lost its entire kitchen staff except the cook, all its laundry maids except one and six of its eight nurses.

During the week following the evacuation only two mail boats left the Island instead of two a day as in normal summer months. Among their passengers, some intended to leave the Island until after the war, others intended to return as soon as they had attended to whatever business it was that took them to England. The normal service of cargo boats was resumed, after nearly a week's interruption, and three hundred thousand baskets of tomatoes were shipped before the disaster of June 28th brought the export of produce to an abrupt end.

On Monday, June 24th, the first working day since the close of free evacuation and incidentally the first since the subsidence of the panic, the Bailiff, speaking as Civil Lieutenant-Governor, broadcast from the loudspeaker installed at the Press Office an exhortation to courage and hope. Later in that day and on each of the four following days Deputy Stamford Raffles, the Information Officer, used the loudspeaker to address those who cared to assemble in Smith Street after the closing of the shops. Sometimes he gave advice emanating from his colleagues on the Emergency Controlling Committee, as, for example, that people should save less perishable food by drinking more milk, because, whereas the Island's milk production was practically as great as before the evacuation, there were now less than half as many people to consume it; but principally he broadcast the latest news officially received of the welfare and whereabouts of the evacuated children. It seems not to have occurred either to those in authority or to any of their numerous critics that there was any danger in causing crowds to assemble in the heart of the town.

On the evening of Friday, June 28th, an exceptionally large crowd assembled because it was known that His Majesty's Procureur was to broadcast. What Mr Sherwill said is not on record. Reports of his speech were crowded out of the next day's newspapers by the chronicling of more sensational events. One of his audience, however, remembered afterwards that, referring to a plane that had flown low over the town on the previous day, he said 'I have been asked if it was a German plane. I can answer – Yes, it was. What of it?'

The answer to Mr Sherwill's question reached the Island within the next ten minutes. The crowd that had gathered in Smith Street had scarcely dispersed when suddenly the whirr of approaching planes was followed by the rattle of machine-gun fire and the explosion of bombs, and dense clouds of dust and high-explosive fumes rose from the neighbourhood of the White Rock. The war had reached Guernsey in earnest!

The German machine-gunners had what they must have regarded as exceptionally fine targets. A mail boat and two cargo boats were being loaded in the harbour and the White Rock was crowded with people who were going to embark and their friends who had come to see them off, besides the dockers loading the ships with tomatoes and the usual throng of people who regarded the White Rock as a very pleasant place on which to stroll on a fine summer evening. It was the crowd at the harbour that principally engaged the machine-gunners' attention, but they fired also on people in St James Street and the Grange, which were more crowded than usual as many people were returning from listening to Mr Sherwill's speech, and on haymakers in the Château des Marais. Another easy target was a double line of produce-laden lorries – it was the height of the season and tomato exporters were trying to make up for the lost week – which extended all the way from the jetty to St Julian's Weighbridge. Some of these lorries were set on fire with the terrible result that some lorry drivers who had sought cover underneath them were burned to death. The haymakers in the Château des Marais escaped injury but in the town twenty-three persons were killed outright and thirty-eight seriously injured – five of whom died later; the number of those whose wounds were slight enough to allow them to go home after receiving treatment was not recorded.

The marksmanship of the bombers was distinctly poor. Part of a salvo of bombs aimed at the gas-works fell on the Fruit Export Store and the rest on the beach near the Long Store. A bomb aimed at the States Water Board's pumping station near the Forest Road fell in front of, and blew the roof off, a house at La Vassallerie. Bombs aimed at the petrol store on the Castle Emplacement hit a house in the Strand, the west end of the slaughter house, and the rocks near Castle Cornet. A few fishing boats and small yachts were the only sufferers from three bombs aimed at the mail boat, the *Isle of Sark*, whose anti-aircraft gunners kept up a steady fire throughout the raid. The other two steamers in the harbour escaped with little if any injury. At what target a bomb which fell near a Martello tower at Vazon was aimed it is difficult to conjecture.

On the whole the damage caused by the bombs to buildings was small in comparison with their number. It was estimated that thirty bombs weighing fifty pounds each were dropped on the town area. On the White Rock fifty-one motor lorries and many taxi-cabs were reduced to scrap-metal. The sheds at the Cambridge berth were gutted, and though a small proportion of their contents was salved the disaster cost the Island a large amount of foodstuffs and other goods ranging in importance from buckwheat to bootlaces.

The raiders also attacked the local steamboat *Courier*. She was on her way from Alderney, bringing salvaged stores and a few people who had remained in that Island after the bulk of the inhabitants left, and was near the entrance to St Sampson's Harbour when a plane sprayed her deck with machine-gun bullets and dropped a bomb that fortunately missed her. The captain beached the ship and when she was aground some members of her crew launched her boat, rowed ashore, and ran away, leaving those still on board, eleven of whom were wounded, to get ashore as best they could. Two men and two women, one of whom was wounded in the leg, swam ashore and were taken to the First Aid Post for bandages, blankets and hot tea. Fortunately for those who still remained on board a young dock hand had more grit than some other members of the crew. He swam ashore and brought back the ship's boat so that all reached the shore. The *Courier* was refloated next day and by order of the Admiralty proceeded to England.

While the raid was in progress the lifeboat was at sea between Guernsey and Jersey. One plane, after leaving Guernsey, attacked it with machine-gun fire, which killed Frederick Hobbs, a son of the coxswain.

Estimates of the number of planes engaged vary between three and nine. Obviously no estimates were reliable. Anyone who was sufficiently calm and collected to count the planes and to be sure that he did not count any plane twice over had something more important to do. Some White Rock officials, for example, improvised splinter-proof shelters with bags of flour. Some lorry drivers, despite considerable danger from blazing lorries and exploding petrol tanks, drove on to the White Rock to remove injured people for whom there was no room in the ambulances. A tribute is due also to the Police, Special Constables, ARP workers and men of St John's Ambulance Brigade who, though off duty at the time, hurried to the White Rock to render what services they could; and a licensed porter who distributed tomatoes, which circumstances had made anybody's property, to people huddled under cover deserves honourable mention for setting an example of coolness.

St John's Ambulance Brigade was short-handed at the time of the raid. Some of its members had gone to Alderney on duty and more had left the Island at the end of the previous week when their services in the evacuation of invalids were no longer needed. If all those whose services were available had stayed in safety until the raiding planes had gone they would have been justified by a general order, issued some time before, that in the event of a raid they were to wait until the 'all-clear' signal before exposing themselves to danger. A number of them, however, disregarded this order – gallant disobedience which cost one of them, Private R. Nicolle, his leg. The following extract from the official report of another of them, Private Margot, gives so vivid a picture of what they found to do when they reached the White Rock that it may well serve as a description of the Brigade's work in general.

> 28/6/40. On duty 6.55pm Took two persons into shelter in Doyle Road. Took one girl into a house. Came to Pollet Sarnia shed. Gave 30 people water and asked them to stay under cover. Saw if Mrs H--- and family were all right. Found the family under the table. Coming out of shop saw invalid pushed by his mother trying to reach Weighbridge. Took them back to Sarnia shed. Gave water to everybody. Went back in direction of Weighbridge and found three casualties in Joe Way's shop. (1) Bullet or shrapnel wound left back shoulder. (2) Bullet wound stomach through bladder, in great pain. Dressed wound. No more bandage left. Ran to ambulance by Weighbridge. Saw Privates Froome and Taylor and Police Constable Bougourd attending casualties. Took bandages. Ran back into shop. Had to jump over a patient. Bombs and bullets were falling close. Second casualty received two more bullet wounds in leg. (3) Attended third casualty. Two wounds in buttock. Back to ambulance. Found Constable Bougourd dying from bullet through head. One casualty dead. Called to public-house. One woman badly injured. Ran back to Boots (Chemist) with Private Froome for bandages. On way back

attending fainting woman. Woman with bad foot. One other man, leg off, open scalp on top of ear. Put Constable Bougourd and two other dead casualties on lorry and went with them to the mortuary. Back to Weighbridge.

At this point Private Margot's report became somewhat incoherent, but it appears that after his return to the harbour he employed himself in removing the dead from underneath burned-out lorries. He concludes the report laconically 'off duty, 12pm'.

Was the raid an act of legitimate warfare or should it be stigmatised as yet one more of those intentional violations of the laws of war, as recognised by civilised nations, of which the German military authorities have from time to time been guilty? At the time that the raid was made Guernsey had been demilitarised and disarmed, so that the only opposition it was possible to offer to the raiding planes was that of the mail boat's anti-aircraft gun which probably did good service in distracting the aim of the bombers. There is, however, some reason to believe that the raiders did not know that we had been disarmed, as there seems to have been some delay in officially informing the German Government that the Channel Islands had been demilitarised; in fact the officer in command of the airborne German troops that landed in the Island two days later told the Bailiff at their formal first meeting that he had not known of it. If on this ground the raid may be regarded as justifiable the targets at which the bombs were presumably aimed – the gas works, the petrol store, the pumping station at St Martin's and the mail boat – must be regarded as perfectly legitimate targets. The destruction of the lorries on the White Rock by machine-gun fire may also be justified as they were laden with food destined for England. There was less excuse for the firing on the ambulance which, when it was hit, was nowhere near the lorries on the White Rock and cannot therefore have been struck by bullets aimed at one of them. It is conceivable, however, that the machine-gunner responsible did not recognise it as an ambulance in spite of its being plainly marked with a Red Cross. It might even be possible – should anyone care to make the effort – to exonerate the shooting of people in the Grange and on the deck of the *Courier*. There is, however, one incident of the raid which the most earnest German apologist will find impossible to justify, excuse, or even palliate. Lifeboats should be regarded by belligerents as especially immune from attack because it is their noble duty to serve, not the people of any individual country, but humanity as a whole. Yet one of the planes fired on the Guernsey lifeboat, killing one of her crew. No sophistry, however ingenious, can excuse that outrage. The machine-gunner cannot have hit the lifeboat by accident when aiming at something else, for the lifeboat was well out to sea and no other target was within range. He cannot have mistaken the lifeboat for any kind of small naval auxiliary vessel for the boats of the Royal National Lifeboat Institution differ so conspicuously in colour and design from any other kind of craft that it is impossible to mistake them. The machine-gunner who fired on the lifeboat must therefore have known well what he was doing and his act must be classed with those acts of *schrecklichkeit* (frightfulness), approved by German war lords when they feel strong enough to defy the international laws that regulate civilised warfare, and perpetrated for the purpose of terrifying civilian populations. In fact the cold-blooded murder of the lifeboat man suggests that the main purpose of the raid was to strike such terror into the hearts of the people of Guernsey as would ensure their docility when the time came to occupy the Island. On the day after the raid an air raid warning drove most people to cover. As no bombs were dropped and no machine-gun fire was heard it was concluded that the alarm had been caused by a German reconnaissance plane sent to report on the extent of the damage caused on the previous day. Some people were so optimistic as to believe that we need not fear any more raids, for that morning an announcement had been published that there would be no more export of tomatoes and other produce, and they thought that Guernsey would not be worth the attentions of the German air force when the Island no longer sent foodstuffs to England.

Those optimists – and they were many – who believed that the Island need not fear German occupation, had the support of an anonymous 'military expert' quoted by *The Star* in that morning's issue. On the subject of the demilitarisation of the Channel Islands the military expert had said 'there need be no fear of the Germans taking any advantage from the British decision to quit. The Nazis could no more hold positions in the Islands than we could defend them.' We were to lose the comfort we derived from that expert assurance in less than forty-eight hours. On the following day, Sunday, June 30th, just before 1pm, another air raid warning was sounded. Again neither the explosion of bombs nor the rattle of machine-guns was heard and so long a time elapsed before the 'all clear' signal was given that many who had gone to their cellars returned to their belated meal. At 8pm that evening air raid warnings sounded again, followed by 'all clear' signals at 10pm. During those two hours Germans had landed on the Island, but few were aware of their presence until next morning when newsboys distributed free copies of *The Star*, across the front page of which was displayed in large letters the headline:

ORDERS OF THE COMMANDANT OF THE GERMAN
FORCES IN OCCUPATION OF THE ISLAND OF GUERNSEY.

CHAPTER IV

GERMANS LAND IN THE ISLAND

The Island had had two air raid warnings on Sunday, June 30th, 1940, Guernsey's last day of freedom. In neither case did those who took cover hear bomb explosions or machine-gun fire, so that few knew until the following day what had caused the warnings.

The first had been occasioned by the approach of four German planes, three of which alighted on the airport while the fourth circled above it, presumably on the watch to guard against surprise. The men that landed from the three planes broke into the airport offices but raced back to their machines and hurriedly took off when the plane that was circling above dropped a flare. Their hurried departure was due no doubt to the approach of two – according to some accounts three – British planes. The few people who saw them expected to witness an air battle but were disappointed. It was asserted, however, that machine-gun fire out at sea was heard soon after the planes had disappeared.

Guernsey's second air raid warning on that historic Sunday was caused by the approach of four large troop-carrying planes. These all came down at the airport. Soldiers, each armed with a rifle, a tommy-gun, a revolver and some hand grenades, alighted from them and searched the vicinity, commandeering and taking to the airport all the cars they could find. The Germans took no steps towards getting into touch with the Island authorities until the Inspector and Deputy Inspector of Police drove up bringing a letter in which the Bailiff invited senior German officers to meet him and the King's Procureur at the Royal Hotel. The senior German officer accordingly drove to the Royal Hotel in the police car, closely followed by half a dozen commandeered cars packed with officers and men, all armed. Machine-guns were set up on each side of the doorway of the hotel after the German officer had entered it, and throughout the interview that followed he sat with a rifle between his knees. The heads of various States Departments were sent for and told that henceforth they must take their orders from German officers detailed to supervise them. Squads of soldiers meanwhile were stationed to guard the Telephone office and the Post Office – where the telegraph apparatus was dismantled – and commandeered cars raced to and fro between the airport and the Royal Hotel. On the front seat of each car sat a soldier who continuously blew a whistle and on each running board stood two soldiers, rifle in hand. All this noise and bustle advertised to people living near the road that the Germans had landed on the Island, but few others were aware of their arrival until on the front page of next morning's newspaper they read the 'orders of the commandant of the German forces in occupation of the Island of Guernsey.'

- (1) All inhabitants must be indoors by 11pm and must not leave their homes before 6am
- (2) We will respect the population of Guernsey, but should anyone attempt to cause the least trouble, serious measures will be taken and the town will be bombed.
- (3) All orders given by the Military Authority are to be strictly obeyed.
- (4) All spirits must be locked up immediately, and no spirits may be supplied, obtained or consumed henceforth. This prohibition does not apply to stocks in private houses.
- (5) No person shall enter the aerodrome at La Villiaze.
- (6) All rifles, airguns, pistols, revolvers, daggers, sporting guns, and all other weapons whatsoever, except souvenirs, must, together with all ammunition, be delivered at the Royal Hotel by 12 noon to-day, July 1st.
- (7) All British sailors, airmen and soldiers on leave in this Island must report at the Police Station at 9am to-day, and must then report at the Royal Hotel.
- (8) No boat or vessel of any description, including any fishing boat, shall leave the harbours or any other place where the same is moored, without an order from the Military Authority, to be obtained at the Royal Hotel. All boats arriving from Jersey or from Herm or elsewhere

must remain in harbour until permitted by the Military to leave. The crews will remain on board. The Master will report to the Harbourmaster, St Peter Port, and will obey his instructions.
(9) The sale of motor spirits is prohibited, except for use on essential services, such as doctors' vehicles, the delivery of foodstuffs, the sanitary services, where such vehicles are in possession of a permit from the Military Authority to obtain supplies. These vehicles must be brought to the Royal Hotel by 12 noon to-day to receive the necessary permission. The use of cars for private purposes is forbidden.
(10) The black-out regulations already in force must be observed as before.
(11) Banks and shops will open as usual.

The purpose of enforcing the existing black-out regulations was at first difficult to understand. We now had no further cause to fear German air raids and the danger that the British Royal Air Force would bomb anything in the Island except military objectives was to most men unthinkable. It was soon obvious, however, that the Germans were in lively fear of British air raids.

On the following day, July 2nd, the following announcements and exhortations were published in the local newspapers:-

(1) The German Commandant has taken over the military powers in the Islands of Guernsey and Jersey. The population is hereby required to retain calmness, order and discipline. If this is assured, the life and property of the population will be respected and guaranteed. The German Commandant is in close touch with the Civil Authorities and acknowledges their loyal co-operation. The German Commandant expects that every effort will be made to adjust the economic life of the Island to the changed circumstances arising out of the evacuation and occupation and to preserve its economic structure and life.

(2) The Civil Government and Courts of the Island will continue to function heretofore, save that all Laws, Ordinances, Regulations and Orders will be submitted to the German Commandant before being enacted.

(3) Such legislation as, in the past, required the Sanction of His Britannic Majesty in Council for its validity will henceforth be valid on being approved by the German Commandant and thereafter sanctioned by the British Civil Lieutenant-Governor of the Island of Guernsey.

(4) The order of the German Commandant will automatically have effect in the Island of Sark on promulgation therein by the German Military Authorities.

(5) The orders of the German Commandant heretofore, now and hereafter issued shall in due course be registered on the records of the Island of Guernsey in order that no person may plead ignorance thereof. Offences against the same, saving those punishable under German Military Law, shall be punishable by the Civil Courts and the Royal Court shall, with the approval of the German Commandant, enact suitable penalties in respect of such offences.

(6) All clocks and watches are to be advanced one hour as from midnight of the 2nd/3rd July, 1940, in accord with German time.

(7) Assemblies in churches and chapels for the purpose of divine worship are permitted. Prayers for the British Royal Family and for the welfare of the British Empire may be said. Such assemblies shall not be made the vehicle for any propaganda or utterances against the honour or interests of or offensive to the German Government or Forces.

(8) Cinemas, concerts and other entertainments are permitted subject to the conditions set out in Order 7 above.

(9) The British National Anthem shall not be played or sung without the written permission of the German Commandant. This does not apply in private houses

in respect of a broadcast (British) programme received therein.
(10) The use of wireless receiving sets is permitted.

There were seven other clauses. They forbade the raising of prices, restricted the sale of intoxicants, prohibited traffic between Guernsey and Jersey, temporarily fixed the rate of exchange between the German mark and the Guernsey pound, and warned us that the 'continuance of the privileges granted to the civilian population' depended upon our good behaviour.

The clause allowing the Civil Government to continue was in accordance with International Law. The extent to which its provisions operated in letter and spirit was to be learned by experience. We found that the Germans respected International Law when it suited them to do so. When it did not they said that military necessity overrode all other considerations.

The adoption of German time benefited us as well as the Germans, because the difficulty of renewing fuel supplies made economy in the use of electric light and gas urgently necessary.

In British Roman Catholic churches the prayer for the King includes a clause beseeching that in time of war he may conquer his enemies (*tempore belli hastes superare*). Very often German soldiers must have heard this prayer. Presumably they did not understand Latin or did not pay attention to the service.

Four months later all radios were requisitioned as a communal punishment for 'the favouring of espionage in the Island'. The order was not drastically enforced and a number of radio-owners had the courage to retain their sets, with the happy result that we were still able to learn the news. The confiscated radios were returned to their owners in December, 1940, but were requisitioned again in June, 1942, this time on the ground of military necessity. Again a number of radio-owners ignored the order, even after the death penalty had been threatened for so doing, and the news continued to pass surreptitiously by word of mouth so efficiently that any item of unusual interest – such as that a Guernseyman, Major Le Patourel, son of a former H.M. Procureur, had been awarded the Victoria Cross – was known throughout the Island within two hours or less of its announcement by the BBC.

Communication with Sark was resumed on July 6th and by the end of August it was possible for those who could obtain permits to travel to or from Jersey.

The value of the mark was eventually fixed at 2s. 1d. German soldiers bought largely from local shops and market-stalls. They were encouraged to do this by a peculiar arrangement. Part of their pay went to their families in the form of separation allowances, part accumulated to their credit in Germany to be drawn when they returned there, and part (in no case less than the equivalent of 25s. a week) was paid to them locally in paper money (*reichskreditkassen*) which was of no value in Germany or anywhere but in German occupied countries. An interesting commentary on this arrangement was made in a leaflet, many copies of which were dropped on the Island by a Royal Air Force plane three months after the German occupation had begun:

> RM 7 = £1.
>
> Invaders of old used to allow their troops to 'live on the country' by frank and open looting. The Nazis, however, have invented a new, more subtle, kind of looting, whereby they make pretence of paying for the goods they steal, with worthless bits of paper.
>
> The Nazis tell you, for example, that the proper rate of exchange is seven marks to the £1. This is complete nonsense. Even at the fictitious rate of exchange quoted in the United States of RM 2.40 to the dollar – a rate of exchange at which no business is actually done – the corresponding rate for you would be about eleven marks to the pound.
>
> Actually, however, the mark has practically no value whatsoever outside Germany – for the simple reason that nobody wants German paper money. It is backed neither by gold nor by goods for export – only by force and fraud.

Shopkeepers did not lose by having to accept German paper money, for it was passed on to the banks at the current rate, and the banks in their turn passed it on to the States Treasury. The Guernsey tax-payer was the loser by this arrangement. Before we were once again free the States Treasury had paid for this worthless paper a sum of approximately £2,000,000.

On the whole and at first sight there seemed nothing particularly tyrannous about the German Commandant's orders. It appeared that so long as the German Forces remained in the Island we were to be subject to a benevolent despotism in which the proportion of benevolence to despotism could be gauged only by actual experience. During the five years of the German occupation the despotism was perhaps more noticeable than the benevolence, but in a review of the period which Jurat Leale made after it was over he was able to say: 'We shall associate the occupation with hunger and cold and homelessness rather than with dramatic arrests and sensational sentences.'

CHAPTER V

"INNUMERABLE AND PRESSING PROBLEMS"

On August 7th, at the first meeting of the States since the German occupation, Mr A. J. Sherwill, speaking as the President of the Controlling Committee, said 'the partial evacuation and then the severance of communication with the United Kingdom have dealt a terrific blow to Island economics and we have had to deal with innumerable and pressing problems, many almost and some quite insoluble, without time to sit back and think, without precedent to guide us.'

The most immediate, though not the most difficult, problem was that of the many people who had been suddenly cut off from their ordinary means of subsistence. These were of two classes: people who lived on pensions payable in England or on dividends drawn from England, who literally did not know how they were to obtain food when the money they happened to have by them was expended; and wage-earners thrown out of work by the sudden cessation of the export of tomatoes, potatoes and flowers, by the evacuation of many employers, or by the pressing need of employers who remained drastically to reduce their expenditure.

The unemployment problem was, however, counterbalanced by a labour problem. There was much work that was crying to be done, because some farms and many greenhouses – potential sources of valuable food supplies – had been left derelict when their owners evacuated, or had lost the labour necessary for their efficient working by the evacuation of men normally employed on them. It was of vital importance that these farms and greenhouses should be restored to working order as soon as possible, as the Island's reserve stocks of food were very low. Stocks of fuel were also very low and the time when we should have no more water, except from wells, and neither gas nor electricity, seemed to be within measurable distance.

Another difficult problem was that of States finance. To quote Mr Sherwill again; 'The cost of the occupation of this

Island by the German Forces falls on the States of Guernsey; the provision of premises, the wages of the civilian personnel, such as interpreters, cooks and various helpers, and the expenses of transport, all these have been directed to be borne out of States funds.'

Two other weighty problems were less pressing. Abandoned houses were in danger of rapid deterioration unless steps were taken to preserve them, and there was still a considerable number of children in the Island for whose education arrangements had to be made. None of the problems was such as could be solved at a moment's notice, but the announcements in the newspapers on July 3rd showed that the various members of the Controlling Committee were actively getting to work on them. The Information Officer published six items of advice to the general public: (1) To consume foodstuffs that would not keep, especially milk, of which the evacuation of more than half of the Island's population had caused a temporary glut; (2) That friends should arrange where possible to share houses so as to economise in light and kitchen fuel; (3) To pay rent and tradesmen's bills as much as possible so as to keep money in circulation (the trading community had of course been hit hard, as few even of the most conscientious evacuees had found time to pay their bills before they left); (4) To treat the German troops with courtesy; (5) To note orders published in the newspapers by the German Authorities and to obey them; (6) Not to purchase anything not immediately required.

The Controlling Committee announced that they had assumed control of the tomato-growing industry and that the tomato crop was States property; that half the crop was to be destroyed, but that no crop was to be destroyed without permission, and growers were to continue their normal work until they received instructions; that the Committee was prepared, while the crisis lasted, to take over and manage the tomato-growing of those owners who wished them to do so – the Committee paying all wages and assuming all responsibilities – and would endeavour to employ the growers on the properties they were accustomed to work.

By the end of July employment had been found for practically all the men – some fourteen hundred in number – who had been thrown out of work by the crisis. It was less easy to find employment for the larger number of women normally employed in tomato-packing, flower-picking and – during the holiday season – in hotels, boarding houses and tea-shops. At a meeting called by Deputy Johns eighty such women volunteered to work on the land and in the following September a number of women found temporary employment at picking blackberries for a jam factory controlled by the States. The rest soon found employment with the Germans, who offered such high wages (at the expense of the States Treasury) that most households were bereft of their maid-servants, a great hardship to elderly ladies unaccustomed to cook for themselves.

Within a week of the assumption by the States of the control of the tomato-growing industry, five head organisers were appointed to oversee its general management. These gentlemen had power to decide what crops were to be grown in greenhouses in which the tomato crop had been destroyed and what staff was to be employed in their cultivation. About two thousand properties came under States management. Of these, catch crops of potatoes, leeks, celery, lettuce and especially beans were sown. The beans became available for food in December and were a very valuable addition to the Island's food supply.

A States Department for the relief of persons whose incomes were normally derived from England came into being on July 9th under the management of Deputy Stamford Raffles. Applicants for relief were invited to answer a number of necessary questions as to the amount of the income they normally received and its source, whether they owned or rented the houses in which they lived and the extent of the assistance they needed. Arrangements were then made in each case with the applicant's bank under which the States guaranteed a specified weekly or monthly overdraft up to a reasonable proportion of the applicant's normal income.

A census made by the Education Council showed that 1,050 children remained in the Island, but only twelve school-teachers were available to teach them, the remainder having left the Island in charge of evacuated children. The Council therefore appealed for the services of people with the necessary qualifications who could spare the whole or part of their time to teach in such schools as it was decided to re-open.

Early in July a census was made of abandoned houses and the States Supervisor, Mr H.E. Marquand, was appointed Custodian of Dwellings. He appointed deputies who were authorised to enter any abandoned house; to arrange for any repairs that were or would become necessary; to hire out or store furniture; to let premises furnished or unfurnished; to hand over any consumable stores to the Essential Commodities Committee; and to cultivate and dispose of garden produce.

Among other articles found in abandoned premises were a large number of bicycles. Owing to the prohibition of the use of private motor cars, the impossibility of hiring taxis and the cessation of the motor bus services, these would have fetched high prices if put up to auction. They were, however, disposed of to those who needed them. Because a number of shops had been abandoned Jurat Pierre de Putron was appointed Custodian of Business and Industry with powers similar to those of the Custodian of Dwellings. One of his first tasks was to arrange for the return to their owners of boots and shoes that had been entrusted for repair to cobblers who had evacuated.

The loss to the States' Treasury of a large portion of the monies due to it through the evacuation, just before quarter-day, of many people who owed payments to the Water Board, Telephone and Electricity Departments and the Income Tax Authorities, and the burden of paying the cost of the German occupation, necessitated both rigid economies and finding some new sources of revenue. The salaries of Civil Servants, who shortly before the occupation had been granted an increase of ten per cent on account of the rise in the cost of living, were drastically reduced. To increase the revenue, matches were taxed at the rate of ½d. a box, the stamp duty on cheques was raised to twopence and a tax of one halfpenny in every sixpence was imposed on the sale of everything except rationed and essential foods, gas, electricity, paraffin, water, fuel, livestock, clothing for children under fourteen, and (by way of proof that the States were amenable to sentiment) children's toys and books not exceeding half-a-crown in value. Some difficulties arose, principally because no detailed decision had been come to as to which foods were essential and which were luxuries. While chickens were still available some vendors charged the purchasers with the tax and others did not; apples and sugar were not taxable but apple jam was; and when a horse and van were sold by auction in one lot it was difficult for the auctioneer to decide the value of purchase stamps that the buyer must pay as the horse, being livestock, was not taxable but the van was. On the whole, however, the tax was very well received. The necessity for it was recognised and it did not fall very heavily on the economical housewife.

It was generally recognised in the Island that there were some people who could not meet all their liabilities. The turnover of many small shopkeepers was reduced by more than half, partly because they had fewer goods to sell and partly because half of their usual customers had left the Island. In general creditors were lenient with debtors. In consequence, some ultra-cautious people paid no debts that they were not compelled to pay. To encourage such as these to pay their proper share of the Island's revenue the States approved an ordinance by which a rebate of 2½ per cent on the first half of the year's Income Tax was allowed. The important problem of supplies could not be tackled until the authorities knew what stocks of essential commodities were in the Island and how many people remained to consume them. To get this information, wholesale and retail dealers were required to render returns of what stocks they had in hand; householders were called upon to report what quantities of coal and coke they possessed; the Assistant Controllers of Unoccupied Dwellings and of Business and Industry compiled statistics as to what stocks had been left behind by evacuees and a census was taken, which showed that the Island still contained nearly twenty thousand people.

Coal had been provisionally rationed at the rate of one cwt.

a week per household. This ration fluctuated in proportion to the amount of supplies obtained from time to time from France. Cooking fat, margarine, malt, hops, salt, tea and sugar were added to the list of rationed foods and the sale of candles and tinned fruit was temporarily suspended as these would be urgently needed in the winter months. The sale of some other groceries, though not rationed, was restricted; when a housewife asked for jam, macaroni, potted meat, cheese or a number of other commodities she was asked how many people there were in her household and she had to be content with as much of that commodity as her grocer thought fit to allow her. Because some housewives tried to buy more than their fair share grocers refused to sell any commodity – unless they had ample supplies of it – to any but their registered customers and to those not more often than once a week.

The imposition by the German Authorities of a curfew between 9pm and 6am was at first no serious hardship, except to those who urgently needed medical attention during the night. Notices appeared in the newspapers urging expectant mothers to arrange to be confined in the Emergency Hospital instead of in their own homes, and soon after the imposition of the curfew, passes were issued to doctors and clergy authorising them to be out of doors at night for the purpose of visiting the sick. At a later date curfew restrictions proved a very real hardship to all food producers. Thefts of rabbits, poultry and garden produce, at first no more than a nuisance, became very serious as food stocks diminished. Islanders, risking arrest for being abroad during forbidden hours, may have been and probably were responsible for some of these thefts, and it is known that some of them were committed by ill-fed French and Spanish labourers imported by the Germans to work on the elaborate defences they constructed, but it is practically certain that the thieves were mostly German soldiers, almost as ill-fed as ourselves, since they alone could be abroad at night unchallenged.

CHAPTER VI

SIEGE CONDITIONS, 1940
SOME ASSETS

The severing of communication with England and the consequent cessation of imports from the mother country left Guernsey ill prepared for siege conditions, though the situation was in some respects better than it might have been.

When the threat of war began to darken in the early months of 1939 the States Committee for Agriculture and Fisheries urged farmers to prepare to grow in 1940 larger food crops than usual. In response to this appeal land in the Island under potatoes was increased in the autumn of 1939 by 26 per cent and that under corn by 60 per cent. We profited also by Jersey's misfortunes. In normal years that Island exported large quantities of main crop potatoes. She could not now export her surplus to England so she sent it to us instead. Our stock of potatoes was therefore very large. To ensure that it should be used economically the Controlling Committee requisitioned all potato crops. The retail price was fixed at one penny a pound – raised later to a penny halfpenny a pound for the better varieties – for table potatoes and two shillings a hundredweight for very small potatoes regarded, in that time of comparative plenty, as fit only for pig food. At this low price consumers were encouraged to eat more potatoes and less bread than was their custom, with the excellent result that the Island's shortage of flour became less serious that it would otherwise have been.

Early in 1939 horticulturalists were urged to produce food instead of flowers and if all had dug up their bulbs in order to grow potatoes and table vegetables in their place much of the hunger from which we suffered in the lean months January to May of later years would have been alleviated. Many flower-growers, however, were reluctant to abandon the growing of flowers which in normal times were exported to the value of £250,000 a year. When the severance of communication with England made it imperative that the Island should be made as self-supporting as possible and called into being a Controlling Committee with dictatorial powers, the Agricultural Officer of that committee was empowered to compel the digging up of the commoner variety of bulbs, and to order that the more expensive varieties of bulbs which he allowed to be left in the ground were to be overcropped with clover, rye, grasses or corn.

Nevertheless flowers continued to be grown on a large scale throughout the period of the German occupation. They could always be bought at market stalls where harassed housewives stood in queues on the chance of buying coarse roots such as are normally considered fit only for cattle-food. And they were grown very profitably, for Germans of all ranks bought them in large quantities and were prepared to pay high prices for them. Irises and tulips of which the wholesale price in normal years was from threepence to one shilling a dozen put from eightpence to two shillings into the pocket of the grower. He received from two shillings to three shillings for gladioli, instead of from sixpence to a shilling, and from fourpence to one shilling and sixpence for daffodils instead of from twopence to tenpence. As bulbs could be left in the ground from one season to the next the flower-grower had, moreover, less wages to pay than the grower of potatoes and table vegetables which had to be replanted every year, and the latter was handicapped by the fact that the prices paid to him were controlled whereas the flower-grower could demand as much as he liked. Again, the stipulation that land in which bulbs were left should be overcropped did not produce as much food as it should, as growing corn was trampled underfoot when the flowers were picked. The seriousness of the food situation was aggravated by the loss, a few days before the German occupation, of two valuable cargoes, one of petrol and another of flour. Both of the ships that brought them were locally owned and, as soon as they arrived in the harbour, their owners, smitten by the panic that prevailed at the time, embarked on them at once with their families and ordered them to put to sea immediately. We badly needed those cargoes.

As soon as it was known how many people remained in the Island the authorities took stock and estimated that, at the normal rate of consumption, no gas – many people had no other means of cooking – would be available after November; that the Island's stock of flour would be exhausted before Christmas; and that early in 1941 we should have no more electricity for lack of fuel to generate it and, incidentally, because the water works depended on power electricity, no more water except from wells. The prospect was grim and the Committee for the Control of Essential Commodities, with the whole-hearted support of most – but not all – of the general public, tackled the problem with energy and an ingenuity of device comparable to that of the famous Swiss Family Robinson.

There was just one form of food that at the time of the German occupation the Island had in embarrassing profusion. In the autumn of 1939 the Home Government had informed a deputation of Guernsey growers that they could make no better contribution towards the national war effort than by producing as many tomatoes as possible. As a result of this advice, when exports abruptly ceased, the Island's greenhouses contained over 2,000 tons of ripe or ripening tomatoes, enough while the season lasted to give three pounds weight of this fruit daily to every man, woman and child in the Island. The market price dropped immediately to sixpence a pound and a few days later to twopence and then to a penny a pound. At that price they would not pay the cost of marketing and many growers exhibited notices outside their greenhouses 'Come inside and help yourself.'

Growers might have saved wages by destroying the tomato plants or leaving them to rot, but this they could do without permission, for the German authorities had ordered that half the plants must be preserved in case it became possible to export tomatoes to Germany and France in exchange for food supplies. It became therefore the duty of the Controlling Committee to ensure that the greatest possible use was made of the tomatoes from the plants that were not destroyed. This could best be done by giving the tomatoes away. People in the country parishes were informed that if they had any difficulty in getting tomatoes for nothing they should apply to their Parish Connétables for information as to the nearest greenhouses at which they could be got and for the benefit of town dwellers who lived at a distance from vineries a number of depots were established in St Peter Port and St Sampson's at which anyone could take as much as he wished of the fruit.

Farmers were urged to feed tomatoes to their cattle, pigs and poultry. This advice proved disastrous as far as poultry were concerned. When a bird that had been fed on tomatoes was killed for the table its flesh was found to be so watery that it was unfit to eat. Cattle were shy of the unaccustomed food but experiments conducted by veterinary surgeons showed that a reasonable proportion of tomatoes added to a cow's fodder increased her milk yield. Farmers were therefore urged to compel their cattle to eat tomatoes by docking their supply of other foodstuffs and when it was found that many were as conservative in their ideas about cattle food as were the cows themselves pressure was put upon them by restricting the sale of oilcake and other cattle foods. Farmers were thus practically compelled to feed tomatoes to their cows, which had to choose between eating them or going hungry, and it was found that after a little while they ate the unaccustomed food greedily.

At first too little use was made of the facilities for getting free tomatoes. As this was probably due to the fact that many housewives could ill spare the time to go and get them, the Committee for the Preservation of Tomatoes – at this time new committees sprang up like mushrooms – employed men to collect tomatoes from the vineries, load them on to hand trucks and offer them from door to door. This scheme proved so successful that by July 12th, 3,377 baskets, or approximately 15 tons of tomatoes had been given away in the Town Parish alone. Only a fraction of the total amount of available tomatoes could be disposed of in this way and other means of disposing of them had to be found. Canning them was out of the question for there was no canning plant in the Island. The public had responded readily to an appeal made by the Committee for information as to methods for preserving them for winter use but unfortunately most of the recipes suggested were too elaborate for the ordinary housewife or specified sugar, of which there was a serious shortage, as a necessary ingredient. Tomato pickling with brine was, however, practicable for those who had sufficient supplies of salt and the Committee for the Preservation of Tomatoes organised a demonstration of the method of doing it which representative ladies in each parish were asked to attend and afterwards pass on the instruction they had received to their neighbours. The Committee also arranged with the Guernsey Jam Company to manufacture tomato purée for sale at cost price, a penny a pint, to all who applied for it and brought their own jars. It was difficult for anyone living at a distance from St Peter Port to profit by this enterprise but it was a great blessing to people living in town. To the average housewife the purée was nothing more than a remarkably cheap condiment; in the eyes of the Health Officer it was a most valuable health-giving food, rich in vitamins that, lacking oranges and lemons, we should badly need in the winter months. So great a quantity of the purée was made that at the end of the year the Guernsey Jam Company still had about thirty tons of it in stock. In spite, however, of all efforts to make full use of the tomato crop so much of it was inevitably wasted that the Medical Officer of Health was obliged to issue a peremptory order that tomatoes dumped as refuse on waste land must be covered with a layer of earth.

Grapes ranked next to tomatoes – but far below them – as the Island's principal greenhouse produce. It was found possible early in October to export a considerable quantity of this fruit to France. In spite of these exports the market was flooded with grapes at prices hitherto unknown to any but the oldest inhabitants. The finest early Muscats were sold for 8d., and Black Hamburgs 2d. a pound. Obviously it was desirable to turn surplus grapes into raisins if it could possibly be done in a climate less sunny than that of the Mediterranean countries, and the States Domestic Expert published advice as to how they could be dried in ovens. As no locally grown raisins came on the market it is to be presumed either that those who followed the advice consumed all the raisins they dried or that the experiment failed. Another experiment worth trying was that of making vinegar from grapes. M. Berthou, the Director of Vimiera, who had a cider press in which grapes could be crushed, undertook to make the attempt with grapes supplied by the Controlling Committee. From 18 tons of grapes he obtained some fifty-six thousand gallons of grape juice. Vinegar making is a slow process, but in January, 1941, M. Berthou announced that by the middle of the year he would have two hundred and sixteen gallons ready for the market.

The free distribution of tomatoes ceased on September 11th, by which time it had become a civic duty to consume as many apples as possible, especially as the profusion and cheapness of grapes had lessened the demand for them as dessert fruit. At an earlier date hedge-trimmers had been officially asked to spare brambles so that there should be a good crop of blackberries, and now the Essential Commodities Committee enabled the Guernsey Jam Company to make blackberry and apple jam by releasing for the purpose enough sugar to make two tons of it. The Health Officer of the Controlling Committee, Dr A.N. Symons, foresaw that, as we were unlikely to be able to obtain any oranges during the winter months, there would then be a serious lack of vitamin-supplying food, which might affect the future life of the Island's infants. He therefore urged those who had long-keeping varieties of apples – such as Bramley's Seedling and Newton Wonder – to preserve them carefully so that at the appropriate time they could be crushed and the juice given to the babies. All the apple-juice thus obtained was used in the maternity ward of the hospital. A suggestion that sugar should be made from apple juice was found to be impracticable as the process would have necessitated the use of more fuel – another scarce commodity – than the sugar would have been worth.

In times of emergency the rights of the individual must be subordinated to the needs of the community and it had become justifiable for the States to requisition private property if by so doing they could benefit the community as a whole. Obviously the first property to be requisitioned was that which had been left behind by those who had left the Island. The men employed by the Custodian of Unoccupied Dwellings removed from abandoned houses and pooled for general use foodstuffs, clothes, bedding, tools, everything worth taking that someone remaining in the Island might need.

A census was taken of all cultivable land, including private gardens, and an intensive food-production campaign was organised. Early in October power was given to the Glasshouse Utilisation Board to take over, on behalf of the States, gardens attached even to occupied houses if they were not being put to good use. Owners of arable land were told by the Farm Produce Board what crops to cultivate and were allowed to cultivate only such crops. Land not cultivated in a proper manner was taken over by the Board. Growers and gardeners were required to hand over to the Parish Organisers any seed that they did not require for their own immediate use and those who needed seed obtained it, if procurable, from the Farm Produce Board. The sale of fertilisers and manures, both organic and inorganic was also controlled. All cereal crops were requisitioned and farmers who needed help in harvesting them obtained it at the expense of the States.

It was found that there was an acute shortage of animal food. Owners of horses, cattle, pigs and poultry were therefore required to register their livestock and such food as was obtainable was allocated to them in proportion to their needs.

To ensure that no one should obtain more than his fair share farmers were ordered to allow the places where they stored their cattle-food to be inspected by men appointed by the Controlling Committee. Because the shortage of cattle-food led to a shortage of milk all bull calves (except such as were selected by the Herd Book Council to be kept for breeding purposes) were ordered to be slaughtered for food within a week of birth.

The slaughter of pigs on the other hand was not allowed except by special permission, both because it was necessary to conserve meat supplies – especially fats of which a shortage early in 1941 was anticipated – and because the Island's stock of salt was not sufficient to allow of any being used for curing bacon.

As early as a week after the German occupation glasshouse

owners who had retained the management of their own properties were asked to sow beans immediately in the place of the tomatoes they had destroyed and a large proportion of the greenhouses that had come under States management were also used for the cultivation of this form of pulse – the staple food of vegetarians. Instead of being picked while the pods were still green the beans were allowed to ripen and were then dried and were available for use in December and the months that followed, when, being rich in proteins, they afforded a very valuable substitute for other muscle-forming foods, such as meat, fish, eggs, and cheese.

The Controlling Committee did not disregard even such a comparatively unimportant food as honey; Mr E.C. Gould was appointed to take charge of all abandoned bee-hives, to market the honey and to pay the money obtained for it into the States Treasury.

To anyone who knew nothing about the subject it must have seemed obvious that one of our chief assets was an inexhaustible supply of fish from the sea that surrounded us. This was far from being the case. Locally caught fish formed only a very small proportion of our food supplies. Due partly to natural but principally to economic causes the local fishing industry had been steadily declining for a generation past, and the Island had had to depend for its main supplies on big fishing-ports such as Grimsby and Milford Haven. The natural cause of the decline was that fish had become scarcer in local waters – notably bream which caught in great quantities as late as 1914 had been found nowhere round our coasts since about 1925. The economic cause was the great increase of British steam-trawlers. Our rocky local waters are suitable only for line-fishing and a line fisherman, hauling fish out of the sea one at a time, cannot compete commercially with steam-trawlers that catch a ton or more of fish every four hours.

The activities of such fishermen as remained were, moreover, severely restricted by the German authorities. During the first few days of the German occupation no fisherman was allowed to take his boat from her moorings. On July 6th fishing boats on the East side of the Island were allowed to put to sea, but not before 7am, to fish within two miles of the shore, and while fishing were to keep close to escorting boats manned by Germans. Probably the official who drafted the order, knowing nothing of the subject, supposed that fish may be caught at any spot over which a fisherman drops his line. He did not know – or did not care – that none of the best fishing grounds were within the specified area. After a while restrictions were somewhat relaxed. Fishing was allowed in small rowing boats without German escort provided they kept within half a mile of the shore, and escorted fishing boats, including those from the West Coast, were allowed to fish anywhere within two miles of the shore. This greater freedom lasted until six men took a boat from Bordeaux Harbour and escaped in it to England. It was then ordered that all fishing boats from all round the Island were to be brought to the Town Harbour and might put to sea from there only. This order made it almost impossible for West Coast fishermen to follow their calling as to do so they had either to come and live near their boats in St Peter Port or walk anything up to ten miles a day to and from their work.

As some offset to the German restrictions the Royal Court on July 13th ordered the suspension of all local restrictions as to the times and seasons when fish might be caught and permitted the marketing of immature shell-fish. The suspension of these restrictions in so far as it permitted the taking of ormers of any size and at any time aroused a strong protest from fishermen. The ormer (Haliolis Tuberculaea) is an edible shell-fish found nowhere in British waters except in the Channel Islands. Ormers are found clinging to the undersides of stones near low-water mark. Half a dozen of them, if full grown, suffice to make a substantial meal. As ormer-gatherers must be prepared to wade thigh-deep no one takes them merely for sport during the winter months – from November to April inclusive – to which season ormer-fishing had hitherto been restricted. Fishermen represented that an exceptionally low spring tide was expected in September when the warmth of the water might tempt many amateur fishermen to go ormering with the probable result that large numbers of immature ormers – less than three inches in diameter – would be taken, leaving few to reach full growth in winter. This protest was very reasonable and a fortnight later the customary restrictions on ormer-fishing were reimposed.

As with other food problems private individuals offered advice to the general public through the medium of letters to the newspapers. One letter represented that the repulsive appearance of the dog-fish did not detract from its value as food. Possibly as a result of this letter dog-fish was offered for sale in increasing quantities until it was to be found on fish-market stalls as often as skate or conger. The writer of another letter said that he had eaten octopus in Italy and saw no reason why it should not be eaten in Guernsey. He did not go so far as to commend it as a delicacy and his directions as to how it should be prepared for the table were vague, but his letter called forth another from a correspondent who not only gave precise direction as to how it should be cooked but also declared it to be as great a delicacy as lobster. Octopus, however, did not appear on the market, possibly because the season during which it is caught is a short one or possibly because of its value as bait.

Fortunately mackerel and later in the summer garfish – better known as 'long-nose' or 'green-bone' – were plentiful, but when the season for these was over only coarse fish such as conger, skate and dogfish came on the market and that very irregularly and in small quantities.

Perhaps the greatest sufferers at first on the numerous occasions when it was impossible to buy fish were cat lovers. At such times elderly ladies might be seen painfully scrambling over the rocks at low tide striving with unsuitable tools in unpractised hands to detach limpets that they might take home, boil and mince for their fastidious pets. Happily for them fish-market stallholders gradually – but somewhat tardily – realised that limpets had become a marketable commodity and the time came when the limpets were almost always obtainable.

CHAPTER VII

SIEGE CONDITIONS, 1940: EXPEDIENTS AND ECONOMIES

It was discovered that the Island's stock of salt was so low that no more than a meagre ration of one ounce per week could be allowed to each person. With an unlimited supply of salt water all round us it was obvious that we ought to be able to obtain all the salt we needed; the problem was how to get it from the sea to the dinner table.

The Controlling Committee had let it be known that they were anxious to receive advice on any matter that concerned them and many people had advice – sometimes valuable advice – to give, but most of these preferred to get credit by imparting their advice in the form of letters to the newspapers. One correspondent triumphantly announced that he had solved the problem; he had evaporated a pint and a half of sea water by boiling it in a frying pan on a gas-jet and thus obtained an ounce of salt which he described as excellent. His letter produced an emphatic protest from the Economics Officer, Jurat the Rev John Leale, who said that as the Island's stock of gas-coal was very low the value of the salt obtained by this method was very much less than the value of the gas consumed in obtaining it. Owners of old-fashioned ovens built in kitchen walls – which retain heat for a long while after the kitchen fire is extinguished – were able to obtain salt from sea water without any additional cost in fuel; they put crocks full of sea water into their ovens after removing the Sunday joint. But this expedient – and the economising of the salt ration by boiling vegetables in sea water – was practicable only for such people as lived fairly close to a beach. For the majority of Islanders salt manufacture as a private enterprise was out of the question.

Fortunately Mr A. Best, who at one time had manufactured iodine on Lihou Island and had obtained salt as a by-product, was able to give practical advice, guided by which Mr S.H. Arnold and Mr S.J. Bragg established a plant on the Castle

Emplacement with which they manufactured salt in bulk. The Model Yacht Pond was emptied, cleaned and divided into sections by low concrete walls. In these sections sea water was evaporated and the resulting salt was swept up and given a final drying under the glass of cucumber frames erected for the purpose. Two kinds of salt were obtained; a fine salt suitable for the table and a coarse salt used in the slaughter-house for the tanning of hides. On the Upper Walk, near the Model Yacht Pond, scaffolding was erected and packed with sloe bushes on to which a windmill pumped sea water. The water dripped into a pan from which it was pumped over the brushwood again and again. The drying effect of sun and wind on the wet brushwood turned the sea water into brine suitable for pickling fish and for other purposes. Within five weeks three hundred gallons of brine and nearly eight thousand pounds weight of salt were produced.

Unfortunately the Castle Emplacement plant was of service only while the sun gave sufficient heat to evaporate the sea water. At the end of September the work there came to en end. The manufacture of salt, however, was continued by the Guernsey Railway Company, the plant of which was near enough to the beach to pump up sea water at high tide. The Company obtained heat for the evaporation of the sea water by bringing again into use its too-long-neglected refuse-destructor. This could not produce as much heat as it had done when it was formerly in use because the rubbish now sent to it was not as inflammable as it had been, thrifty housewives preferring to save wastepaper and rags instead of putting these into their dust-bins. Nevertheless it gave enough heat to produce salt at an average rate of five pounds an hour and had some to spare for the generation of a useful amount of electricity.

Before the German occupation – primarily in order to economise shipping – household coal had been rationed to householders at the rate of four hundredweight a month. A month after communication with England was cut off the ration was reduced to three hundredweight and was allowed only to householders who had less than ten hundredweight in stock.

Householders were required to report what stocks of coal they had in hand. This order placed some strain on the honesty of the more fortunate, as a week before it was made Jurat Leale had forecast a possibility that holders of large stocks of coal might be compelled to share with their less fortunate – or less provident – neighbours. Housewives were officially urged either to send their joints and stews to be cooked at the nearest bakery or to use hay-boxes, and unofficial advice was given by correspondents who wrote to the newspapers explaining how anthracite can be made to burn in open grates, how fire-bricks could be made by anyone who could obtain the necessary fire-clay and how waste-paper could be pulped to burn in the form of briquettes. People who thriftily pulped their waste-paper may have regretted it later when there was a shortage of waste-paper for the lighting of fires.

Coal was supplemented before winter set in by wood fuel. Very soon after the German occupation the Bailiff, acting under authority given him by the Defence Regulations, requisitioned all the trees in the Island. No one was allowed to fell trees except persons authorised by the Fuel Controller and he was empowered to fell any trees which in the opinion of his technical adviser were suitable for fuel.

Tree-felling began on July 25th but the number of men employed on it was restricted by the number of cross-cut saws, hammers and wedges available. Mr R.H. Johns, head of the Labour Department, appealed to the public to hand over any such tools they might possess but apparently the whole resources of the Island were insufficient. It was, however, found possible to import some tools from France and within two months the number of men employed in felling and cutting-up trees grew from seventeen to two hundred. At the end of September the distribution of logs began. The price was half-a-crown a hundredweight a week – if the coal-merchants could deliver them. A minor result of the general use of wood-fuel was that such stocks of bellows as shop-keepers possessed were soon exhausted.

Lumps of peat are often washed up on the Vazon beach by

winter gales but the few who knew where deposits above high-water mark were to be found did not reveal the secret until a lady found and passed on to the Controlling Committee a map of Guernsey on which forty years earlier a local scientist, Mr Collenette, had pencilled the position of an accessible peat deposit. Here, three feet below ground level, a seven-foot deep peat bed covering about fifteen vergees (nearly four acres) was found and exploited. The peat was not ready for use until the following year when depots at which it could be purchased were established. Though it was of very inferior quality the supply was exhausted in a few days.

Because paraffin, fuel-oil and electricity were all needed for pumping at the Waterworks the public were urged to use rainwater or well water as far as possible, instead of water laid on from the reservoirs, and the Economic Officer, Jurat Leale, appealed to people to limit themselves to two baths a week with a maximum depth of two inches in the bath, whereupon someone who had lived in semi-desert country wrote to the newspapers describing how the whole body can be efficiently washed with a basinful of water. Of those who followed his directions some may have been actuated by public spirit but more probably did so because the Gas Company, acting under orders from the Controlling Committee, had disconnected their gas-geysers. Few people cared to use more than a very moderate amount of bath water if it had to be carried laboriously from kitchen to bathroom.

Besides prohibiting the use of gas-geysers the Controlling Committee forbade the use of gas-fires in houses that had fireplaces adapted for the burning of solid fuel. To save fuel needed in generating electricity the public were urged to use electric irons as little as possible, to replace high-powered lamps with others of lower power, and not to make undue use of their radios. As another practical step towards economising electricity, neighbours were urged to share sitting-rooms after dark and householders who had accommodation to spare were asked to invite friends to share their houses. Some people whose homes were in the country moved into the houses of friends in or near town, but these were probably actuated less by public spirit than by the inconvenience of living far from town at a time when private cars could not be used and no bus services were available.

Our stock of paraffin was lower than that of any other essential commodity. Farmers, as food producers, had first claim on it for driving their tractors. The Water Board also needed it to drive the pumping engines. Housewives who depended on it for lighting and cooking had also a claim on it, but so scanty was the reserve stock that for a while their claim had to be disallowed. At worst the housewife suffered nothing worse than serious inconvenience for she could arrange with a neighbour to cook her food for her and, while summer lasted, she and her household could go to bed by daylight.

The fuel shortage was felt least by those who lived in old country cottages. In the days when the lack of decent roads made difficult the transport of coal from the harbours country people burned brushwood, furze, cowdung and dried seaweed under *trepieds* in the yards outside their houses. *Trepieds* came into use again until the German Authorities saw fit to forbid the burning of fires out of doors. The order was subsequently modified to allow outdoor-cooking between 11am and 7pm.

Because the Germans had commandeered all the Island's motor-buses and a large number of commercial vehicles, country-dwellers accustomed to visit town once or twice a week were obliged to use pedal-bicycles, to walk or to stay at home, and even such tradesmen as were allowed to keep their vehicles were allowed so meagre an allowance of petrol that they could deliver, and that with difficulty, only such goods as were too heavy or too bulky to be carried by hand. Licensed porters, deprived of their lorries, used hand carts instead. Cycles found in abandoned houses were sold by the Custodian of Unoccupied Houses to those whose need of them was greatest. Horse-drawn vans fitted with rows of seats extemporised with planks laid on packing-cases to some extent took the place of motor-buses and ran – or rather crawled – on market days between the town and the parishes of Torteval and the Vale.

Old fashioned horse-drawn vehicles – landaus, broughams and governess-cars – which for a generation past had lain idle in outhouses were seen on the roads again. In town childless housewives borrowed perambulators in which to carry home their parcels and many good Samaritans whose houses adjoined the steep roads leading up from the town placed their private garden seats on the public pavements outside their gates for the benefit of anyone who cared to use them – a great boon to elderly people whose breath was short and whose shopping bags were heavy.

The Germans suffered no inconvenience from lack of motor-transport. It was apparently beneath the dignity of a German officer to be seen in public using his legs, and the marching powers of the common soldiers must have deteriorated during their stay in the Island for they were brought in motor-coaches from their quarters into town when they visited it either on duty or for recreation. Very often a large motor-bus might be seen with one solitary German private as passenger – a galling sight to a householder who had not been able to get his coal ration because of his coal-merchant's shortage of petrol!

As a result of the transport problem it was decided that fifteen members of the States should suffice to form a quorum. The Island's three public laundries were amalgamated and depots were established to which – and from – laundry parcels had to be carried by their owners. Depots for the sale of bread were also established from which customers had to fetch their bread instead of having it delivered, an arrangement which compelled people to get their bread from the nearest depot instead of from the baker of their choice.

Presumably with the idea of helping in the direction of flour economy the German Authorities organised a demonstration by a German baker of the making of rye-bread. It was attended by a number of master-bakers but with no result sufficiently marked to be apparent to the general public. Whether they profited by the German baker's instructions or not the bread they continued to give us, though certainly different from what we had been accustomed to in peace-time, was as good as could reasonably be expected. Sometimes it was gritty with sharp particles of husk but it was certainly very much better than the sour glutinous stuff that we had to eat in the latter part of the war of 1914-18. On the whole it was good, sometimes in fact so good that many people preferred it to the whiter bread such as was commonly eaten in normal times. Bakers were ordered to economise fuel by baking only three times a week and to economise flour by requesting customers when obtaining their bread to declare how much they would require at the next baking. By this means the baker knew exactly how much flour to use and had no fear that bread would be left on his hands and wasted.

Our meat-ration was reduced from two to one shillingsworth a week for each person. Customers had no choice as to the kind of meat or joint they received and the quality varied greatly: sometimes it was excellent, sometimes so tough as to be fit only for soup. Offals – to use a word that was good respectable English until Victorian fastidiousness denied its use to all but butchers – such as kidneys, liver, ox-tail, etc, and sausages containing less than 50 per cent meat were not rationed but were difficult to get as the supply was very small. When the meat-ration was first reduced it was fairly easy to supplement it with poultry at the controlled price of 1s. 7d. a pound for roasting, and 1s. 3d. for boiling fowls. This was because the scarcity of poultry food compelled poultry-keepers to kill and place in cold storage a large number of their birds. When this supply was exhausted it was still possible to buy poultry of an inferior quality but even this supply failed before winter set in.

The food value of wild rabbits was not overlooked by the Controlling Committee. They could not be shot for all shotguns had been confiscated, but it was thought that they might be netted and as early as July 10th the Agricultural Officer published a request to all owners of ferrets to look after them well as they would be needed in the winter. Yet when winter came no wild rabbits came into the market. This was not due to any scarcity of rabbits for many owners of vegetable gardens complained of the serious damage that rabbits were doing to them. It was partly due to an order issued by the German Chief of Military Administration in France that although German troops might hunt anywhere without paying any indemnity to landowners, no others might hunt except landowners and these only with the Commandant's permission; but principally it was due to the fact that the Germans, in their efforts to make Guernsey an impregnable fortress, had planted land mines all along the cliffs where wild rabbits were to be found. Food was not so scarce as to make rabbits worth catching at the risk of death from concealed dynamite. The islands of Herm, Jethou and Brecqhou – on which there were no land mines – were overrun with rabbits and the German Authorities promised that a certain number of men from each Guernsey parish would be allowed to visit each of these islands in turn and catch rabbits for sale on the Guernsey market. The promise, however, did not materialise further than the granting of a permit to a poulterer to land the rabbits when they arrived.

Some of the suggestions offered to the Controlling Committee were adopted : others did not stand the test of practical experiment. It was suggested, for example, that oats and barley should be sown in greenhouses in August to afford poultry food for the winter. It was not hoped that the seed would ripen but that the poultry would eat it green after it had formed. It was contended that fowls kept in a greenhouse, besides feeding themselves on the unripe oats and barley, would be very useful in manuring the ground and destroying insect pests. This suggestion proved to be not as valuable as it seemed because of the great range of temperature in the greenhouses; the sharp decline from midday heat to midnight cold affected the fowls' health.

Another attractive suggestion was that electric current could be generated by taking dynamos from unused motor-cars and connecting them with windmills. The suggestion was discussed at length in the newspapers by several electrical engineers and eventually it was announced that experiments were being made but it is to be supposed that they did not prove successful as the general public heard no more of the matter.

A proposal that for the sake of economy water used for

boiling potatoes, instead of being thrown away, should be saved and used several times for the same purpose met with no response either from the Controlling Committee or apparently from the general public!

CHAPTER VIII

SIEGE CONDITIONS, 1940:
NO REAL HARDSHIP YET

The Controlling Committee's most acute anxieties were allayed when it was found possible to trade with France.

On August 14th with the consent of the German Authorities the Committee's Agricultural Officer, Mr R.O. Falla, left the Island for Granville on a mission to buy and send to Guernsey such stocks as he could get of what we most needed and, because seeds to enable us to grow more food were needed more than anything else, he was accompanied by a seed expert, Mr W.G. Hubert. By instruction of the Field Commandant a motor-car was placed at Mr Falla's disposal when he reached Granville and a German official was detailed to accompany him on his tour through Northern France and give him what help he needed. On September 3rd Mr Hubert returned to Guernsey with the welcome news that he had bought sixty tons of seeds of various kinds, and that Mr Falla hoped soon to send flour, cattle-fodder and chemicals. Supplies of meat, flour, coal, coke and fertilisers soon began to arrive in the Island at fairly regular intervals – supplies never large enough to satisfy our normal requirements but sufficient to avert distress.

Besides these commodities Mr Falla occasionally sent small consignments of goods less vitally necessary but nevertheless urgently needed. A supply of horse-shoe nails arrived opportunely at a time when, owing to the increased use of horses for transport purposes, there were scarcely any left in the Island. With them came some cross-cut saws which made it possible to increase the number of men engaged in felling trees for fuel. Other goods sent included agricultural implements, medical supplies, paraffin, sugar, leather – badly needed for boot-repairs – oil cakes, onions and tinned milk – very useful after fresh milk was rationed and French butter – sold and used as cooking fat. One small consignment of lemons raised hopes – that did not materialise – of more to come.

These imports were paid for to a certain extent with exports of local produce, principally grapes but also tomatoes and green beans grown under glass. Other exports of a kind that could not be officially included in trade returns were cameras, watches, civilian clothing, dress material, linen and especially – until local stocks ran out – coffee – all eagerly bought from local shops by German soldiers, who paid in paper money which, though worthless on the world's money markets, was worth its nominal value in France and so served our purpose.

For a short while before and after the German occupation began the Island was embarrassingly rich in milk because although some cows had been killed by their owners at the time of the panic, the number thus lost had been more than made up by others salvaged from Alderney. Early in July the Controlling Committee urged the public to drink more milk and late in August it was announced that the States Dairy was experimenting in cheese-making. The superabundance of milk did not, unfortunately, last long enough for the experiment to have a fair trial but in due course enough Guernsey-made cheese to give one ration a head was released by the Food Control Committee. Just before the occupation the States Dairy had advertised that it wished to find four thousand new customers for butter, but the arrival of the Germans relieved them of any anxiety in this respect, for they consumed it in large quantities, besides, in all probability, posting it to their homes in Germany.

Those who had expected that milk would continue to be abundant had not taken into account the Island's acute shortage of cattle-food. By the end of September the yield had decreased so gravely that milk had to be rationed. Half a pint of whole milk and the same quantity of separated milk was allowed to children under fourteen, pregnant and nursing mothers and invalids; all others had to be content with separated milk only and no more than a daily half pint at that. An exception was made in favour of cow-owners who were allowed to retain half a pint a head of whole milk for themselves, members of their families and resident employees; presumably the Controlling Committee did not wish to put an undue strain on the honesty of those who, having the first handling of the milk could, had they wished, have ignored the milk-rationing order almost with impunity. At first the quality of the separated milk was very inferior, but after a while it markedly improved. No explanation was given but it was hinted by those who professed inside knowledge that the States Dairy had found that it had control of more cream than had been anticipated and had decided to improve the quality of the milk rather than make more butter which the Germans would probably appropriate.

The shortage of poultry-food was so acute that many birds had to be killed, with the result that eggs soon became difficult to obtain. The current price in the first week of the occupation was 2s. 9d. a dozen but a week later the Controlling Committee, presumably to prevent profiteering, fixed the maximum price of 1s. 9d. a dozen. At that price, owing to difficulties of transport, none came on the market, poultry-keepers preferring to preserve their eggs. The maximum price was therefore raised to 2s. 6d. a dozen, later to 3s. and eventually to 3s. 6d. a dozen. Even at this price they were difficult to obtain and very soon the address of a poultry-farmer who was willing to sell eggs to those prepared to call for them at his farm became a valuable secret to be imparted only to intimate friends.

Bacon, though rationed at only three and a half ounces per head per week, was exhausted before the end of July.

A week after the occupation began the weekly sugar ration was reduced from eight ounces to six ounces and householders were allowed their choice of tea, coffee or cocoa: the tea ration was reduced in August from three ounces to two and at the end of September to one and a half ounces; the alternative coffee ration from four to three ounces and the alternative cocoa ration from two to one and a half ounces. The weekly ration of salt was increased from one to two ounces a head, when imported stocks reached the Island. German soldiers were not allowed to buy rationed foodstuffs except under official military requisition but, judging by the large quantities of coffee they bought, presumably to send to friends in Germany, it seemed that they found little difficulty in wangling official requisitions, and still less in altering the figures on these documents. Butter or margarine – four ounces – and cooking fat – two ounces, sugar, tea, coffee, cocoa, and salt were the only groceries that were rationed, but there was a serious shortage – only temporarily relieved by stocks salvaged from abandoned houses – of practically every commodity in which grocers deal. To ensure a fair distribution of unrationed groceries the Controlling Committee, on August 10th, enacted that purchasers must give their retailers a certificate to the effect that they did not possess more than one month's normal supply of the commodity purchased, and that retailers who did not feel satisfied as to the truth of the certificates offered were to report to the Essential Commodities Committee, who might order an examination of the prospective purchaser's store cupboards. This cumbrous and very irritating order was still-born. Retailers ignored the letter but obeyed the spirit of it by refusing to serve any but their regular customers, by restricting these to what they regarded as a reasonable week's supply of any commodity and by requiring their customers to buy their week's supply in one purchase. This unauthorised arrangement worked very well.

Shopping lists dwindled week by week. Weekly purchases of cheese, while local stocks lasted, were restricted to two ounces for each member of a family. Then for a while cheese was unobtainable. Later supplies of cheese, Port Salut and Camembert arrived from France at irregular intervals. Grocers continued to restrict the sale of the Port Salut, because it would keep, and of the Camembert also except when, as sometimes happened, the latter had reached the stage of over-ripeness at which it reeked of ammonia. At that stage the demand for it was small and those who knew that the fault could be remedied by cooking the cheese were allowed to purchase as much as they liked.

The sale of invalid foods was forbidden unless authorised by medical certificate. The sale of soap was restricted to an allowance of four ounces for each person per month and housekeepers were officially urged to economise by having clothes washed at public laundries. Proprietary brands of tooth-paste and shaving-soap were replaced, by the enterprise of local chemists with locally manufactured equivalents, when the necessary ingredients were obtainable, and sold in cartons originally intended for ice-cream, of which the local stocks seemed to be inexhaustible.

Very soon after the German occupation began only one bottle of wine or six bottles of beer were allowed to be sold at one time. By the end of the year wine was still obtainable, but stocks of bottled beer were exhausted by the end of September. The brewers announced that they hoped to be able to continue the supply of draught beer but that its quality would deteriorate. Their hope was fulfilled, possibly because the quality deteriorated so much that it ceased to attract any but the most confirmed beer-drinkers.

The purchase of more than five cigars or fifty cigarettes at anyone purchase was forbidden and tobacconists were officially urged to refuse to sell to those whom they suspected of hoarding. The edict was quite unworkable. As there were no less than thirteen tobacconists in St Peter Port alone there was nothing to prevent a selfish man buying from them all and thus obtaining over six hundred cigarettes a day, and tobacconists, so far from refusing to sell to customers whom they suspected of hoarding, actually advised them to buy largely and hoard on the reasonable ground that the Germans were buying cigarettes in such large quantities that stocks were rapidly diminishing. Smokers who followed this advice had reason to congratulate themselves when early in November tobacco was rationed by order of the German Commandant. The weekly allowance was two ounces of pipe tobacco and either twenty cigarettes or five cigars and this to men only; women received no tobacco-ration cards. The Germans were also rationed but on a more lavish scale. They were allowed to buy as many cigarettes or cigars and half as much pipe tobacco every day as Islanders were allowed in a week; furthermore, it was decided that in the event of scarcity Germans were to have preference over Guernseymen.

Chocolate was also a commodity that the Germans bought in large quantities. Its value as a long-keeping concentrated food seems to have escaped the attention of the Controlling Committee. Many people bought it to store but most of these conscientiously restricted their purchases to four ounces or thereabouts a week until it became known that Germans were buying it in quantities of two or three pounds at a time. At once Islanders followed the example of the Germans but a few days later all stocks of chocolate remaining in the shops were requisitioned by the German authorities for sale in soldiers' canteens, despite a strong protest from the Essential Commodities Committee, which dared to declare that it was undignified to rob children to please grown men.

As it behoved everyone to make his clothes last as long as possible the Information Officer on July 12th published excellent and detailed advice on the care of boots and shoes and soon afterwards, with a view to their repair when necessary, the public were officially urged to save old motor-car and motor-cycle tyres for the purpose. Before the end of July clothing was added to the list of rationed commodities.

The shortage of everything normally-purchasable prompted a number of suggestions from the general public such as that rhubarb leaves might be used to remove stains from the hands and that dried tea-leaves might be smoked instead of tobacco but in those early days of comparative luxury the only advice at all widely adopted was that a substitute for coffee could be obtained by roasting parsnips and grinding them into powder. Of those who made the experiment some said that 'parfee' (the name coined for parsnip-coffee) was delicious; others condemned it as positively nasty. Before the German occupation was over we had learned to use – but not necessarily to like – many kinds of substitutes.

The Essential Commodities Committee celebrated the Christmas festival by allowing everyone to have eighteenpence worth of meat instead of a shillingsworth, six ounces of butter instead of four, and four ounces instead of two of cooking-fat. This concession together with the release of what was left in the Island's stock of currants and raisins made the traditional Christmas dinner possible and a consignment of oranges from France was probably just large enough to allow of one being put into the Christmas stocking of every child remaining in the

Island.

By the end of the year some desirable but not vitally necessary articles such as mustard, pepper, aspirin, bottle-corks, mothicide, mouse-traps, hair-pins and knitting needles, had become difficult or impossible to obtain. (Some of these articles were imported at a later date; others we had to do without.) But, thanks to the foresight of the Essential Commodities Committee, the energy of its buyers in France and the care taken by at least the greater part of the general public to avoid waste, no one had as yet suffered any real hardship, and prospects for the next few months seemed considerably brighter than anyone had at first dared to hope.

CHAPTER IX

NARRATIVE, 1940

From the entirely selfish viewpoint of people interested in their own safety and comfort we in Guernsey were, during the German occupation, more fortunate than many people in Great Britain. We suffered more hardship from shortage of food, fuel and other essential commodities, but our lives were practically as safe as if no war were in progress, because, except for the very slight danger of being hit by falling German anti-aircraft shell when British planes passed overhead, we enjoyed complete immunity from air raids. The fact that Germans had established themselves in our Island as conquerors gave most of us, of course, a feeling of irritation and humiliation, but our thoughts on that score were overlaid by the very difficult problems created by severance of communication from England, by the obligation to provide house accommodation for the Germans and by the difficulty of protecting our property from individual German thieves. The government of the German authorities was on the whole mild, the behaviour of the German officials we were obliged to come into contact with was in most cases civil, and so long as we did not too flagrantly disobey a large number of official orders we were free to live our lives almost as we chose. Football and cricket matches were resumed. Amateur dramatists were allowed to give public performances so long as they were careful to stage nothing that might hurt the Germans' very touchy feelings. Organisers of concerts had to submit their proposed programmes to the German authorities but permission to perform was always given provided that the programmes did not include music by Mendelssohn or any other Jewish composer. We lived under government by decree and almost the only grievance we had against the decrees was that many of them were extraordinarily silly. On the whole we soon got accustomed to regard the Germans in our midst as nothing much worse than unpleasant blots on the landscape.

From time to time the monotony of our lives was relieved

and our hearts were cheered by rumours of some hostile act performed by the British against the Germans among us. No two accounts of any of these acts ever exactly coincided because, though much could be learned by inference, the German authorities scarcely ever permitted any reference to them to be published in the local newspapers. What the Guernsey public knew of them was based mainly on rumour, and any attempt to arrive at the exact truth by collating and sifting the rumours was as unsatisfactory as would be the reading of a detective novel from which some pages – especially pages revealing the most important clues – were missing. Yet if no mention was made in these pages of events, the truth of which it was impossible entirely to substantiate, this attempt to give a true, unbiased history of the German occupation of Guernsey would be even more misleading than it would be if every rumour were to be recorded and presented as unchallengeable fact; for it is beyond doubt that a great part of many of the rumours proved to be true in essence though probably inaccurate in detail. The reader must judge for himself how much of each account of British hostilities against the German forces is the product of the imagination of sensation mongers and how much is true.

Take for example a rumour that spread through the Island as early as July 15th, just a fortnight after the arrival of the Germans. It was said that a party of British marines had landed – some said at L'Ancresse, others said at St Martin's Point – and had cut the submarine telegraph cable. Scorn was thrown on the rumour by people who, having some knowledge of telegraphic apparatus, contended that the cutting of a submarine cable, to be effective, must be done some distance out to sea, as if cut on land it could be easily repaired. Instead of wilting, however, the rumour became more detailed. It was said that, presumably to delay interference while they were at work, the landing party had built a barricade of stones across the road some distance to the west of Doyle Column, that a German patrol had discovered the obstruction early in the morning, had accused the occupant of the nearest house of having built it and had compelled him to remove it; and, further, that our police, having had orders to investigate the matter, found a clip of Bren-gun ammunition lying on the ground close to where the barricade had been. More rumours on the same subject were current. It was said that a man who lived on the seaward side of Doyle Monument had been awakened very early in the morning by a small party of British soldiers who, after asking him whether there were any Germans in the neighbourhood, cut all telephone wires in the vicinity; and that later in the morning of that day, when the falling of the tide had uncovered the sands at Petit Port, machine-guns and British military uniforms had been found lying on them.

The obvious inference to be drawn from all these rumours was that a British armed party had landed at Petit Port at about the time of highwater – which on that particular morning was at 2.23am; Greenwich time, one hour and a half before sunrise – and that when it left it had to leave in such a hurry that some members of the party had abandoned their weapons, stripped off their clothes and swum out to whatever vessel was waiting to take them away. All doubt that a landing had actually been effected seemed to be dissipated by a rumour that several of the Island's leading officials had been strictly cross-examined by the German authorities and had had some difficulty in satisfying them that they had had no communication with any invaders.

It was next rumoured that two of the British party who could not swim had been left behind and had surrendered; that they had been taken by car under escort to the German headquarters at the Royal Hotel; that the Guernseyman who drove the car had had an opportunity of talking to them; and that they had told him that a party had come from England in a motor patrol launch and had landed in a collapsible rubber boat, but that during re-embarkation the rubber boat had been torn on a jagged submerged rock and had sunk and its occupants, being heavily loaded with bombs, had narrowly escaped drowning. After that rumour got about, only the most obstinate sceptics continued to disbelieve that a British armed party had landed on the morning of July 15th and departed a few hours later. Unfortunately they seemed to have left behind them no evidence as to the object of the landing or the extent to which it had been successful. For lack of this one feared that they had not achieved their object. When the Island was liberated it was learned that the raiding party had been commanded by Captain Cantan, formerly of the Royal Guernsey Light Infantry. One objective was to capture Germans presumed to be in Jerbourg Baracks which, however, proved to be empty.

Throughout the period of their occupation of the Island the German authorities kept us as far as they could in ignorance of what they were doing. They did not, for example, until long afterwards, let us know in what way our lives would be endangered if we ventured into forbidden areas on the South Coast, but when the prohibited area was extended to a point north of Fermain Bay and fishermen were warned that when mooring their boats there and at Bec du Nez they must not use the landing steps it was reasonable to guess that land-mines had been buried in various places. This proved to be the case. One day early in September residents of the Village de Putron heard a loud explosion and soon afterwards saw a German officer and a woman, both bleeding profusely, return to a car they had left above Le Becque Battery. In October a land-mine was exploded between Fermain and Jerbourg, killing three Germans and wounding one. A Guernseyman who was on the cliff above at the time said that the uninjured members of the party were slow in going to the assistance of the wounded man because after each step they took they paused and consulted a paper, presumably a plan showing the exact whereabouts of the land-mines.

Not until October, 1941, did the German authorities officially announce that mines had been laid in the prohibited areas. On the 21st of that month the local newspapers published new regulations made necessary by the 'heavy mining' of the Island. The landing of any 'watercraft' (including fishing vessels of all kinds) except at the harbours of St Peter Port and St Sampson's was forbidden. All cliffs, and all beaches except the bathing places at La Vallette were put out of bounds. All areas proclaimed by notice boards as mined areas were ordered to be evacuated and the cultivation of the land within such areas was forbidden. No dogs were to be allowed out of doors except on leash.

The prohibition of access to beaches was a serious matter for it made impossible the collection of limpets, which by this time supplemented the meagre food-ration of many people, and, which was much more important, it prevented the gathering of seaweed badly needed now that it was difficult to import artificial manure. It became obvious, however, that by no means all the prohibited areas were dangerous to enter, for permission was given from time to time to gather seaweed from some of the principal beaches such as Belgrave Bay, Grand Havre, Cobo and Vazon, and some owners of land in the prohibited areas were given permits entitling them to continue the cultivation of their fields. Only three Guernseymen were killed by land-mine explosions, one at Chouet Peninsula, one at Grandes Rocques and one at Pezeries. How many Germans fell victims to German land-mines it is impossible to say, but it is certain that there were considerably more than three.

Soon after the visit of the British reconnaissance party on July 15th it began to be whispered, by people who would have been better advised to keep their mouths shut, that British spies were on the Island. It was said that a woman living at Icart hid food every evening in a gorse-bush and found next morning that it had been taken. A more definite rumour and one that should certainly not have been circulated was that two Guemseymen known to be in the British army – Lieutenants Mulholland and Martel – had been seen in civilian clothes cycling on a main road. Later it is said that these two officers had surrendered voluntarily to the German authorities. Soon afterwards it was learned that Mulholland's mother, Mrs Michael, and Martel's sister, Mrs Le Masurier, had been arrested and taken to France on a charge of having harboured these two officers. This was followed by an official proclamation exhibited in shop windows to the effect that two British officers had landed in the Island for the purpose of reconnoitring, that they had stayed with their relatives 'without the German authorities having been notified', that the relatives were Mrs Ada Le Masurier (the proclamation had 'Adale Masurier, née Martel') and Mrs Dorothy Michael, née Moorhouse, and that 'in order to stop any support by the civilian population of further English reconnaissance attempts on the occupied British Channel Islands, orders were issued by the competent Chief Command that both women must be transferred to a place situated on the mainland of France at least 15 km. away from the coast, and that there they must report daily to the Feldkommandantur'. A retired British army officer of high rank who knew that Mulholland and Martel were in the Island was at the time of their arrest engaged in trying to arrange for their escape back to England in a fishing-boat. They had been put ashore during the first fortnight of the German occupation and were to have returned to England with the reconnaissance party that landed at Petit Port on July 15th, but somehow had the misfortune to fail to make contact with it. When arrested they had been in the Island about three weeks. They were imprisoned in Castle Cornet for one night, then taken by aeroplane to France, where they were treated as ordinary prisoners of war. Unfortunately they surrendered just too soon. During the night following the day on which they surrendered a Guernseyman in the British Army, Sergeant Ferbrache, was landed in the Island, went to Mrs Michael's house and said that the boat that had brought him was waiting to take Mulholland and Martel away.

On being told he was too late he went away and as nothing further was heard of him it was confidently supposed that he at any rate got away safely.

It must be admitted that the arrest and deportation of Mrs Michael and Mrs Le Masurier was justified by the Laws of War and indeed that they were very leniently treated. Mrs Michael's husband was allowed to join her in France soon after she had been taken there, and both women were allowed to return to Guernsey in January, 1941.

In the supplementary orders issued on 2nd July, 1940, it was promised that 'the Civil Government and Courts of the Island will continue to function as heretofore, save that all Laws, Ordinances, Regulations and Orders will be submitted to the German Commandant before being enacted'. The Commandant did not, however, deny himself the pleasure of appearing in public as the Governor of the Island. Sometimes he attended meetings of the States to which he had had himself summoned in the traditional manner and at which he sat in the Lieutenant-Governor's customary seat. This must have been somewhat galling to most members of the States but it probably gave him a delicious sense of importance. It soon seemed, however, that the German authorities considered that when any case was brought into our courts in which German interests were concerned the scales of justice should be weighed in their favour. This idea was suggested by a case the unusual features of which should give it a prominent place in the history of Guernsey jurisprudence – the trial of a man for an offence that was not illegal at the time that his offence was alleged to have been committed.

On July 31st, within a month of the beginning of the German occupation, at eleven o'clock in the morning the Royal Court passed an Ordinance making it an offence to utter any words inimical to the German military authorities or soldiers which would cause a breach or mischief between the people of Guernsey and the German authorities in occupation. The maximum penalty for such an offence – either twelve months' imprisonment or a £500 fine or both imprisonment and fine – was harsh, but it was certainly advisable that some such order should be made. A curious feature of the case was that it was obviously rushed through the Royal Court at the instigation of the German authorities to give power to the Police Magistrate to punish an offence of the kind alleged to have been already committed. Normally the Police Court does not sit in the afternoon, but at 3pm on the same day – less than four hours after the passing of the Ordinance – the Acting Magistrate tried the late Mr Collins, manager of Messrs Le Riche Ltd, on the charge that on July 29th (two days before the Ordinance was passed) he 'uttered speech likely to bring about a deterioration in the relations between the German forces in the Island of Guernsey and the civil population of that Island'.

Evidence was given that a German had come into Le Riche's shop and had lodged a complaint as to the non-delivery of some goods, that an assistant who could speak some German left the work he should have been doing and offered his services as interpreter, and that later the accused, Mr Collins, had privately told that assistant to confine himself to his regular duties, at the same time pointing out that the office of States Interpreter, who could be summoned at any time when his services were needed, was only a few yards away. The accused's specific offence, according to His Majesty's Comptroller, who prosecuted, was that he had told the interfering assistant that in future he was not to talk German to soldiers who came into the shop. Mr Collins denied the allegation. He said that the assistant concerned had formed the habit of leaving his proper duties in order to stand beside any other assistant who happened to be serving a German customer, and that he had, therefore, told him not to waste time but to carry on with his own duties. Six witnesses were called for the defence and only one – the assistant who had been snubbed – for the prosecution. His Majesty's Comptroller agreed that the statements of the shop assistant, who was the one witness for the prosecution were confused and uncorroborated and the Acting-Magistrate very properly dismissed the case as not proved.

A curious feature of the case was that the name of the shop-assistant, on whose evidence the prosecution solely relied, was not mentioned in the reports of the case that the newspapers published. No explanation of this omission was given but it is reasonable to suppose that the German authorities gave instructions that it should be omitted. If by so doing they wished to save the man from the odium among Guernseymen that he had earned, they entirely failed to do so. Within a few hours his name became known to the whole Island.

Another curious feature of the case was that the newspaper reports of it did not state on whose instructions His Majesty's Comptroller had prosecuted. Apparently the German authorities did not wish their connection with the affair to be made public, but that they had instigated it was, of course, quite obvious to anyone who took the trouble to think. That the German authorities were dissatisfied with the Police Magistrate's decision is clear from the fact that they subsequently conducted all cases of the kind themselves in a way that violated fundamental British ideas of justice. Their trials of Guernseymen against German authority or against individual Germans were conducted in secret, sometimes without allowing the accused to be present at his own trial or giving him an opportunity for self-defence.

Once and once only did a German in his private capacity sue in a Guernsey court. Then a soldier brought an action against a firm of jewellers for an overcharge and won his case.

Among the orders first issued by the German Commandant was one that all British soldiers, sailors and airmen must report themselves. Forty-two officers and men, who had been in the Island on leave when the Germans came, obeyed the order and were shipped off to France on August 1st. In the meanwhile they were imprisoned in Castle Cornet. They were treated with consideration. They were allowed to fish from the breakwater and to bathe under escort, and sometimes they were marched up to the Fort Field where they played football against their German guards. They were allowed to receive visitors and twice a week they could obtain permission to go into town where their dress – knee-high top boots, blue coats and flannel trousers – advertised them as prisoners. On one occasion one of them, 2nd Lieutenant McLeod, was allowed out all day on parole to play in a cricket match. As the steamer that took them away left the harbour they sang 'There'll always be an England' and 'Auld Lang Syne'. At the last moment before the ship left one soldier, Private Goupillot, was released and allowed to go to his own home on the ground that he was unfit for further military service. He had been badly shell-shocked in Flanders, had been in hospital in England, and had returned to the Island on sick-leave late in June. While employed in the cook-house at Castle Cornet he had been distressed to see a Union Jack in German possession. He contrived to steal it, together with some documents that he thought might be of value to the British on the day of departure, and marched out of the Castle with them concealed under his clothes – a creditably courageous act on the part of a nerve-shattered man. When the Island was liberated he handed them to the officer in command of the first British troops to land in the Island.

On August 9th a single plane made a tip-and-run raid on the

airport at noon and five hours later a series of attacks was made by a number of planes. According to BBC broadcasts the single attack was made by a medium bomber which saw between forty and fifty German aircraft on the ground. Of these it wrecked one troop-carrying plane besides spraying anti-aircraft batteries with machine-gun fire. The later attacks were made by a Coastal Command patrol. By the time it arrived unfortunately the undamaged planes had fled but the hangars and a petrol dump were set on fire.

The fire-brigade was summoned but, not being zealous to save enemy war material, they responded with less than their usual alacrity. Firemen who arrived at the fire-station at the run were allowed ample time in which to regain their breath before a start for the airport was made. On the way there the driver of the fire-engine drove at a cautious pace and when he saw that the British planes were returning halted under cover of some trees until they had gone. The hangars were well alight before the fire-engine reached them. By that time the British planes were returning and the firemen ran for cover, leaving the German soldiers to make what use they could of the fire-engine. Had they not done so they would almost certainly have suffered for the fire-escape lorry was badly damaged by bomb-splinters. Later on the same evening a German plane crashed in a lane near the airport.

Our newspapers did not venture to make any direct reference either to the raids or to the crashing of the plane but *The Star* published advice from the Chief Air Raid Precautions Organiser that in the event of an air attack all persons within sight or hearing should take cover and the *Evening Press* published the following letter from the President of the Controlling Committee:-

> Sir,
>
> It appears that a number of people went to the aerodrome last evening on a sight-seeing expedition and it occurs to me that this may be repeated, perhaps on a larger scale, to-morrow. Sight-seeing in the vicinity of an aerodrome is a pastime against which I

advise most strongly. So, sightseers, please keep away from it.

Yours faithfully,
A. J. SHERWILL.

It was the policy of the German authorities to keep us as far as possible in ignorance of any damage done to Germans by British action, but on this occasion, probably because the BBC had broadcast an account of the raid, the German Commandant published the following official statement on August 12th:-

> Contrary to English reports of Saturday evening, the airport at La Villiaze is not extensively damaged. Only one German soldier was killed and one wounded on Friday by the British bombardment and no airplanes were destroyed. On the same evening four other soldiers were killed and three wounded by a German airplane which was obliged to make a forced landing on the airport. The damage to property was confined to a few barrels of petrol; and a little wooden hut was burnt.

Throughout the Occupation there was always a wide discrepancy between the news broadcast by the BBC and the news given to our newspapers by the German authorities. It is interesting to compare the Commandant's statement with statements made by reputable islanders who were in position to speak with authority.

According to the Commandant the material damage was confined to a few barrels of petrol and a little wooden hut, but Mr Oliver, the Fire Brigade Chief, told curious enquirers that a line of barrels, each containing five gallons of petrol, was destroyed, that three planes in a hangar were damaged and that the hangar that was set on fire was still burning on the morning after the raid. According to the Commandant only four Germans in all were wounded but it was noticed that ambulances made repeated journeys between the airport and the Victoria Hospital, which the Germans had taken for their own use. Moreover, that hospital's German doctor, who asked the States Medical Officer for anti-tetanus serum, seemed dissatisfied when he was given sufficient for the inoculation of forty wounded but said that he would make it suffice. According to the Commandant only four Germans in all were killed, yet the Dean of Guernsey was called upon to read the burial service over five coffins and Canon Hickey buried several others with Roman Catholic rites. Moreover Guernseymen working at the airport stated that some uncoffined corpses were taken away by plane and that others were buried at the airport without either coffins or funeral rites. Eventually it became known that twenty-seven Germans were killed and seventeen wounded by this raid.

On several subsequent occasions when any considerable number of Germans were killed by British air raids soldiers of the rank and file were hurriedly buried without ceremony in unconsecrated ground. This gave rise to a suggestion that the German authorities were endeavouring to keep Heaven socially select by reserving consecrated ground for officers only. If that suggestion be libellous the fault lies with the Germans for endeavouring to keep secret matters in which Islanders had a perfectly reasonable curiosity.

One result of the raid was that services ceased to be held at the Forest Church and other places of worship in the neighbourhood of the airport. Banns of marriage which should have been read at the Forest Church were read instead at the church of St Pierre-du-Bois.

Everyone in the Island must have wished that our relations and friends in England could know that the treatment that we were receiving from the Germans was better than reports of German brutality in Poland might have led them to suppose. Apparently the German authorities shared that wish, for they asked Mr A.J. Sherwill to make a gramophone record of an address to evacuated Islanders which they promised should be broadcast from a German wireless transmitting station. It began:-

This is His Britannic Majesty's Procureur in Guernsey, Channel Islands, speaking to the people of the United Kingdom, and in particular to those who left Guernsey and Alderney during the evacuation which preceded the German occupation.

I imagine that many of you must be greatly worried as to how we are getting on. Well, let me tell you. Some will fear, I imagine, that I am making this record with a revolver pointed at my head and speaking from a type-script thrust into my hand by a German officer. The actual case is very different.

Continuing, Mr Sherwill said that the Bailiff and all other Island officials were being treated 'with every consideration and with the greatest courtesy' by the German military authorities, that the Island Government was functioning, and that churches, chapels, banks, shops and places of entertainment were open as usual. He referred to the innumerable problems that had resulted from the sudden and entire severance of communications with the United Kingdom, spoke of the establishment of the Controlling Committee and instanced as an indication of the success of their efforts the fact that there was little unemployment in the Island. Continuing he said:-

The conduct of the German troops is exemplary. We have been in German occupation for four and a half weeks, and I am proud of the way my fellow islanders have behaved, and grateful for the correct and kindly attitude towards them by the German soldiers. We have always been and we remain intensely loyal subjects of His Majesty, and this has been made clear to, and is respected by, the German Commandant and his staff. On that staff is an officer speaking perfect English – a man of wide experience, with whom I am in daily contact. To him I express my grateful thanks for his courtesy and patience.

The address ended on a personal note. Mr Sherwill sent a message of 'love and good wishes' to all Guernsey schoolchildren, wished 'God speed' to all men of military age, who had left the Island to join His Majesty's forces and sent 'fondest love' to his own children whom he named by their Christian names. Finally he asked the British Broadcasting Company to transmit the message and the daily papers to publish it.

A few people resented Mr Sherwill's taking advantage of his opportunity to address his own children while other people could send no loving message to theirs. These critics did not realise that his mention of his children by name had its use as tending to prove that his address was genuine and not a fake invented by a German propagandist.

If it had been possible for us to send uncensored messages to England few would have described the conduct of the Germans in quite such flattering terms. Still it was desirable that some such message should be sent. It was true in the main, and if it had been less sugar-coated the Germans would probably not have transmitted it. It was broadcast from Bremen twice at least. Listeners in Guernsey heard it on August 24th and again on August 30th, preceded by the historically untrue statement that the Germans were the first people to invade the Channel Islands since 1066 A.D.

In September the trial of a man charged with having attempted murder at the time of the general panic was made difficult by the absence on service in England of the man whom it was alleged he had tried to murder. Medical evidence showed that the accused man's mind was unhinged at the time and that he had believed that he was shooting at a German. This evidence, supplemented by the fact that the absent witness was the only person who had seen the shot fired, secured the accused's acquittal.

About the middle of September it was rumoured that nine men had escaped in a fishing-boat from Havre Bordeaux. A fantastically incredible part of the rumour was that a British destroyer had arranged to pick them up. Yet in essence the rumour was true as Guernsey fishermen soon had reason to know. An official order, obviously intended to give the German authorities fuller control of the Island's boats, was issued on September 26th to the effect that 'all boats in the Island whether moored around the coast or on dry land must be brought to the harbour of St Peter Port by October 1st at latest'.

This order was followed on September 28th by a notice inserted in the local papers by the President of the Controlling Committee.

NOTICE.

It must now be known to a good many local inhabitants that some eight persons recently left this Island in a boat with a view to reaching England.

As a direct result, drastic control of boats has been instituted by the German authorities, resulting in fishermen in the northern and western parts of the Island being unable to follow their vocation and depriving the population of a very large proportion of the fish obtainable.

Any further such departures or attempts thereat can only result in further restrictions. In other words, any persons who manage to get away do so at the expense of those left behind. In these circumstances, to get away or attempt to get away is a crime against the local population, quite apart from the fact that the German authorities will deal very severely with persons who are caught making the attempt.

In the event of a repetition of any such incident there is a grave possibility that, by way of reprisal, the male population of the Island will be evacuated to France.

The Controlling Committee views such incidents with the utmost disfavour for they tend to negative all the efforts which are made in the interest of the local population to preserve good and courteous relations with the German authorities. To any who may be contemplating running away (for that is what it is) we urgently address the order to put it out of their heads as an action unworthy of Guernseymen.

I am officially informed that, before the incident, the local German Command had been at pains to communicate to their headquarters the co-operation of the Island authorities and the exemplary behaviour of the whole of the civilian population and for their part, they hope no further incident will compel them to take the drastic action which would follow the departure of any other boat.

A. J. SHERWILL

Some critics of the notice were inclined to resent the statement that an escape from the Island was to be condemned as 'running away' and 'an action unworthy' of Guernseymen, but it was realised by the more level-headed that Mr Sherwill had an exceedingly difficult task in his position as liaison officer between the German authorities and the population of the Island. Moreover, since the German authorities obviously knew about the notice before it was published, it is possible that they instructed him to issue it.

We learned particulars of the escape when on October 7th and again on October 15th British planes dropped a leaflet which, besides other news, contained the following:-

> ESCAPE FROM GUERNSEY.
> EIGHT REACH BRITAIN.
> London, September 27th.
>
> A party of eight men have successfully escaped from Guernsey to England in a 20-ft. boat. The London Press is headlining their adventures.
>
> They left Guernsey under cover of darkness and rowed half a mile before using the motor. When they were about two miles out four flares were dropped by three German 'planes flying over them. One fell only twenty yards from the boat, but they were not seen.
>
> Just after passing the Casquets their engine broke down, but the repairs were finished in four hours and

they eventually sighted Start Point, the landmark for which they were making.

The party consisted of Mr Frederick Hockey, 47, a signalman employed by the harbour administration at St Peter Port, three of his sons, Frederick (25), George (21), and Harold (16), who were engaged in tomato growing, and Messrs. William Mahy, Percy du Port, William Dorey and Herbert Bichard, independent growers.

The plane that dropped leaflets on October 7th dropped also a few copies of the *Daily Sketch* and *Daily Mirror* which gave prominence to the escaped men's adventures and a somewhat exaggerated account of conditions in Guernsey under the Germans. According to local report the escaped men took with them a log-book, appropriated from the Deputy Harbourmaster's office, containing records of all ships that had entered or left the harbour since the German occupation and also a complete set of local newspapers published during the same time.

The first occasion on which leaflets were dropped was on September 24th. British planes made two raids that morning, one about an hour after midnight and another two hours later, doing considerable damage and dropping copies of a leaflet headed 'News from England. No.1. Distributed by the RAF'. Beneath the heading was: 'A Message from His Majesty the King. The Queen and I desire to convey to you our heartfelt sympathy in the trials which you are enduring. We earnestly pray for your speedy liberation, knowing that it will surely come.: George R.I.' There followed accounts of British bombing in Germany and targets in occupied countries, of the growth of the manufacture of planes in England, of financial contributions from the Empire towards the cost of the planes, of the rise of Free France under General de Gaulle and of help from America. Inset were reproductions of three cartoons and a photograph of the King and Queen inspecting damage done by German raiders to Buckingham Palace.

The leaflets were dropped in many parts of the Island but owing to lack of wind did not scatter well, consequently comparatively few people were able to secure copies. From an early hour German soldiers were busily employed in collecting them, even climbing trees to retrieve copies stuck in the branches. On Vazon racecourse they had to be particularly active because there the leaflets fell over a wide area and they were frequently obliged to run, brandishing their revolvers, in chase of Guernseymen who had picked some up. People who witnessed the scene said that it looked like a lot of adults playing the children's game 'Tom Tiddler's Ground'. Besides picking up leaflets the soldiers searched a number of people whom they suspected of having secured some. One man had to congratulate himself because the insides of his socks were not examined. It was reported that a milk-roundsman who had the luck to pick up a bundle of the leaflets found a ready sale for them at two shillings apiece and it was said that as much as five pounds was offered for a copy. That morning everyone in town looked exceptionally cheerful. Though few had seen the leaflet and fewer still possessed one all were cheered by the unnecessary but nevertheless welcome sign that England had not forgotten us.

Two days later the following notice was published in the local newspapers:-

> The attention of the public is drawn to the fact that leaflets which were dropped on this Island by a British 'plane on the night of the 23rd-24th September, 1940, come within the definition of 'enemy propaganda material' contained in the German Proclamation dated 29th July, 1940.
>
> It is therefore an offence, to hand on such leaflets or to communicate their contents to others, and it is the duty of persons in possession of such leaflets to deliver them to the Feldkommandantur, Grange Lodge Hotel.
>
> 25th September, 1940.
A. J. SHERWILL

The proclamation referred to threatened fifteen years' imprisonment for circulating enemy propaganda. It is not known how many possessors of documents were so docile as to surrender them to the German authorities. One lady, in fact, a Miss Collas, wrote a defiant letter to the Commandant saying that if she had a leaflet she would not surrender it as it would have been sent to her by His Majesty the King. She signed the letter but omitted to give her address. In order to trace the offender a German official with the aid of a local directory visited everyone in the Island of the same name and initial and made them write specimens of their signatures for comparison with the signature of the offending letter. By this means the culprit was discovered to be a lady over eighty years of age whom the Commandant contented himself with reprimanding.

On the morning of September 28th many men, while on their way to work, were rounded up by German soldiers and kept herded together for several hours, throughout the day all lorries on the roads were stopped and examined, and many houses were searched by German soldiers carrying fixed bayonets. In accordance with their usual custom the German authorities gave no explanation for this activity but it was rumoured, soon afterwards, that three men, of whom one had been captured, had been dropped on the Island by parachute and that the armed soldiers were searching for the other two. Next it was learned that the captured man was Captain Parker of the South Lancashire Regiment, and that his father, Lieutenant-Colonel Parker, had been arrested and imprisoned in Fort George. Colonel Parker while under detention was subjected to a strict cross-examination as to his son's mission in the Island but was able truthfully to say that he knew nothing about it, as under the circumstances he was the last person in the Island whom his son would have visited. He was detained for two days only, during which he was treated with perfect courtesy, but he was not allowed to see his son who was taken away to France. Nothing further was heard of the other two men, so it may be assumed that, if there were two other parachutists, they eventually found means of returning to England.

CHAPTER X

NARRATIVE, 1940

On October 15th British planes made a very effective raid. After machine-gunning a gun-crew at Pleinmont they dropped bombs on the airport. Unverifiable reports stated that fifteen Germans were killed at Pleinmont and five at the airport. Next morning the Guernseymen employed at the airport were refused admission and were told that they were to return to their homes till the following day. No reason was given for granting them this unexpected holiday, but they supposed that the Germans did not wish them to see how much damage had been done there. But the damage was on too large a scale to be kept wholly secret. That day no less than nine lorries – there may have been more but no more than nine were counted by any one observer – went from the airport to the White Rock carrying the wreckage of German planes.

Such raids always cheered us but this one was particularly welcome because the planes dropped the leaflets, referred to in the previous chapter, which gave us the news of the safe arrival in England of the men who had escaped by boat from Havre Bordeaux. Many people obtained copies and cheerfully took the risk of fifteen years' imprisonment for possessing and passing on 'enemy propaganda'.

The escape of the Guernseymen had naturally rankled in the minds of the German authorities. On October 12th the newspapers published an exchange of letters on the subject between the Island Commandant and Mr Sherwill in his capacity as President of the Controlling Committee. The Commandant, after formally announcing the appointment of a Commandant for the Channel Islands with headquarters in Jersey, said smooth things about 'the pleasant relations which have hitherto existed between Occupying Forces and the population'. Then in less sugary vein he said that he could not tolerate conduct which might militate against the interests of the German Reich such as the escape of eight islanders to England 'as it is by no means unlikely that information of military importance may reach England in such manner'. Continuing, he said that it was possible that there were still British soldiers in the Island, either having stayed behind at the time of the evacuation or having since entered the Island, threatened punishment for anyone who afforded assistance to any such soldiers or who engaged in espionage or sabotage, announced his intention of fixing a date by which all members of the British Armed Forces still in hiding were to report and gave a specific promise, quoted here in full because the exact wording of the promise was made important by later events:-

> Those reporting up to that date will be treated as prisoners of war, also no measures will be taken against their relatives who had assisted in hiding them. Those members of the British Forces who may be found after this time limit must expect to be treated as agents of an enemy power, at the same time those who have been aiding them will have to take the consequences.

In his reply, Mr Sherwill said that the Commandant had given tangible proof of his goodwill towards the Island Administration and population, expressed appreciation of the responsibility which rested on him in the execution of his duty, and assured him that the Island Authorities and he himself would continue their endeavours to ensure that no incident should arise which might imperil the correct and courteous relations which existed between the German military authorities and the Island Administration. Passing on to 'the departure of a boat-load of persons from this Island' he said that the Island Authorities deplored the incident and would have prevented it had they been aware of it, and called attention to the notice which he had published on the subject in the newspapers of September 28th and to the fact that, until relieved of the responsibility, he had instituted police watchings of the bays and harbours. He accepted unreservedly the Commandant's statement that no civilian might participate in any military activity without incurring the gravest penalties.

He referred to the grave perplexities of the problems with which the Island Administration had to grapple and said that nothing would embarrass it more than that this Island should be the scene of any activities forbidden by the laws and usages of war. He described as a generous gesture the Commandant's assurance that any personnel of the British Armed Forces who surrendered within the time limit that was to be fixed should be treated as prisoners-of-war and that no measures would be taken against any of their relatives who might have given them assistance. Mr Sherwill then suggested the publication of his and the Commandant's letters so that everyone should realise as fully as did the Island Administration the consequences of illegal actions. He then spoke of the confidence he derived from the fact that it was 'possible – though only in the Channel Islands – for a German officer and a British official to enter into friendly correspondence, to engage in full and frank discussions and to exchange courtesies'. Finally, Mr Sherwill asked the Commandant to let him know of any happening to which he might take exception and asked that he might be permitted 'to intercede on behalf of anyone who, unwittingly, or without appreciation of the consequences' might offend against the German Military Code.

Many Guernseymen thought Mr Sherwill's letter too suave and conciliatory. These did not realise that the more he succeeded in winning the confidence and goodwill of the Germans – at a bitter cost no doubt to his own feelings – the more successful he was likely to be in any intercession he might have to make on behalf of his fellow islanders. They would have been more charitable had they known that at the time of writing the letter he had already, by his loyalty to individual islanders, brought himself within the shadow of the French prison in which at a later date he suffered.

On October 19th the Commandant followed his letter of October 12th by issuing the following notice:-

> Members of the British armed forces in hiding in Guernsey and persons who are assisting them in any

way must report at the Island police-station, St Peter Port, at the latest by 6pm on Monday, 21st October, 1940.

Members of the British armed forces obeying this order will be treated as prisoners of war and no measures will be taken against persons who have assisted them.

Any member of the British armed forces who may be found after this time limit must expect to be treated as an agent of an enemy power. Also all those who have assisted in hiding such persons or in any other way will have to take full consequences of such actions.

The Bailiff called attention to the notice in a letter addressed 'To the People of the Island of Guernsey', published in the newspapers alongside the Commandant's order. He most strongly urged all Guernsey citizens to take careful notice of the announcement, adding 'It is absolutely imperative that all should comply with this order without delay. If this be not done the consequences will be most serious'.

Six men obeyed the order on the same day. Most of them were expecting their discharge papers when communication with England was cut off and therefore had not considered it necessary to surrender at that time. They were all imprisoned and sent to France where, for aught we knew to the contrary, they were treated as prisoners of war in accordance with the Commandant's promise.

On October 21st, within the period of grace allowed, two more soldiers, 2nd Lieutenant Nicolle and 2nd Lieutenant Symes, surrendered. These two officers were on a somewhat different footing from the others. Both had been on service in England at the time of the occupation. Nicolle landed at Le Jaonnet Bay at midnight on July 7th/8th from a submarine which took him back to England three days later. Among other qualifications that he had for the special service duty entrusted to him was that he was a fine swimmer. This was fortunate, for the small boat that should have landed him capsized in the breakers, leaving him to swim ashore. Lest his drenched clothes should arouse suspicion he stripped after landing and dried them on a gorse bush before making his way to his parents' home. Again when returning the submarine's boat was capsized three times before he got aboard. He returned to Guernsey on September 4th, landing at Petit Port from a motor launch and on this occasion Symes came with him. They expected to be taken off three nights later but the motor launch did not come. They waited for it until daylight then and on several successive nights, staying at the appointed place as long as they dared. It is not unreasonable to suppose that when Captain Parker was sent to the Island, part of the mission entrusted to him was to get into touch with Nicolle and Symes and tell them what arrangements had been made to take them away.

Nicolle and Symes could not offer the German Authorities the same excuse as the others for their presence in the Island. Yet, though they were clearly engaged in espionage, they were justified in considering that the Commandant's promise, conveyed in the letter to Mr Sherwill which was published on October 12th, would apply to themselves and their relatives, for it seemed made quite definitely to soldiers who either stayed behind at the time of the evacuation or who had since entered the Island. The German High Command either did not take this view or did not consider itself bound by the Commandant's promise, for at some time during early November – we got the news only by hearsay as the Germans kept the matter as secret as they could – thirteen islanders related to these two officers or having some close association with them were taken to France and imprisoned there. No explanation was given but we could guess at the reason when on November 4th a proclamation ordering the surrender of all wireless sets was preceded by the statement that 'the favouring of espionage in the Island of Guernsey makes further measures necessary'.

Those arrested were: – Nicolle's parents, Mr and Mrs E. Nicolle, his uncle and aunt, Mr and Mrs Frank Nicolle, and Miss Jessie Mariette, his fiancée; Symes' parents, Mr and Mrs Louis Symes; his fiancée, Miss Mary Bird; her father, Mr Wilfred Bird, and her brother, Mr Walter Bird; Mr William Allan, groundsman at Elizabeth College cricket-ground; Mr H.E. Marquand, States Supervisor, and Mr A. J. Sherwill, His Majesty's Procureur and President of the Controlling Committee. Mr and Mrs E. Nicolle had harboured their son. His uncle, aunt and fiancée had known of his presence in the Island and were guilty of the German crime of not betraying him to the authorities. Symes had hidden in the house of his fiancée's father, Mr Bird, so that he, his son and his daughter were guilty of harbouring a British agent. Mr Allan had allowed the two officers to hide in a shed on the cricket field when, one day, after waiting at Petit Port in vain to be taken away by the patrol boat, full daylight came before they could reach the houses in which they had sheltered. On the occasion of Nicolle's second visit to the Island his father was staying at Grandes Rocques with Mrs Nicolle as the former was on sick-leave from his duties in the States Office and had been ordered there to recuperate. In order to be able to look after their son they wished to return to their home in St Peter Port and that they might do so without attracting attention Mr Nicolle asked Mr Marquand to recall him to his duties. Mr Marquand consulted Mr Sherwill on the matter, so that both these gentlemen knew of 2nd Lieutenant Nicolle's presence in the Island and were thus guilty of failing to denounce him to the German authorities.

Uncertainty as to the fate of the thirteen persons whose arrest had followed the surrender of Nicolle and Symes made the customary Church prayer 'for all prisoners and captives' more poignant than usual for Guernsey people during the last two months of the year. Then on December 24th, coupled with the announcement that our wireless sets were to be returned to us, came the inexpressibly more welcome news – saddened by a rumour, which unhappily proved to be true, that the father of 2nd Lieutenant Symes had died in his French prison – that the prisoners were to be released and returned to the Island.

The news came in the form of an official German proclamation:

1. The findings of the Legal Investigations have

proved conclusively:
(a) During the night from the 3rd to 4th September, 2nd Lieutenant Nicolle and 2nd Lieutenant Symes having landed in Guernsey in civil clothing with a reconnaissance order are guilty of espionage.
(b) Emile Nicolle, Elsie Nicolle, Frank Nicolle, Hilda Nicolle, Louis Symes, Rachel Symes, Wilfred Bird, Walter Bird, Elise Bird, William Allan and Jessie Mariette have given refuge and assistance to the two officers. They have therefore been guilty of high treason and having lent assistance to espionage.
(c) Mr Sherwill has, before the publication of the notice, made declarations contrary to the best of his knowledge and acted against his appointed duty of information. He has therefore been guilty of favouring the above and acting disloyally towards the German Inselkommandant.
(d) All the parties concerned have attempted to mislead the German Authorities even after having reported themselves in accordance with a notice of October 18th, 1940.
2. In accordance with the German Military Law and in agreement with the Hague Convention the penalties provided for are the following: – Espionage: death penalty. Assistance to espionage: penal servitude up to fifteen years. Favouring: imprisonment up to one year.
3. In spite of aggravating circumstances, the German Military Authorities have treated the above-mentioned cases 1 (c) and (d) with full consideration to the assurances given in the notice of October 18th, 1940. No Martial Law condemnation will take place. All the persons concerned will be exempt from punishment. After

conclusion of the investigation proceedings, 2nd Lt. Nicolle and 2nd Lt. Symes will be sent to a camp as prisoners of war. The other persons concerned will be brought back to the Island. The matter is therefore settled.
4. Mr Sherwill will be released from his office as further co-operation with the German authorities is no longer possible.
5. The wireless sets confiscated in the Island of Guernsey will be returned to their owners for use until further notice.
6. All the above measures have been taken in the expectation and under the condition of a perfect loyalty on the part of the Island Authorities and population in the future. Any disloyal or illegal behaviour will result in immediate counter measures. The whole community would bear the consequences of individual misconduct.

SCHUMACHER,
Oberst und Feldkommandant

Some comments suggest themselves. If Nicolle and Symes were liable to the death penalty, as they undoubtedly were by the accepted laws of war, their sentence was very lenient. If the others were liable to penal servitude, which is perhaps more doubtful since, though some of them were questioned and cross-examined none were brought to trial, their treatment, too, was lenient. This lenience may be attributed by some to policy, to a desire on the part of the Higher German Command to make us regard German rule as exceptionally benevolent. But there is reason to believe that it was due to representations made by the Guernsey Commandant who had pledged his word on October 12th that if British soldiers at large in the Island surrendered they should be treated as prisoners of war and no measures would be taken against persons who had assisted them. In fact it is stated – not officially but on good authority – that the Commandant had intimated to higher authorities that if Nicolle and Symes were shot and the others sentenced to penal servitude he would demand to be relieved of his command.

The use of the words 'high treason' and 'perfect loyalty' was of course ridiculous. High treason is the violation by a subject of his allegiance to his sovereign and none of those accused owed any allegiance whatever to the German Fuehrer. By International Law 'People in occupied territory remain the subjects of their sovereign and continue to have patriotic duties to their country' (*Manual of Military Law*. Chap. XIV. VIII. Paragraph 356) and the suggestion implied in the paragraph 6 of the Commandant's proclamation that anyone, who at some future date might have the opportunity and the courage to serve his lawful sovereign by harbouring a British agent, would be deterred from performing this duty by fear of losing his wireless set illustrates the German's inability to understand the mentality of any people but themselves. Incidentally it should be noticed that the punishment of the whole community (by the confiscation of wireless sets) for the 'war-crime' of a few was contrary to International Law which lays down that 'no collective penalty may be inflicted on the population on account of the acts of individuals for which it cannot be regarded as collectively responsible' (*Manual of Military Law*. Chap. XIV. VIII. Paragraph 385).

Besides 'releasing' Mr Sherwill from his office as President of the Controlling Committee, the German authorities demanded also the dismissal of Nicolle's father and uncle from their respective posts under the States.

How the Germans were able to implicate as many people as they did in the charge of harbouring Nicolle and Symes will probably never be known, but as each person arrested had to undergo prolonged and very astute cross-examination it may be supposed that one or more unintentionally revealed more than was intended.

Perhaps we shall never know whether any more British agents landed in the Island after the surrender of Nicolle and Symes or whether the British Government then abandoned all attempts to obtain information from Guernsey during the rest of the period of the German occupation. Its attempts up till then had not been wholly unsuccessful. Nicolle carried news to England and Sergeant Ferbrache escaped out of the Island after his failure to establish contact with Mulholland and Martel. If the rumour was true that three men landed here by parachute in September, two of them were not heard of again, so presumably got safely away. On several occasions it was rumoured that British landing parties had kidnapped and carried off German sentries and once it was reported that a British submarine came to the surface alongside some fishermen who were hauling their crab pots and obtained from them news of the Island.

Early in October owners of motor vehicles, except such as were already requisitioned by the German authorities or essential for the maintenance of economic life, received orders to have them overhauled, their batteries charged and their lighting installation put in order so that the Germans could buy them. In view of the fact that after the war motor vehicles would probably be very costly and very difficult to buy, few owners can have been willing to sell their cars, quite apart from the knowledge that by selling them they helped the enemy, but they had no option in the matter. Some owners guardedly sought advice from motor mechanics as to how they could most effectively so damage their cars as to render them temporarily unserviceable. The possibility that this might be done seems to have occurred to the German authorities for on October 28th an order was published threatening fines and imprisonment to anyone who did anything to his car that would nullify or diminish its utility.

On November 11th an order was issued forbidding the activities of Unions, Societies, Meetings, Processions, and wearing of distinctive uniforms and emblems, the display of flags and similar activities. On the following day an exception to this order was made in favour of Italian subjects 'in connection with the Fascist party emblems'. No concession was made to any followers of Sir Oswald Mosley who might happen to be in the Island. Under this order clubs were closed and even such non-political activities as whist and euchre drives were banned.

The last air raid of the year was very well timed. For some

time previously Guernsey workmen had been employed on the airport on the building of hangars. The first they built was knocked down by a gale. By the end of November a second was practically completed except for the painting of the exterior. This was done under the direction of an expert camoufleur who succeeded so well in making it look like a greenhouse containing growing plants that those who saw it described it as a work of art. The last finishing touches were put to it on the morning of December 16th. The workmen were then called into the hangar and officially thanked for the good work they had put into the job. For some time past one or more British reconnaissance planes had passed over the airport every day and it seems that the Royal Air Force had been watching the growing of the hangar with interest, for during the men's dinner hour a plane dropped a stick of bombs on it and smashed it flat, then machine-gunned Germans racing for the air raid shelter, killing ten and wounding seven others. Unfortunately three Guernseymen were also casualties. Though expressly forbidden to go into the hangar during the dinner-hour they had done so to enjoy a quiet game of euchre. One was killed, one slightly wounded and one shell-shocked. Probably the raid was timed to take place during the dinner-hour so that as little harm as possible should be done to our people. Had the raid taken place later in the day it might have been still more effective for the German Commandant and the principal members of his staff had intended to inspect the new hangar that afternoon.

On November 18th four British airmen, whose plane had been forced down by a thunderstorm somewhere in mid-Channel, landed at Portinfer from a collapsible rubber-boat in which they had been afloat for forty-eight hours. They were in a pitiable condition from hunger and cold and their feet were so swollen that their boots had to be cut from them. A man living near by, who was afterwards threatened with deportation on a charge of concealing the rubber dinghy, took them to his cottage and telephoned to the Controlling Committee, who reported the arrival to German Headquarters and to the St John's Ambulance Brigade. The former sent men to arrest the airmen but an ambulance car was first on the scene. It picked them up and was driving away when some German soldiers formed a cordon across the road to bar its passage. The driver, anxious to keep the airmen out of German hands as long as possible, put on speed instead of stopping and the soldiers opened out to let the ambulance pass. The airmen were taken to the Emergency Hospital and put to bed there and Doctor Gibson, on the plea that they were not in a fit condition to be moved, obtained a promise from the authorities that they might stay there until they had recovered their strength. The promise was broken a few hours later when soldiers, in spite of protests, arrested the airmen, made them leave their beds and took them to the Victoria Hospital as prisoners-of-war. A few Guernseymen had, however, had opportunity of talking with them and, it is said, had learned from them that it was already known in England that we had been deprived of our wireless sets. If this report was true it gave gratifying evidence that by some means or other the Home Government was kept closely in touch with Island affairs.

The confiscation of our radios had been announced by proclamation four days before and had been carried into effect by postmen and others conscripted for the task. The penalty threatened for disobedience to the order was announced as a fine of 30,000 Reichsmarks or not more than six weeks' imprisonment. As the local value of the Reichsmark was at the rate of 9.60 to the pound sterling the threatened fine was no less than £3,125, an enormous sum in comparison with the alternative of imprisonment, and a fine that very few people in Guernsey could have paid.

Deprivation of war news was a grievous punishment likely to create despondency, nerve strain and kindred evils. Nevertheless we had at the outset one source of comfort. The German propaganda that our newspapers were compelled to publish was always of a kind deliberately meant to depress us, but we knew that much of it was untrue and we could be confident that, thanks to it, we should always know the worst; if some major disaster had happened to British arms the German propagandist would certainly not have denied himself the pleasure of telling us about it. We found, however, that we were not so entirely cut off from news as we had feared. For a few days we received it from the men employed in stowing away the confiscated radios at various depots. They were not so docile as not to profit by the opportunity afforded them by the sets they were handling of listening to the news at the appropriate times. This news, of course, they passed on to their friends and those friends had other friends. And even after the confiscated radios had all been stored away news mysteriously continued to circulate. The temptation to seek to verify any piece of news by demanding who was the authority for it had to be resisted both because of the punishment threatened for anyone who retained his radio and also because of the somewhat vague threat that any news not emanating from the German authorities was 'enemy propaganda' the circulation of which was punishable by fifteen years' imprisonment.

Very soon what may be described as an underground news service came into being. People learned whom they might confidently ask for news and few of those who received it were so selfish as not to pass it on to others. There was at first a tendency to doubt the authenticity of the news that circulated but when it included matters of less vital importance than war news – such as that of floods in Jamaica, an item that would not have occurred to anyone to invent, one felt that they were originally reported by someone who had actually heard a British broadcast. After a while one discovered that in a number of banks and other places of business it was possible to be shown a typewritten summary of the latest news. Discretion had to be used in asking for it. If a German soldier, or an unrecognised civilian who might be German, was within earshot the correct thing to do was to ask permission to consult a price list or a list of securities. One was then invited to the back premises where the news could be copied without fear of detection. Later this news agency developed so greatly that the news-sheet was mimeographed. News distributed in this manner bore evidence of having been taken down in shorthand and was therefore more reliable than news reported from memory.

It was eventually discovered that news not recorded on the mimeographed sheet had sometimes been inaccurate and that the error had always been in the direction of too great optimism. This can readily be understood. A man or woman who deliberately risks imprisonment in order to hear the war news is of the stuff of which optimists are made and optimists, when passing on news, have a tendency, of which they are possibly unconscious, to exaggerate good and minimise bad news. It did not matter in the least that we were sometimes led to believe that the news was better than it actually was; on the contrary it cheered us up and helped us to live through an anxious time with stout hearts. A report that their Majesties the King and Queen had been killed by bombs dropped on Buckingham Palace caused some anxiety, but as the disseminator of this news item was careful to state that it emanated from Bremen no one was unduly distressed.

On December 20th those who went to wherever they were accustomed to go to read the daily news-sheet found that it no longer circulated and it was whispered that the public benefactor who had been supplying it had reason to believe that he had come under the suspicion of Gestapo agents. Nevertheless we continued to receive less trustworthy but by no means wholly inaccurate war news and five days later our confiscated radios were released.

It may be imagined with what delight we heard once more the booming of Big Ben itself and could listen to news of undoubted authenticity from the British Broadcasting Corporation. Yet, because forbidden fruit is sweet some of us felt that a certain spice had gone out of life when we no longer had to get news by stealth and could discuss it without furtively looking sideways for possible eavesdroppers. Life became more placid – but much less exciting.

It now became possible to make guarded enquiries – asking for no names – as to how we had obtained the news during the weeks when all news that did not come from a German source was contraband. It was said that some of it came from people employed by German civilians who used their employers' radios without, and in some cases even with, their employers' consent. Some of it came from Deputy Custodians of Abandoned Houses who had managed to avoid surrendering radios from houses under their charge. Some people, too, had had the courage to retain their radios in defiance of German orders. One radio was lowered down a well and raised to ground level at the appropriate times; another was kept below the moveable floor of a dog-kennel occupied by a truculent-looking bull terrier; a third was kept in a crevice in a quarry and no doubt there were others in equally ingenious hiding places.

Our thanks to those patriots had to be unspoken. A debt that could be openly acknowledged – and was formally expressed by the Bailiff through the medium of the newspapers – was due to the postmen, constables of parishes and volunteer helpers who worked throughout Christmas Day and Boxing Day to return radios to their owners as speedily as possible.

Others also laboured to make the Christmas season as cheery as in the circumstances it could be made. A fund was raised to give a Christmas present to every school-child remaining in the Island. So many toys were given that the organisers decided to devote a considerable part of the eighty pounds subscribed to the purchase of clothing for children who needed it. Christmas entertainments were organised in the country parishes and the manager of the Regal Theatre invited eight hundred children to an entertainment at which the exhibition of three suitable films was interspersed with community carol-singing and followed by gifts of oranges and sweets.

The year ended on a less jovial note. On December 30th the States were addressed by the German Commandant who, presumably with his tongue in his cheek, spoke of his warm wishes for the success of the work on which they were to deliberate, and of his own interest in the future security of the Island and asked that the co-operation of the Islanders that had been forthcoming in the past should be continued and extended to the German authority. He then left the building and the States proceeded to elect Jurat the Rev. John Leale to be President of the Controlling Committee in the place of Mr A.J. Sherwill whom the German authorities had deposed from that office for his neglect to co-operate with them to the extent of betraying his fellow islanders to them. Having got through this and other routine business the States approved with as good grace as possible the doubling of our Income Tax and other exceptional taxation rendered necessary by the presence in the Island of our unwelcome visitors.

CHAPTER XI

NARRATIVE 1941

Early in January, 1941, the local Post Office's stock of penny stamps was exhausted. To take their place twopenny stamps were allowed to be cut diagonally and the halves used as penny stamps, but this could be only a temporary measure and on February 18th locally-printed penny stamps were issued. They were coloured red and the design was the Guernsey coat-of-arms – minus the laurel wreath – between the words 'Guernsey postage'. At a later date halfpenny stamps with the same design but coloured green were issued.

The Guernsey stamps were so eagerly bought by German stamp-collectors that the supply of paper suitable for their production would soon have been exhausted if the Commandant had not issued an order that no one might buy more than ten at a time.

Towards the end of the month the Island was thrilled by a rumour that a lady had received a letter from England. Already a few messages of a most unsatisfactory brevity had reached some islanders through the agency of the International Red Cross Committee at Geneva. The exciting feature of this rumour was that it was said that the letter was delivered in the ordinary way through the agency of the Post Office and that its envelope bore the Guernsey postmark, the inference being that someone sent by the British Military Intelligence Department to gather information in Guernsey had contrived to land somewhere on the Island and had posted the letter in a local pillar-box.

At the end of January Mrs Le Masurier and Mrs Michael, who had been deported to France for harbouring the two British officers who had been put ashore to reconnoitre, were brought back to Guernsey and released, an act of clemency for which due credit must be given to the German authorities.

On or about February 14th a party of fifteen Frenchmen who had escaped from France by boat landed on the Island, under the impression that they had reached the English coast. They were arrested and sent back to France.

At about the same time a silly practical joke led to the detention of Mrs Sherbrooke, the wife of an officer on service in England, on a charge of having made signals from the roof of her house to British agents concealed in the bushes of her garden. She was not imprisoned but was strictly confined to her house in the charge of a series of German officers, one by day and one by night, who took up their quarters in her drawing-room. As she was not allowed to use her telephone and a sentry was posted at her front door to forbid entrance to the house her friends did not know of her plight till one of them chanced to enter her house by the back door over which no guard had been set. The Germans naturally questioned Mrs Sherbrooke's two maidservants as to her alleged hostile activities. They broke down under cross-examination and admitted that the charge brought against her arose from an anonymous letter which they themselves had concocted as a joke. Mrs Sherbrooke was therefore released from arrest, but the maidservants were sentenced to imprisonment, one for nine months in Jersey and the other for six months in Guernsey. It should be added that the German officers appointed to be Mrs Sherbrooke's temporary gaolers carried out their duties with tact and consideration. The practical joke had given the German authorities a great deal of trouble. Every night for some considerable time before Mrs Sherbrooke's detention they attempted to catch her and the non-existent British agents in the very act of communicating with each other. During these nights it was not British agents but German police who hid in the bushes in her garden. It was natural that they should resent being put in a ridiculous position by others. Sometimes they made themselves ridiculous and did so on at least two occasions during March, 1941.

Early in March the curiosity of people passing the Motor House garage in St Julian's Avenue was aroused by the sight of two fully armed German soldiers on guard at each door. After a few days the guard was reduced to one armed sentry. Towards the middle of the month the duty of guarding the garage doors was handed over to the Island Police. It then became possible, if one knew the policeman on duty and made the enquiry tactfully, to ask why he was stationed there. The explanation given was that the duty of the guard was to prevent the removal from the upper floor of the garage of a midget aeroplane built before the war broke out by the proprietor of the garage, who had left the Island at the time of the evacuation. This was coupled with the information that the manager of the garage, Mr Bell, had been imprisoned by the German authorities for not having reported the existence of the plane on July 2nd, 1940, when it had been ordered that all weapons were to be surrendered. This threw some light on a proclamation from the Commandant that had been published in the newspapers of March 5th (about two days after the posting of the armed guard):-

> There is occasion to again call attention of the population to the fact that the retention of weapons (including hunting-guns) or of implements of war of every description is punishable according to martial law.
> The population is herewith requested to search every nook and corner of their premises for weapons and implements of war. They are to be delivered to the Controlling Committee of Guernsey at once.

Below this proclamation was printed a notice signed by the Bailiff which stated that the phrase 'implements of war of every description' included aeroplanes and parts thereof.

Presumably the German authorities were afraid lest some supremely reckless individual might attempt to steal the plane and escape to England in it; but to any Guernseyman of average intelligence it seemed that any such attempt would be certain to fail at the outset because, small though it was, the aeroplane could not be transported from the Motor House to any level area large enough to enable it to take the air in any vehicle smaller than a large lorry the passage of which through the town with so bulky a load would have been certain to attract the attention of even the most unobservant German. Obviously the German authorities were taking no risks, though later they allowed the duty of guarding the Motor House to be relegated to bored special constables. At last it occurred to some exceptionally intelligent German that the aeroplane could be made useless by the removal of its propeller. This was done and on March 28th the guards were released from their futile duty. At about the same time the manager of the Motor House was released from prison, where he had been confined in a dark cell without being given a chance to say anything in his own defence but was offered his liberty if he would inculpate any States official.

While our local police and special constables were performing, under German orders, duties which might safely have been entrusted to a child in a perambulator, the German authorities were making themselves ridiculous in another direction. On March 19th our newspapers published on their front pages a Bekanntmachung in large type and below it the following translation:-

> Feldkommandantur 515.   Jersey, March 18th, 1941.
> On account of an act of sabotage I order in agreement with the Island Commandant of Guernsey the following:
> 1. The curfew hour for the civil population is fixed from 9pm to 7am
> 2. The States of Guernsey have to report daily in writing to the Inselkommandantur, starting on March 19th, 1941, until 12 o'clock noon, 60 men, 18 to 45 years of age, who are used in accordance with the Island Commandant's order for performing guard tasks during night time.
>
> I specially draw attention to the order of the Chief of Military administration in France relative to protection against acts of sabotage dated October 10th, 1940, and published in the local newspapers on November 28th, 1940, and particular attention to the most severe penalties stipulated therein for contravention of supervision tasks.

The Field Commandant,
(Signed)
SCHUMACHER, Colonel.

The English of the translation was imperfect but it seemed clear that someone in Guernsey had been so bold as to commit an act of sabotage and that sixty men of the Island had to suffer in consequence. We had been warned against sabotage. In the hope, no doubt, of keeping us docile the German authorities had from time to time placarded the Island with posters telling us that some named French patriots had been 'fusilated' for cutting telephone cables or *'pour avoir commis des actes de violence contre un Militaire Allemand*' or for 'favouring the actions of the enemy by wilfully supporting England in the war against the German Empire'.

There were, no doubt, men in the Island bold enough to welcome an opportunity of 'wilfully supporting England in the war against the German Empire' if there had been a chance to do some damage important enough to make the risk of death worth while, but as there were no munition works in the Island that was practically impossible. We could have done many things that would have irritated the Germans but nothing that would have perceptibly hampered their war efforts. Considerable speculation, therefore, arose as to the nature of the alleged sabotage. Rumour said that a telephone cable had been cut. This suggested three thoughts to the mind of the average person: if it was not known who had cut it there was no proof that it had not been cut by some disgruntled war-weary German soldier; if by 'cable' was meant one of the many slender telephone wires that the Germans had laid from tree-branch to tree-branch in many parts of the Island, the 'cutting' may have been accidental as these were often festooned from one branch to another in so slipshod a fashion as to make accidents to them very probable; thirdly it was felt that it was a pity that anyone who had the courage to commit an act of sabotage did not wait until he had a chance to damage more valuable German property.

Few people believed that any act of sabotage had been

committed and there was a general wish for further information. That this would be forthcoming seemed to be promised in a Billet d'Etat published in the newspapers on March 20th which announced that the States had been specially convened 'to hear particulars of the act of sabotage which has resulted in the order that the evening curfew hour shall revert to 9pm, and to condemn all such acts'. Interest as to the alleged act of sabotage drew so large a crowd to the Royal Court that many had to sit on the stairways of the public galleries. Only two speeches were made: the first by the Bailiff; the second by the President of the Controlling Committee.

The Bailiff said:

> Gentlemen,
> I have called you together at short notice, which I am empowered to do, on a very serious matter which has arisen in the last few days and which I desire to bring to your notice as well as to that of the whole population of this Island. A few days ago an ill-disposed person or persons deliberately and maliciously cut a telephone cable in two places in the neighbourhood of the Airport which belonged to the German Military Authorities and thus performed an act of grave sabotage. Such an act was not only stupid but criminal, as it involved those who were participating in it with the penalty of death, and it also brought the population of the whole Island under the grave displeasure of the German authorities and in danger of the loss of their liberties.
> I think you will all agree with me that since the occupation the German authorities, both military and civil, have treated us with humanity and consideration and have gone out of their way on several occasions to help us in these difficult times, and it is our duty and obligation to co-operate with them in carrying out their Orders and Regulations. Those of us who have had to meet German officers from time to time have

always been treated with courtesy and consideration. I will therefore ask you and the people of this Island to govern themselves in such a way that there will be no recurrence of such an incident as that to which I have just referred. Such incidents only make the task of those in authority more difficult, and the Controlling Committee of the States, who are faced with such grave economic problems for the well-being of the community, should not be hampered in their work by these criminal acts. I should also like to add that it is the duty of any individual who has any information with regard to the perpetration of this act of sabotage to inform the Police immediately, as unless the culprit is brought to justice we do not know what further penalties the population may incur.

I may say that I am glad that the great majority of the inhabitants have conducted themselves with propriety and dignity in these difficult times and it is only a very few who do not appear to have realised the grave situation in which the people of the Island are placed by such a senseless act of sabotage, which places not only the property but the very lives of the islanders in danger. I can assure you that I will take all possible steps to bring the perpetrators of such acts to speedy justice, so that the safety of the population as a whole may be safeguarded. I am also sure you will wish to join with me in a declaration of the abhorrence of this and any similar acts which I hope will not recur.

I should like to inform you that the duty of providing the required guard for night duty has been imposed by the German authorities on the five parishes nearest the Airport.

Our German-controlled Press stated that the speech was received with loud applause from the body of the States and the public gallery. It was, on the contrary, listened to in strained silence followed at its conclusion by a murmur of talk. This was natural as many of his hearers must have doubted whether they had heard the Bailiff's words correctly. It was not until the publication of his speech in the local papers that all knew beyond doubt that he, a Guernseyman, had said that he would take all possible steps to bring one or more of his fellow-Guernseymen to justice – 'justice' in this context meaning punishment, possibly very severe punishment at the hands of people with whom our country was at war; and that he had also said that it was the 'duty' of any individual who knew anything about the 'culprit' to betray him to the police. The speech aroused much adverse comment among Islanders who made no allowances for, and had no means of fully realising, the very difficult position in which the Bailiff was placed. If a private individual for the sake of his own self-respect, adopted a truculent attitude towards Germans with whom he came in contact, that was his own affair. If he was punished for it, nobody suffered but himself. But it was the Bailiff's duty to subordinate his own feelings to the welfare of the Island as a whole and do his utmost to keep the Germans in a good temper. It was certain that the Germans would read his speech. It was even possible that they had dictated it. Its tone tended to conciliate them but it also conveyed a very emphatic warning to Islanders. The Bailiff knew that the Germans had selected the names of fifty leading men who were to serve as hostages, if occasion arose, for the good behaviour of their fellow-Islanders, and they had warned him that if sabotage continued they would deport twelve of these to a concentration camp. If he had been allowed to make this public, comment on his speech would have been more charitable.

The only other speaker at this States meeting was the President of the Controlling Committee, Jurat the Rev. John Leale. On the subject of the alleged sabotage he said that the States had 'the right as well as the duty to condemn such acts, as on the one hand utterly foolish, for they do no sort of good to anyone, and on the other hand as wicked, because they bring in their train inconvenience and maybe suffering imposed on everyone'.

Some people may have considered that, as we Guernseymen

still owed allegiance to His Britannic Majesty, we had at least the right, if not the obligation, to hamper the enemy's war efforts if we found any opportunity of doing so. Mr Leale spoke as one of the 'safety first' school of thought, but there was much to be said in favour of his point of view and he was perfectly justified in advancing it. The same cannot be said in favour of the remarks with which he introduced his speech. He said:

> In June of last year, any of us who wished to do so could have left the Island. Two very large vessels left on the Saturday evening of evacuation week; one of them practically empty, the other entirely so. We stayed here knowing full well that German troops could, without any resistance, occupy the Island whenever their Command ordered them to do so. Our staying here meant that we accepted that position and were prepared in the event of occupation to act as good citizens.

The bare historical facts contained in the first three sentences of that statement were true. The inference that Mr Leale drew from them was far from true. He inferred that during what he aptly called 'evacuation week' all had ample opportunity calmly to consider the matter and by deciding to remain in the Island deliberately accepted the danger of finding themselves obliged to submit to German rule. The truth is that during a considerable part of that week lack of leadership had given rise to a state of panic in which it was difficult for anyone, especially for the less educated members of the community, calmly to consider anything at all. As shown in Chapter II, at no time during the panic did anyone in an official position give the public any emphatic warning that a German occupation was probable. It is true that in an unofficial impromptu speech made on the spur of the moment in response to a sudden demand His Majesty's Procureur, Mr A.J. Sherwill, referred to the possibility of a German occupation but distracted attention from that danger by saying that the important issue was the danger of food shortage, and it was for that reason that the children were being evacuated. It is true, too, that Mr Leale did, in a speech to the States on the afternoon of June 21st, speak of the possibility that the Germans might occupy the Island, but he did so only for the purpose of stressing the futility and danger of resisting them if they should come. The speech came almost too late to influence anyone's decision on seizing the opportunity for free evacuation or staying in the Island, for it was not made till the afternoon of the Friday in evacuation week and was not published in the Press until the morning of Saturday, the last day on which free evacuation was possible. The Island obtained the leadership it so sorely needed when at that States meeting on Friday, June 21st, on the motion of Mr Leale, the Emergency Controlling Committee was appointed. The influence of that Committee was definitely directed towards persuading Islanders to stay in the Island by means of the slogans placarded all over the Island by its Information Officer. If the danger of a German occupation had been as widely advertised as were those slogans Mr Leale's inference that everyone in the Island realised the risk of coming under German domination would have been amply justified.

Amongst recalcitrant members of the community that inference aroused strong resentment, which in turn gave birth to aspersions against Mr Leale's character that were monstrously unjust. In an anonymous lampoon, privately but widely circulated, he was accused of having used his personal influence to persuade people not to evacuate because he feared that if too many working people did so the value of his property in the Island would deteriorate. As a general rule anonymous attacks on a man's character should be put into a newspaper basket instead of being given even more publicity than their authors tried to obtain for them, but in this case it seems necessary to mention the subject in order to show on how small a foundation the aspersions rested.

The lampoon, written in ungrammatical doggerel, based its accusation on the fact that at the time of the evacuation Mr Leale addressed a crowd of people, waiting at the White Rock to embark, and urged them to return to their homes. It was not an orderly, easily-controlled crowd such as normally waits to pass a ticket-collector, but a mob of excited people nerve-strung with anxiety because it was obvious that there were too few ships in harbour at the time to accommodate all who were waiting to embark. It is, therefore, not surprising that Mr Leale was imperfectly heard and not fully understood. Many, apparently, thought that he urged them not to leave the Island, whereas what he did advise them to do was to go home and return next day when more ships would be available. Few, of course, knew that he gave this advice at the earnest request of the Sea Transport Officer in charge of the evacuation, who feared that the crowd might get out of hand and rush the ships then in harbour with the certainty of perilously over-crowding them and the very grave danger that some would be trampled on in the scuffle, injured, and perhaps killed.

To return to the alleged act of sabotage: International Law clearly states that 'no collective penalty may be inflicted on the population on account of the acts of individuals for which it cannot be regarded as collectively responsible'.[2] Yet part of the penalty inflicted by the German authorities – the extension of curfew hours – fell on the whole community and the rest fell very unevenly on part of the male population. Those who bore the brunt of it were sixty men, chosen from the Forest parish and the four adjoining parishes, who had to spend the night, from 8.30pm till 8.30am, at the Airport, where for two hours in every six they had to walk to and fro along the length of a telephone wire which they held in their hands. While doing this they were not allowed to talk or smoke and a policemen was detailed to see that they carried out their task, the ridiculous nature of which clearly shows that it was intended to humiliate – like making a naughty child stand in a comer of a room.

A fortnight later the 'telephone guard' was dispensed with and the former curfew hour restored. By this time a theory was generally held, by those who had examined what little evidence there was, to the effect that the wire had been cut, possibly without the driver's knowledge, by the sharp edges of a covered

2   *Manual of Military Law* 1914. Chapter XIV. Section VIII. Paragraph 385.

delivery-van driven through the lane across which the wire had passed. No explanation was given by the German authorities as to why the penalty had been remitted but the remission may have had something to do with a report that a cow had been caught in the act of chewing another German telephone wire and that the offence had been promptly reported to the German authorities. The Commandant, however, saved his face, when announcing the rescinding of the order, by threatening that 'in the case of a repetition of such acts of sabotage considerably stricter measures will be taken'. Soon afterwards it was known that another German telephone wire had been cut. As it was in a residential area this time it could not possibly have been the dastardly act of an aggressively patriotic cow, but, as the Inspector of Police was able to prove, on the evidence of a German sentry, that the cutting – or breaking – must have happened during curfew hours when none but Germans were out of doors the matter was allowed to drop.

It was suggested earlier in this Chapter that the German authorities may have dictated the speech that the Bailiff delivered on the subject of the alleged sabotage. This theory is strengthened by careful examination of the following notice published above the Bailiff's signature in our newspapers of August 11th, 1941:-

> Attention is called to the fact that, under the Order relative to Protection against Acts of Sabotage, dated October 10th, 1940, any person who hides or shelters escaped prisoners-of-war shall be punished with death. The same applies for the hiding or sheltering of members of enemy forces (for instance, crews of landing aircraft, parachutists, etc.). Anyone lending assistance to such persons in their escape is also liable to the death sentence.

In this Order there are two examples of bad English. The words 'the same applies for' should be 'the same applies to' and 'anyone lending assistance to such persons in their escape' should be 'anyone lending assistance to the escape of such persons'. Such mistakes seem unlikely to have been made by an educated Englishman, especially by a lawyer, the exercise of whose profession demands punctilious exactitude in the use of words, but they might easily have been made by a German with a considerable, but not a perfect, command of the English language. Moreover the use in the notice of the words 'enemy forces' where clearly British forces is meant would be pardonable to a German but inexcusable to an Englishman. It is not unreasonable, therefore, to suppose not only that this notice was drafted by a German but also that other notices that appeared from time to time over the Bailiff's signature and even the speech that he made to the States on the subject of the alleged sabotage was drafted by some member of the German staff.

This theory suggests another. It may be that the German authorities believing that we might more contentedly heed advice from our leading officials than direct orders from themselves – inspired many of the public utterances of the Bailiff and the successive Presidents of the Controlling Committee.

On the 4th July the Bailiff published the following warning:-

> I have been informed that the letter 'V' has appeared written up in public places in the Island, that this matter is regarded very seriously by the German authorities, and that the person or persons who have done this are breaking a military order and rendering themselves liable to severe punishment.
>
> Moreover should the culprit not be discovered, the population may be penalised in the same way as in the case of acts of sabotage.
>
> The culprit or culprits must be discovered within 72 hours of the publication of this warning. May I warn my fellow Islanders against committing these foolish acts, which accomplish nothing but merely bring grave consequences in their train?

This modern version of 'Dilly, Dilly, Dilly, Dilly, come and be killed' did not have the designed effect. No culprit or culprits were discovered within the specified 72 hours.

The writing on walls of 'V' (the initial letter of the word 'Victoire') by French patriots who wished by this means to support and stimulate the morale of their fellow-countrymen began in occupied France and was introduced into Guernsey partly by French members of the crews of ships that brought our supplies from Granville, and partly by listeners to wireless reports who heard of the practice from the British Broadcasting Corporation's Overseas Service. At first it showed no signs of becoming popular; few indeed knew that it had been adopted in Guernsey at all until the Bailiff's warning told them of it; and it would probably have died a natural death as soon as the novelty wore off if the German authorities had been wise enough to ignore it. But what might have been only a spark burst into flame on the publication on July 9th in the *Gazette Officielle* columns of the local newspapers of another notice over the Bailiff's signature:

> A reward of £25 will be given to the person who first gives to the Inspector of Police information leading to the conviction of anyone (not already discovered) for the offence of marking on any gate, wall or other place whatsoever visible to the public the letter 'V', or any other sign or any word or words calculated to offend the German authorities or soldiers.

The public did not know that on this occasion the German authorities had threatened to deport 25 leading Islanders to a concentration camp and speculation arose as to whether, if paid, the money would come out of German funds, or the Bailiff's pocket, and at once there began what may well be called 'The Battle of the Vs', a battle waged by us with lighthearted futility and by the Germans with the ponderous strength of a blacksmith swatting flies with a sledge-hammer. Whereas before the offer of a reward careful search was needed to find the offending letter written anywhere, it could now be found in so many places, generally written in chalk in letters a few inches high but in some cases in paint in letters four feet high and three inches wide, that special constables were sent out with buckets and sponges to obliterate them, wherever it was possible to do so. V's cut out of paper or cardboard were dropped in the street, left on shop-counters, slipped into folded newspapers and pushed through the letter-boxes of houses occupied by Germans. Those who possessed or could buy brooches bearing the letter V wore them. People greeted each other in the street by holding up the right hand with three fingers folded so that the thumb and the forefinger made the prescribed letter. Men carried spent matches in their waistcoat pockets and, on finding a temporarily unoccupied motor-car standing alongside the pavement, bent one of them into the shape of a 'V' and dropped it on to the seat of the car where the German occupant would see it on his return.

On the suggestion of the BBC Overseas Service a variation of the game was adopted. It happens that in the International Morse Code the letter V is represented by three short strokes followed by a long one. People knocked on doors with three light taps followed by a heavy one and in shops – especially if a German happened to be among the customers – knocked out the dottles from their pipes on the heels of their boots with similar taps. It was pointed out by the British Broadcasting Corporation that in Beethoven's famous Fifth Symphony – which represents Fate knocking at the door – the knocking is represented by three short notes and a long one. At once the symphony enjoyed an unusual popularity. Those who had gramophone records of it frequently played it, taking care to open their windows so that passing Germans might hear and perhaps reflect that Fate was knocking at Germany's door.

A Mr P. Robilliard planted sunflowers in the form of huge 'Vs' with a background of other crops, thus making a sign that could be plainly seen from the air.

Because at the time the power of the Royal Air Force was becoming more marked each week it occurred to some that the letters RAF might take equal rank with the letter 'V' as calculated to offend the German authorities. These letters appeared on walls in public places and one man had the happy idea of exhibiting at his front gate the notice:

>VVanted
>Rabbits
>Also
>Fowls

The Germans scored their first victory in the Battle of the 'V's by discovering, through the agency of their own police, that a French resident, M. de Guillebon, while discussing the matter, had chalked a 'V' on the saddle of his bicycle. He was allowed to be legally represented at his trial and his advocate afterwards privately expressed the opinion that the German court, consisting of a President and two assessors, were patient and painstaking in their conduct of the case and that they tried it fairly according to German ideas of justice. It should be mentioned, however, that M. de Guillebon was tried under the German penal code of which he had no knowledge, and that he was not allowed to consult his advocate until they met in the Court room just before the Court sat. He was found guilty of 'organisation of anti-German feeling' and sentenced to a year's imprisonment in France.

The day after the trial the German authorities tried to gain another victory in a way that was tantamount to an admission of defeat. They tried to deprive the letter 'V' of the significance it had in our eyes by appropriating it for their own use. Germans stencilled a design of the letter enclosed in a laurel wreath on the doors or walls of the houses they occupied and in order that we should understand that the use of 'V' in such cases did not indicate sympathy with the Allied cause our newspapers were made to publish on July 23rd an article entitled 'Vs – German Victories on all fronts', which informed us that 'V', the initial of the word 'Viktoria' (victory) was the sign of the certainty of a German victory in the struggle for Europe (no mention was made of any contribution towards this victory that might be made by Italy or any other of Germany's allies), that it was to be found in all the streets of innumerable cities on the Continent, that in Holland hundreds of thousands of people wore little 'V' brooches, that in Prague the name of the main thoroughfare had been changed from 'Volkstrasse' to 'Viktoria Street', that aeroplanes were dropping small 'V' tokens all over Poland, and that in Paris the letter 'V' was to be found on the Eiffel Tower and on all the most famous buildings.

The purpose of the article was, apparently, to make us believe that the inhabitants of all German-occupied countries had suddenly and spontaneously adopted the letter as a symbol of their enthusiasm for the cause of their temporary overlords, but it did not explain to us why the Germans themselves used as a symbol of German victories the initial letter of the word 'Viktoria' that is nearly English and nearly French but nowhere near German.

Word was at once passed round by the Guernsey Underground News Service that the letter 'V' stencilled on houses occupied by Germans signified 'Verminous' and three days after the appearance of the article in the newspapers many people found in their letter-boxes envelopes containing strips of paper on which were mimeographed an unofficial but very satisfactory theory: 'The German word of Victory (Sieg) begins with 'S'. The use of the 'V" by Germans suggests to us the word 'verloren' which means LOST, and the wreath suggests a funeral wreath.' If it were true that the Germans regarded the adoption of the 'V' sign in all other German-occupied countries as a compliment to themselves we might well have supposed, after the publication of the article, that the German authorities in Guernsey would have no objection to our adopting it. We should have been wrong. On July 26th two notices were published, one over the German Commandant's signature, the other over that of the Bailiff. As both notices conveyed the same information and warning it is unnecessary to quote them both. The Commandant's is given here because it was somewhat more detailed and much more amusing.

The signs 'E.V.' and 'V' have been drawn in black by unknown perpetrators of the civil population at four points along the road leading from St Martin's to the airport, in the neighbourhood of the Beaulieu Hotel, on walls and in the roadway. In one case a street-number-sign-board of the German forces has been besmeared with the sign 'E.V.', which action is judged as damage to a contrivance of the German forces and therefore explicitly as an act of sabotage.

The Island Police have not yet found out the perpetrators. Therefore the people living in the vicinity, who are suspects in the first place, have to suffer for their guilt.

The Field Commandant has ordered the following measures:

1. The wireless receiving sets of all civilians living within a radius of 1,000 metres from the Beaulieu Hotel are confiscated until further notice and to be collected. The sets must be delivered by 6pm on 26th July, 1941.
2. Two men each of St Martin's are to stand sentry from 10pm to 6am at the besmeared street-number-sign-board and at two more signboards.
3. The measures in accordance with (1) and (2) are carried out by the States authorities.
4. The Field Commandant reserves to himself further measures in case the perpetrators should not be found out in future either.

It is probable that the punishment mentioned in (1) was decided on because Germans needed wireless receiving sets for their own use. On June 26th an order had been published ordering all householders who were in possession of more than one mains wireless receiving set to surrender one of them to the Controlling Committee. Perhaps the response to that order had disappointed the Germans. At any rate the radios confiscated on this occasion were never returned to their owners. As soon as they were collected they were handed over to individual Germans who needed them.

No doubt the variant 'E.V.' had been adopted by the 'unknown perpetrators' because they wished it to be definitely understood that English 'Victory' not German 'Viktoria' was meant. By this time it was noticeable that all German soldiers of the rank and file were wearing the letter 'V' embroidered on the left sleeves of their tunics, for a reason given on the propaganda pages of both our newspapers on July 29th.

THE BIG 'V'

VIKTORIA – Victory, shouted the soldiers of Frederick the Great after they had won the battle.

'Glorious – Victorious' are the words of enthusiasm of one of the most popular German military songs. 'Victorious' is also the cry which the German soldiers of the war of 1941 have adopted to express their unshakable confidence of victory. Proud of the victories gained by their comrades on the Western front, the German soldiers have now begun to display the 'V' on their tunics, on their lorries and on the doors of their barracks.

THE LETTER 'V' CAN ONLY BE ATTRIBUTED TO THOSE WHOSE COLOURS HAVE NEVER BORNE RETREAT; BUT ONLY VICTORIES, CLAIM THE GERMAN PEOPLE.

Again it was not explained why the soldiers of Frederick the Great celebrated the winning of a battle by shouting a word that, whatever language it belonged to, was certainly not German.

On August 3rd Guernsey police called at all houses within an area of which Amherst Schools, then occupied by Germans, was the centre, to take the names of men whose ages made them eligible for guard duty over the school notice-board to which had been pinned a cartoon more likely to offend the German authorities than any number of 'V's. It was a very clever drawing of a Spitfire hotly pursuing a German plane, the pilot of which was exclaiming 'Himmel! Another Luftwaffe victory.' A mysterious feature of this incident was that, beyond the warning of men in the vicinity of the schools that they might be needed to go on guard over the notice-board, nothing was done. The cartoon did not evoke any more official threats from the German authorities and no punishment was inflicted. The real explanation seems to have been that the German police in the course of their detective work, discovered that the cartoon had been drawn and pinned to the notice-board by a German.

That was the last incident in the Battle of the 'V's. It was abandoned on our side not from fear of reprisals but simply because the novelty of it wore off. Had the German authorities ignored it from the beginning it would probably have died down much sooner, but by showing unmistakably that it hurt them they prolonged it. There is little satisfaction to be gained by hitting a giant who shows no signs of consciousness that he has been hit.

Some weeks after the occupation began a German newspaper published a boastful article which, besides making a number of assertions that were quite untrue, said that the Germans had fortified the Island against both air attacks and landings. Certainly they did fortify the Island, and very heavily, but they failed by a long way to make it invulnerable.

Early in January, 1941, a report circulated widely throughout the Island that a party of British sailors or soldiers had landed at L'Ancresse, captured and carried away five soldiers, including one officer, and left no trace behind them except a note which said, 'If you won't invade us we must invade you'. The story may be pure invention. Obviously if true it was a German who first told it, but this is not incredible for already many Germans, disgusted and disillusioned, liked to hear and tell of British successes, and if the story was an invention the inventor showed prophetic powers, for two months later the BBC told us of an exactly similar capture of some Germans stationed on one of the Lofoten Islands of Norway.

The general truth of reports of a number of air raids on the Island during 1941 cannot be doubted, though as a rule no two reports exactly agreed as to details. On February 15th many people heard the sound of bombing in the direction of the Corbière and later it was rumoured that a six-inch gun there had been attacked and nine Germans killed or wounded. On May 9th a plane flew right across the Island, killing twelve Germans at L'Ancresse and forty at Jerbourg with machine-gun fire. On May 13th five British planes flew over the Island, doing nothing hostile but badly frightening the crew of an anti-aircraft gun who, to the delight of some Guernseymen spectators, bolted for cover when they saw the planes coming.

On June 1st gunners at Jerbourg and on June 3rd troops marching along the Fort Road were machine-gunned by raiding British planes. The circumstances attaching to a minor raid on June 2nd might serve for the basis of a sensational magazine story. A plane that, to judge by the noise it made, was suffering from engine-trouble, dropped a stick of bombs in Torteval parish. The bombs fell nowhere near any military target, so it may be supposed that the pilot jettisoned them to relieve his plane of their weight and thus enable it to regain height. Though they actually fell on dry land they fell so close to the sea that it seemed as if the pilot of the plane had wished them to drop in deep water. One of the bombs failed to explode but broke open on falling. Subsequent examination by Germans disclosed that its case contained not only several varieties of explosive but also a highly elaborate mechanism.

We had recently heard from the British Broadcasting Corporation that the Royal Air Force was using a new type of bomb from which great things were expected and therefore had reason to fear that the unexploded bomb might be one of the new pattern. If it were, the failure of the bomb to explode was a tragedy for the British, because the Germans, by examining the mechanism, might learn from it a valuable secret that the Royal Air Force would wish to keep for their own. On the other hand it was possible to believe that the bomb was not meant to explode, that in fact it had been so made that it would break open without exploding, and that, in order to put the Germans on a false scent as to the secret of the new British bomb, it

NARRATIVE 1941

had been specially made and entrusted to a RAF pilot to drop somewhere in Guernsey where Germans would find it and that the pilot had instructions to behave in such a manner as to give the impression that he was compelled to drop it to get rid of its weight but was anxious to drop it somewhere out of German reach.

On June 7th a flight of British planes bombed a gun near the Candie Road between St Andrew's and the Castel and another gun on the Vazon racecourse. A bomb also fell near, but failed to hit, an ammunition dump in St Pierre-du-Bois. Troops were also machine-gunned and casualties on this occasion were so heavy that the Germans held a special memorial service for those killed in the raid. It was known that States workmen were employed to dig a grave capable of holding twenty-eight corpses. Anti-aircraft fire on this occasion was vigorous. One Guernseyman was wounded by falling shrapnel and much damage was done to greenhouses.

On June 9th all the sirens in the Island were tested. By a ludicrous coincidence no sooner had the 'all clear' signal been sounded than a daring reconnaissance raid was made by a plane that flew from the south-west of the Island to the town and then turned northward. The pilot did nothing hostile. Instead he waved his hand to a team of gunners as he passed over Pleinmont and saluted some officers sitting on the verandah of the Royal Hotel. Anti-aircraft gunners were caught napping. Not until the plane had passed over L'Ancresse and was disappearing in the northern sky were any shots fired at it.

On September 18th some British planes came overhead and were met with very heavy anti-aircraft fire which did no perceptible damage to them. They also did nothing hostile but they dropped copies of the *Daily Mail* and *Daily Mirror* with the Stock Exchange prices marked to let us know that War Loan and similar securities stood at a premium. On the following day we had two raids, each made by a single plane. On both occasions more newspapers were dropped, but machine-gun fire was also opened on troops drilling, causing – according to a German soldier's estimate – at least eighty casualties. A day later

131

a plane flew over and neither caused nor attempted to cause any casualties but dropped some silk handkerchiefs labelled 'For the women of Guernsey' and some Craven A cigarettes, presumably for whoever had the good luck to find them.

On September 23rd ships in St Peter Port harbour were machine-gunned. Among the casualties, estimated at eighty killed and wounded, were two Guernseymen employed by Germans at the White Rock. This was a spectacular raid because so many people could see it, but the most spectacular raid of the year was made on September 8th. A convoy of tugs, barges and a floating-crane had come down the Great Russell Channel, rounded Jethou and was off St Martin's Point when about sixteen British planes flying with their tails to the sun attacked it, sinking two barges, slightly damaging others and severely damaging one of the tugs. From the number of visits to the White Rock made by ambulances and the fact that the operating theatre at the Victoria Hospital was alight throughout the following night it was supposed that there were many wounded. A belief that some officers were among the killed was based on the fact that many wreaths were ordered from local florists. It was also believed that the dead of other ranks were buried at sea.

For some reason best known to themselves the Germans feared an invasion that night. All troops were kept on the alert and the sea-front was strongly patrolled. No invasion occurred but towards midnight a single plane dropped photo-flares about the Little Russell Channel between Herm and St Peter Port. Searchlights failed to locate it but anti-aircraft fire was discharged at random and some of the patrolling soldiers fired their rifles hopefully into the void.

Many raids were of such short duration that the departing planes were out of range before the anti-aircraft guns came into action. On the occasions when they did come into action greenhouses and other properties suffered from falling shrapnel but no damage that was perceptible to people in the Island was ever done to any raiding plane during 1941 or in any subsequent year.

Because they found our planes so difficult to hit, the A.A.

gunners on the Island were probably elated by local evidence that the Royal Air Force was at any rate not invulnerable. On March 15th, 1941, two British airmen whose plane had crashed in the sea landed from their rubber-boat and surrendered to the Germans. Three days earlier an airman in difficulties baled out after heading his plane seawards so that it should not crash on land. He landed at L'Eree, made himself comfortable for the night in an unoccupied cottage and gave himself up next morning. It was reported, with how much truth it is impossible to say, that the first Germans he encountered offered to surrender to him supposing him to be the first-comer of an invasion of parachutists.

On Christmas Eve the Press officer gave us an example of German humour at its worst. The Vicar of St Stephen's, Rev Hartley Jackson, had written a Christmas message to his congregation and sent it to *The Star* for publication. When a proof of the message was submitted in the ordinary way to the Press officer he so altered it that when published it contained the sentence 'The recognition that Christ was born into the world to save the world and bring peace on earth is the need of Britain and her Jewish and Bolshevik allies.' On Christmas morning Mr Jackson made an indignant and courageous protest from the pulpit against this outrage. No official notice was taken of his protest but it is possible that his boldness was resented and that it was punished by the harsh treatment that he received when nine months later an order came from 'higher authorities' that certain British subjects were to be sent to Germany.

On New Year's Eve throughout the Island the German troops indulged in a drunken orgy, and on the stroke of midnight they discharged their firearms promiscuously. Shortly before midnight occupants of the Collings Road States Houses had been visited by some Germans, still comparatively sober, who offered them wine and warned them not to go out of doors after midnight on account of the danger of being shot. Unfortunately one man, George Fisher, did go out of doors and was accidentally shot. It is significant of the extent to which our newspapers were under German control that neither *The Star*, which reported the

Coroner's verdict that Fisher died from 'excessive haemorrhage caused by a bullet-wound', nor the *Evening Press*, which reported the tragedy, published the name of the man, a non-commissioned officer, who fired the shot that mortally wounded Fisher. One of the occupants of the Collings Road States Houses said that he was so drunk when he fired his revolver that he could hardly stand but the *Evening Press* tactfully said he was 'completely unnerved by the shock', and added that he had been arrested by the German police pending a thorough investigation by the German authorities. What was the result of that investigation we were never allowed to know.

CHAPTER XII

NARRATIVE 1942

The outstanding events of the year 1942 were the confiscation of our wireless sets, the deportation of a number of people to German internment camps, and the trial and imprisonment of most of the Island police.

How absolutely our newspapers were under German control appeared in their reports of a daylight raid made by three Beaufort bombers on January 17th, 1942. The bombers came from a north-easterly direction, dropped bombs on shipping in the harbour and flew off, machine-gunning troops in Castle Cornet and Fort George as they went. Neither of our newspapers had ever mentioned any former British air raids on the Island – of which there had been at least twenty-five since the occupation, not counting mere reconnaissance raids – but three days after it happened both of our newspapers mentioned the raid, apparently for the purpose of discrediting the veracity of the British Broadcasting Corporation's news reports. The two accounts were not in identical words but they resembled each other so closely as to show that the writer of each of them was given a general outline of what he was to say. Both accounts laid stress on the unfortunate fact that more civilians than Germans were killed (the civilians were with one exception imported foreign labourers); both emphasised that one of the killed was a Guernseyman, a crane driver named George Tucker; and both made the incorrect statement that this was the first raid made by British airmen on St Peter Port harbour. As mentioned in the previous chapter, shipping in St Peter Port harbour was machine-gunned on September 23rd, 1941.

A comparison of the exact wording of the two version of this incorrect statement is enlightening. *The Star* said:

> Although one Islander, at least, lost his life and other workmen were victims, a certain section of the public seemed to derive some satisfaction from the

fact that after the lapse of eighteen months, the RAF had made their first raid, lasting only a few seconds, on the St Peter Port harbour.

The *Evening Press* said:

> Some people were apparently thrilled that the RAF had finally made their first attack on St Peter Port harbour, although one Guernseyman at least was among the victims of the raid.

Note that in one version was written 'a certain section of the public seemed to derive some satisfaction' and in the other 'some people were apparently thrilled'.

Both accounts contained an unwarranted attack on the veracity of the British Broadcasting Corporation, which had simply stated that Beaufort bombers had attacked shipping in the Guernsey harbour and machine-gunned troops on the Island.

The Star said:

> On Sunday morning, and later that day, the BBC news commentators endeavoured to magnify the result of the raid, but listeners reflected on the fact that the casualties among the German personnel were comparatively insignificant compared with those caused among the civilian labourers.
>
> It occurred to them that if this was the manner in which the BBC dealt with the local raid, about which they were in a position to know the facts, broadcasts about similar events on the Continent might be similarly exaggerated.
>
> With that in mind, the public will in future regard news of RAF activities with scepticism, not to say doubt or disbelief.

The *Evening Press* said:

> Much stress was laid on this raid by the BBC in their broadcast report, but, judging by the obviously minor results achieved – the proportion of German casualties being relatively small in comparison with those of civilian labourers – one wonders whether other much-boosted raids on the Continent and elsewhere achieve the results which the BBC would have us believe. This would now appear to be somewhat doubtful.

The casualties inflicted by the raiders were, as nearly as could be ascertained, one Guernseyman, eight Germans and twenty Frenchmen killed by the bombing and some fifty Germans killed or wounded by machine-gun fire in Castle Cornet and Fort George. Among other results of the raid that both accounts minimise were three cranes wrecked, a steamer of 8,000 tons sunk at the Southern Railway's berth on the jetty, a large munitions steamer holed in the bows, the back of a barge broken, and the sides of several other barges perforated with bomb splinters.

The Germans always endeavoured to keep us in ignorance of any damage done to them by British planes, but they could not hide from us what had been done to these vessels for the broken-backed barge was towed into the inner harbour with her forehold flooded, the steamer that still floated was brought to Albert Dock where any passer-by could see that the hole in her bows was at least eight feet in diameter, and as for the steamer that was sunk, because only her fore part was flooded, her stem rose with each tide and could be seen at high water high above the level of the jetty. We therefore had all the opportunity we needed for assessing the extent of what the *Evening Press* was made to describe as 'obviously minor results'.

It is conceivable that a British journalist, if he happened to have a mind poisoned by anti-British hate, might take advantage of our newspapers being under German control to write for publication an account of this particular raid and to seize the chance to relieve his embittered mind by belittling the Royal

Air Force, sneering at his fellow countrymen and impugning the veracity of the British Broadcasting Corporation. But it is quite inconceivable that two such journalists, after neglecting to record any of the previous raids that the RAF had made on the island, should, three days after it had happened, be inspired by this particular raid to write, spontaneously and independently, accounts of it in which the same bare facts were chosen for record, the same misstatement made, the same important details as to the damage done to the shipping ignored, the same sneer indulged in, and the same attack made on the veracity of the British Broadcasting Corporation. Such coincidences do not occur in real life. Anyone who read both accounts must have realised that they had the same source and that that source was the mind of the German Press officer. In causing them to be published the Press officer defeated his purpose. So far from sowing in our minds doubts as to the truth of the news given us by British broadcasts he confirmed what we already knew – that the anti-British propaganda published each day in our newspapers, though often amusing, was not to be credited as true. Incidentally he reminded us that among other cherished British institutions of which German rule had deprived us was the freedom of the Press.

On March 3rd, 1942, an advertisement appeared in the local papers inviting applications for employment as auxiliary police. No official explanation was forthcoming at the time, but it was rumoured that a number of the Guernsey police were in prison, having been caught in the act of stealing foodstuffs from a German store. Later, rumour gave place to certain knowledge, for on April 22nd the imprisoned policemen, eighteen in number, were brought to trial before a German court. Although it was their usual custom to withhold from the Guernsey public all information as to trials of Guernseymen before German courts, the German authorities, for some reason or other, wished to obtain the fullest possible publicity for this particular trial, for not only was it fully reported in the local newspapers but the public were even admitted to the Court while the trial was in progress.

The trial was held in the Police Court. It was decorated for the occasion with a Swastika flag hung behind the presiding judge's seat and he and his two assessors gave the Nazi salute as they took their seats. Mr A.J. Sherwill, who at the time was still debarred by the Germans from exercising the duties of King's Procureur – he was allowed to resume them on June 27th – represented the prisoners.

The trial lasted for two and a half days. It was proved that most of the accused policemen, taking advantage of their freedom to be out of doors unchallenged during curfew hours and of the immunity from suspicion that their uniform gave them, had for months past been systematically stealing German foodstuffs. It is probable that many people regarded thefts of enemy property as less disgraceful than thefts from our own people, but such sympathy as may have been felt for the accused on these grounds evaporated when it was proved that they had robbed not only their German enemies but also their fellow-Islanders by stealing foodstuffs from the Essential Commodities Committee's stores, meat from the Meat-market and spirits from local wine and spirit merchants.

They were also charged with the theft of firewood from a stock imported by the Germans and stacked in the open space surrounding what had formerly been St Paul's Methodist Church within a few yards of the Police Station. No German sentry had ever been posted over the wood and so little care had the Germans taken to guard it that occasionally children might be seen in broad daylight carrying off pieces small enough for them to carry. The temptation to steal it was great, for the ration of fuel allowed by the Essential Commodities Committee was pitifully meagre, so much so that many Islanders, including virtuous ladies of recognised social position, unblushingly admitted having stolen sawn timber from German contractors. It was unreasonable to expect a policeman on duty in the Police Station to shiver through the long hours of a cold winter's night when he could get as much firewood as he liked by walking across the road. So trivial was the theft of firewood in comparison with the theft of foodstuffs that the German authorities would have shown a better sense of proportion if they had considered the maxim *de minimis non curat lex* and disregarded it altogether. Yet they regarded this petty pilfering with such solemn gravity that the sole charge brought against one of the police was not that he had stolen wood but that, knowing that other police had stolen it, he had failed to denounce them. This particular policeman was the only one of the eighteen to be acquitted. It transpired during his trial that the others had been careful to keep him in ignorance of their thefts because of his reputation in the Police Force. The sentences passed on the seventeen who were adjudged guilty ranged from one of four weeks' imprisonment for the theft of firewood only to one of four and a half years' imprisonment passed on the ringleader who had organised the robberies, run the least risk of detection and taken the largest share of the plunder. It should be recorded that the Presiding Judge's conduct of the case seemed to be careful, competent and fair-minded; he showed only slight signs of impatience when one of the counsel insulted his intelligence by making statements so palpably false that they would hardly have deceived a child.

On June 6th ten of the convicted police were tried by the Royal Court for the theft of foodstuffs belonging to individual firms or to the Island as a whole. One was acquitted; the others received sentences of from three months to sixteen months' hard labour.

On June 13th the culprits were shipped out of the Island to serve their terms of imprisonment in France. From the fact that they were made to march handcuffed through High Street – which was not on the direct route to the steamer in which they were to travel – and that the time chosen was that at which the High Street was usually thronged with Saturday afternoon crowds, it was supposed that whoever had charge of the prisoners at the time meant deliberately to humiliate them.

Why did the German authorities give the fullest possible publicity to this particular trial? On a number of occasions Guernsey men or women had been tried before German courts for a variety of offences, for retaining radios or cameras after their surrender had been ordered, for assaulting Germans, for abusing them or even for having been overheard to speak of them as 'bloody Germans'. But on no other occasion were members of the general public allowed to be present at the trial of offenders, nor were the newspapers allowed to make any reference to such trials. In fact it seemed, whenever the Germans tried and punished anyone, that they wished to keep both trial and punishment as secret as possible. Arrests, of course, could seldom or never be kept secret. If a man were arrested at his place of business his colleagues knew about it; if in his home his family knew; if in the street there were probably some bystanders who witnessed the arrest, but until he regained his freedom it was only by chance that anyone knew of what he had been accused or to what punishment he was sentenced.

One would have supposed that the German authorities acted against their own interests in keeping their penal administration so secret. If they wished to deter us from disobeying their orders or doing anything that was against their interests surely the publication of the punishments awarded to offenders would have tended in that direction. What else were the punishments for? Vindictive punishment, that is, punishment the object of which is simply revenge, no longer forms part of the policy of any civilised State. In modern civilised countries punishment has two objects and two objects only – to reform the offender and, by letting his offence and its punishment be known, to deter others from following his bad example. We may leave out of consideration any idea that the Germans felt any interest in the reform of those they punished, especially as the offences for which they were punished were not as a rule breaches of any code of morals, and as they did not take the obvious steps they should have taken if they had wished to deter us from offending, we are driven to the only other alternative and must suppose that the punishments were merely vindictive. If this is the case, Nazism, breaking away from the practice of modern civilised beings, reverted by an atavistic process to the barbarism of the Middle Ages. Yet this idea hardly fits in with known facts, for those who had been imprisoned did not after their release complain of unduly harsh treatment.

Another puzzling circumstance is that the Germans were not consistent in their policy of secrecy. When Mrs Le Masurier and Mrs Michael, as related in Chapter IX, were deported to France for harbouring British agents, their names, the nature of their offence and the punishment awarded them were widely proclaimed both by poster and by announcements in our newspapers. When the Nicolles and others were deported to France and imprisoned for exactly the same offence the Germans exercised all possible secrecy when taking them away, but when they brought them back and released them they issued a proclamation specifying their names and the charges on which they had been tried. The object of this proclamation, however, seems not to have been to deter us from harbouring British agents so much as to advertise clemency.

An announcement that all wireless sets in the hands of the civilian population were to be confiscated again was published on June 8th. On the following day it was announced that this was not in any way a punishment of the civilian population but was for purely military reasons. The military reasons were not stated but they must have been obvious to anyone who had listened to recent broadcasts of the Overseas Service of the British Broadcasting Corporation.

These had led us to believe that an allied invasion of the Continent was imminent and had invited us to assist the invaders by sabotage and other ways. We were promised that at the right moment we should be told by the British Broadcasting Corporation exactly what we could most usefully do. Naturally the Germans did not wish us to be told how best we could help defeat them, so, of course, they did what they could to prevent us hearing any more British broadcasts. The confiscation of our radios, therefore, was not only an obviously necessary precaution but even an entirely justifiable one. True it was not permitted under the Hague Convention, but if those who drafted that convention had realised that wireless receiving sets might become weapons even more valuable than wireless transmission sets they would certainly have approved their confiscation.

The advertised penalty for disobedience of the order to

surrender radios was at first either a comparatively light term of six weeks' imprisonment, or, alternatively a staggering fine of 30,000 reichsmarks, equivalent to £3,205 2s. 6d., according to the official German valuation of the reichsmark. There can have been few people in the Island who could have paid such a fine, but enough stout-hearted people disobeyed the order to keep the whole Island supplied with all the news of real importance. Some of these merely listened-in and told others as much as they could remember having heard. Others while listening-in took notes which they afterwards elaborated, typed, and circulated among friends in whose loyalty and discretion they could trust.

On December 23rd another announcement threatened those who retained their radios with imprisonment with hard labour or, in serious cases, the death penalty. Even after the threat of death penalty, stout-hearts – to whom the Island's debt of gratitude is incalculable – retained their radios, received the news and passed it on to others, and those again to others.

When confronted with an emergency for which they were not fully prepared the Germans were apt to lose their heads. It was noticeable when in May, 1941, a magnetic mine was dropped on the shingle near Fort Saumarez. Everyone living within six hundred yards was made to evacuate the area immediately, though later those who wished to do so were allowed to return at their own risk to remove cattle and collect necessaries for the night. Not until late on the following day did it occur to the German authorities to have the mine rendered harmless. Again in the latter part of November, 1942, gunners at Jerbourg opened fire on an approaching German ship that they did not recognise, killing fifteen officers and men, including a General believed to have been coming to Guernsey on an important mission, and wounding between seventy and eighty others; and an occasion when German gunners shot down German planes is recorded at the end of this chapter.

Perhaps because they knew themselves to be temporarily unfit to cope with unforeseen emergencies, the Germans in Guernsey took the most elaborate precautions against any predictable mishap that might occur; even when the chances of its occurring were remote. After the raid on Dieppe – news of which circulated through our underground news service before the Germans here heard of it – elaborate preparations to resist a raid on Guernsey were made. The use of the telephone service was denied to the general public, a number of roads were closed, making it impossible for many people to get to their work or places of business or to fetch the day's ration of milk, Guernseymen employed at the airport or in German canteens were sent home, all foreign labourers were confined to their billets (where they amused themselves by truculently singing *La Marseillaise* and shouting 'Come On Tommy') and all Germans who at the time were serving terms of imprisonment were released. Similar precautions were adopted when later in the year it was known that American troops had landed in North Africa. From November 9th until November 30th all troops were kept on the alert. Coast roads were patrolled day and night by men who constantly peered seawards through binoculars. All Germans not on patrol duty had to be in their quarters by 6pm and – so it was stated by those in whose houses they were billeted – were not allowed to undress at night or even to remove their boots.

The work of fortifying the Island on a grandiose scale went on throughout the year. Tunnels were dug and gun emplacements constructed by imported Arab, Spanish and French labourers under the direction of French, Belgian, Dutch and German technicians of the Organisation Todt, a sort of non-combatant sapper corps colloquially known as the O.T. The labourers were well paid at the rate of a mark (2s. 1d.) an hour, but badly housed and very poorly fed. Some of them, according to their own account of themselves, had been recruited by press-gang methods and consequently were sullen and disinclined to do any more work than they could possibly help. As might be expected many fell foul of their German overseers and were punished. Accounts of German brutality towards the foreign labourers were never precise and could not of course be verified, but they came from so many fairly reliable sources that there can be little doubt that they were substantially true. On one occasion protests against ill treatment developed into a riot at the Airport in the course of which a German soldier was killed. The Frenchman who killed him was arrested and shot two days later. On another occasion a labourer of unspecified nationality struck on the head with a spade a German who was bullying him, splitting his skull open. The labourer was shot on the spot by an officer of the O.T. Men who flatly refused to work were deprived of their rations and were driven to live precariously by begging from Islanders who had garden produce to spare, by rummaging in dustbins (where very little that was edible was ever to be found), but principally by theft. Such men did not return to the billets assigned to them but slept in sheds, outhouses and whatever shelter they could find. The German authorities took little interest in these vagrants and the task of rounding them up fell on the Island police, who sometimes arrested and handed over to the O.T. officers as many as a dozen in one day. The Organisation Todt used a number of what had been private houses for the incarceration of vagrants and other offenders among the imported foreigners.

Because the houses were not suitable for use as prisons and because the O.T. gaolers were inefficient or negligent, prisoners frequently escaped, were arrested again by the Island police, imprisoned again and escaped again. This happened so often that our police, in the words of one of them, got 'sick and tired of catching them'. Negligent is too mild a term to apply to the O.T. gaolers. It came to the knowledge of the Island police that they frequently released prisoners at night on the understanding that they were to return before daybreak and share whatever they had been able to steal.

Vagrants and prisoners were not the only foreigners who stole growing crops. All had great inducement to steal: they were provoked to it by the meagreness of the rations supplied to them; rendered, by the hardness of their lot, reckless of whatever punishment might befall them; and tempted by the ease with which they could rob, for owners of gardens and greenhouses were debarred by curfew restrictions from guarding their property at night.

It was seldom possible to apprehend a thief, but on one

occasion the local police caught a foreigner in the early hours of the morning carrying a heavy sackful of immature potatoes that he had stolen from a greenhouse. On investigation at the scene of the robbery it was found that the thief, having no tools, had torn up the potato plants by the haulm and picked one or two of the largest tubers from each. By this method he had destroyed perhaps twenty times as much food as he had stolen. That is but one recorded case out of hundreds that were not recorded.

It was principally to the owners of garden produce that the foreigners were an unmitigated nuisance, but in one respect all people of moderate means had cause to resent their presence. As their lodging was free, and their food, such as it was, provided for them and as it was almost impossible for them, as for anyone else, to buy clothing, they could afford to regard their wages, which would sometimes amount to as much as £5 a week, as pocket-money, and did in fact spend much of it on the costlier varieties of fruit and vegetables, thus driving the price of these up to a level where it was beyond the reach of the average householder's pocket. One might often see in the market-place a foreigner whose clothes were almost falling off him buy half a dozen peaches at two shillings apiece and eat them all on the spot. It was a somewhat galling sight for a thrifty housewife who would have liked, but could not afford, to give her family some treat to vary the monotony of their meals.

As the foreigners were closely herded into houses in the poorest quarters of the town and as many of them belonged to a class of Frenchmen whose habits are grossly insanitary, few disbelieved a rumour in November that an epidemic had broken out. That there was an epidemic was never directly admitted by the authorities but certain facts could not be hidden. For a few days Cornet Street and Allez Street, both of which were principally inhabited by foreign labourers, were closed and when traffic was once more allowed to pass through them it was noticeable that some houses were being fumigated and that the occupants of others, including some houses in Hauteville, were in quarantine – sentries stood at their doors to prevent those who were billeted in them from mingling with others.

At the same time notices in German, English, French and Spanish appeared outside shops and picture-theatres forbidding entrance to foreign labourers and members of the Organisation Todt. The epidemic lasted throughout the greater part of the winter and all doubt of its nature was dispelled in the following February when the Health Services Officer published a warning that typhus fever is mainly, if not solely, transmitted by vermin, coupled with an invitation to anyone infected with lice to apply to the Sanitary Authorities at Lukis House in order that they themselves, their clothing and their houses should be freed from that dangerous condition. On March 1st an order was published giving the States Medical Officer power to compel anyone whom he had reason to believe might be verminous to submit himself, his clothing and his premises to cleansing treatment.

On Tuesday, September 15th, the following notice was published :-

> By order of the higher authorities the following British subjects will be evacuated and transferred to Germany:
> (a) Persons who have their permanent residence not on the Channel Islands, for instance, those who have been caught here by the outbreak of the war.
> (b) All those men not born on the Channel Islands, from 16 to 70 years of age, who belong to the English people, together with their families.

On the following day a form was published which all concerned were directed to fill in and take or send to the Greffe, stating name, birthplace, date of birth, number of dependents, occupation and place of employment.

As the German authorities very seldom took really energetic and efficient steps to enforce the orders they issued it occurred to many people that it might be worth while to run the risk of disobeying this order also. Word got about, however, that the Germans, meaning this order to be strictly obeyed, were preparing lists, from the duplicate identity cards lodged at the Greffe, of all those to whom this order applied and that those who neglected to fill in the form would be imprisoned as well as deported. There was therefore nothing for it but for those affected to shrug their shoulders and face the uncertain future with upper lips as stiff as might be.

Next day, Friday, 18th, German soldiers accompanied by Island police served notices – for which they demanded receipts – on those whose ill fate it was to have been selected for deportation. Coupled with each notice was advice to the recipient to take only so much luggage as he could carry, to take at least one blanket, and food for the journey, and to pack trunks with additional clothes and blankets to be forwarded later. Money might be taken but not more than ten marks per person.

Some people, though liable to deportation, were exempted from the order at the request of the Bailiff or someone else of standing in the island. On the ground, for example, that rigid enforcement of the order would deprive the Island of nearly all of its Church of England clergy, the Dean of Guernsey applied for those whom he considered could least be spared. His request was granted in most cases but not in all. He had applied for the exemption of the Vicar of Saint Stephen's, Rev Hartley Jackson. This was refused and Mr Jackson received notice to prepare for deportation. Mr Jackson's doctor, supported by the Health Officer, then represented to the Commandant of Guernsey that Mr Jackson was an invalid, that he needed special diet such as he would be unlikely to get in an internment camp, and that he was not physically fit for the fatigue of the journey to Germany. The representation was fruitless. An appeal was made to the Jersey Commandant, to whom the Guernsey commandant was subordinate, but without success.

Nobody so much as tried to assign a motive for the forcible carrying off of a number of people. The most plausible theory suggested was that for some unfathomable reason Germany intended to hold them as hostages and that the German authorities supposed that the British Government set a higher value on English-born, than on Guernsey-born, British subjects.

(It became known that British subjects who had had the luck to be born in Southern Ireland were not served with deportation notices). If this theory were correct it might be supposed that in the eyes of the German authorities one English person was of just as much value as another. But if so why did the German authorities insist so obstinately that Mr Jackson was to be deported? When the question arose in people's minds it was remembered that – as mentioned in the previous chapter – on the previous Christmas morning Mr Jackson had commented vigorously from his pulpit on the offensive alteration that the German Press Officer had made in the wording of his Christmas message. The obvious conclusion was drawn that the refusal to exempt Mr Jackson from deportation was due to petty spite.

It was fervently hoped that by some means or other the British Government would learn of the deportation, and when it became known that two fishermen had escaped from the Island it was hoped that they knew of the deportation order before they got away so that they could inform the British authorities of it when they arrived in England. Soon afterwards a German officer called on Mrs Bichard, the wife of one of the fishermen, and told her that her husband must be presumed to be drowned as his boat had been found drifting and empty. Experienced fishermen, however, do not fall out of their boats, especially in such fine weather as was prevailing at the time. If the German's statement that the boat had been found empty was true it seemed probable that the fishermen had been picked up by some British vessel which, rather than be hampered with it, had turned the boat adrift.

A feeling spontaneously arose among those fortunate ones who were to remain in Guernsey that it was their manifest duty to do anything in their power to mitigate the hardships of exile for those who had to go. This feeling found expression both among public officials and private individuals. It was announced that the first batch of exiles was to leave the Island on Monday, 21st September, barely three days after they had received orders to get ready, and the second was to follow two days later. Whatever could be done for them had to be done quickly.

The help that public officials were prepared to offer the exiles was published in the *Evening Press* on Friday the 18th in a number of announcements. The general effect of these was that the Custodian of Dwellings and Gardens was prepared to take charge of the homes and personal effects of those who wished him to do so, and to arrange for the harvesting of their crops and the future cultivation of their land, and that the Controller of Clothing and Footwear had arranged for the States Shoemaking Department to be open throughout the following Sunday for the repair of the boots of those whose usual cobblers were too busy to serve them, and for the Essential Commodities offices at the Ladies' College to be open throughout the Sunday for the supply of clothing to those desperately in need of it.

An editorial in the same issue of the *Evening Press* announced that 'the wife of a leading Islander' had suggested the probability that many children would be evacuated whose parents had neither sufficient warm clothing for them nor the means of supplying it, and had announced that her husband was prepared to subscribe what the *Evening Press* described as 'a considerable amount of money' for that purpose. This call to private individuals to play their part met with a response of which the Island might justly feel proud. The Bailiff promptly initiated a fund, known as 'The Bailiff's Fund', by which the sum of £1,813 12s. 7d. was raised for the purchase of necessities for exiles. But many individuals were not content merely to give money. Some, and their number included a few who themselves were to be exiled, gave their services – so many in fact did so that offers of help had to be refused from all but the first-comers. Many more gave what was even more valuable than money or personal service. They gave clothes: not just the clothes they could easily spare – for at this stage of the occupation all wardrobes were so seriously depleted that no one had clothes they could easily spare – but clothes that they could sacrifice without making themselves destitute.

Announcements in Saturday's *Star* made it known that *The Star* office, and the Children's Emergency Bureau, as well as the Ladies' College, would be open throughout Sunday for the receipt and distribution of clothing. The Children's Bureau coupled an appeal for the help of needlewomen who would offer their services without a moment's delay with a statement that it would make a continuous 'day and night effort to meet all possible needs'. And the Electricity Controller announced that electric current might be used during prohibited hours 'so that helpers may get on with their job as rapidly and uninterruptedly as possible'.

At the Ladies' College on Sunday morning clothing was on sale to exiles. Much of it had been given by private individuals, the rest had been requisitioned from shops by the Controller of Clothing and Footwear. At this period of the occupation the stocks of most shops were so seriously depleted – many boot-and-shoe shops had in fact closed down altogether – that the Controller had been able to get little new clothing or footwear. Most of what he had requisitioned he got from the many barter-shops that had sprung into existence, at which second-hand clothing was sold on commission on behalf of its owners. Acting under powers conferred on him the Controller put his own price on the goods he requisitioned and paid in no case more than 90 per cent of their original cost price, instead of the 200 per cent which in some cases the vendors had asked. The price at which most of the clothing was sold, especially that which had been given by private individuals, was left to the judgment of the voluntary helpers, the majority of whom had experience as shop-assistants. Many who had come to buy could afford to pay the full amount asked. Some could not, for earners of weekly wages usually replenish their wardrobes with an article at a time and find difficulty in meeting an unexpected emergency out of a single week's wages. For such as these generous deductions were made. Boots that in normal times would have cost twenty-five shillings – for which perhaps fifty shillings had been asked at a barter shop two days earlier – were sold for ten shillings or less. Buyers who could not afford to pay full value were in fact invited first to choose what they needed and then to pay what they could. In some cases clothes were given away as freely and with as little suggestion of alms-giving as perhaps, an hour before, they had been given by their original owners. Unfortunately, in one respect, it was impossible to dispense with a precaution that makes the receipt of alms distasteful to a self-respecting man. Contemptible people are to be found in every community and Guernsey has its full share of them. Some people who, not being under orders to go into exile, had no claim whatever on the Island's generosity, saw in the misfortunes of others a chance to replenish their wardrobes at little or no cost to themselves. So many of these applied for clothing under false pretences that it became necessary to require applicants to produce their evacuation orders as proof that they were entitled to assistance.

As first arranged the exiles were to leave the Island in two batches, the first on Monday the 21st, the second on Wednesday the 23rd of September. The Gaumont Theatre was the assembly point. Country residents were brought by motor buses at the expense, not of the Germans, but of the States. Town residents had to go on foot. At the Gaumont all were medically examined, and on reaching the White Rock they had to pass a barrier beyond which friends who had come to see them off were not allowed to go. But before passing the barrier each was given, at the expense of the States, a basket containing food for the journey and on the White Rock a meal was supplied to be eaten before embarking. As an example of the thoroughness of the arrangements for the comfort of the exiles it is worth mentioning that above the counter at which they received their baskets of food was a notice 'If you have forgotten toilet soap or razor-blades please ask for them'. Both toilet soap and razor-blades were, at this period of the occupation, luxuries difficult to obtain.

The caterer commissioned to provide the meal on the White Rock had done his best to give it a festal character. In the first place, though Monday was a meatless day he was able, with the consent of the Food Controller, to supply a hot meat stew. Secondly he gave each person a hard-boiled egg. The eggs were not paid for by the States but were the personal gift of the caterer himself, Mr F. Stroobant, who himself was to be one of the exiles. Three days before, he had advertised that he had immediate need for a thousand eggs and was prepared to pay 8/- a dozen for them. As it became known for what purpose the eggs were wanted it is probable, in so generous a mood were many people at this time, that he did not have to pay for all that he received. Finally he served the exiles with ham sandwiches – a treat indeed! – few of those who enjoyed them can have tasted ham for two years or more. The provision supplied for the journey was also of a comparatively luxurious character. Each person received 2 lbs of bread, ¼ lb of butter, ¼ lb of cheese, one tin of sardines, 2½ ozs of liver paste, ½ lb of biscuits and ½ lb of chocolate. In addition to this, children under the age of three received half a pound of rusks, and men received a generous supply of tobacco and cigarettes.

But there was nothing luxurious about the steamer on which the first batch of exiles embarked. She was a small cargo vessel with no sleeping accommodation whatever except that provided for the crew, and no place in which it was possible even to sit in comfort except one small saloon in which there were settees large enough to seat about a score of people. A more or less self-appointed committee assigned this saloon to mothers of young children – one child was only fourteen days old. The sanitary arrangements on board, though adequate for a crew of not too fastidious seamen, were entirely unsuitable for two hundred people of both sexes accustomed to the ordinary decencies of civilised life, and the closet could not be reached except through the saloon assigned to the mothers of young children. To give an edge to the general discomfort it was known that a gale was blowing between Jersey and St Malo, the port to which they were bound.

After a night of acute discomfort the steamer was still at her moorings. Her captain, realising how great would be the danger of broken limbs among the exiles when his ship, with no cargo to steady her, met the full force of the gale, had refused to sail until the weather improved. During the course of the morning the exiles were allowed to disembark and return to their dismantled homes for the time being. Two days later they left on a better equipped steamer than that on which they had first embarked. Their presence on the Island for those two days created, of course, a need for emergency measures in the food control office. The second batch of exiles, scheduled to leave on Wednesday, 23rd September, finally got away on Sunday the 27th. They left at midnight and people living near enough heard them singing 'Auld Lang Syne' and 'God Save the King' as the steamer cleared the harbour.

It was rather surprising – and not a little gratifying to those of us who loathed renegades – to see among the second batch of exiles two Quislings who had ratted from their loyalty to their Mother-country as soon as the Germans arrived in the Island and ever since had been notorious as toadies and lickspittles, lavishingly entertaining German officers, not because of any perverted but honest pro-Germanism, but avowedly for what they could gain by thus prostituting themselves. They seemed to have gained little in the long run. One of them even had to submit to the indignity of being searched at the barrier. The other sought, at the last moment, to re-establish himself in the eyes of his compatriots by trying to give the impression that he could have escaped exile had he chosen to do so. Just before reaching the barrier he addressed the crowd assembled to bid God-speed to the exiles. 'They said I was German. Now they will know that I am British', he said, and passed through the barrier with the proud air of one who prefers imprisonment to dishonour.

Another batch of exiles was deported in the following year. On January 27th a number of men received orders to present themselves and their families at the Regal Theatre for medical examination. Those found to be physically fit were deported on February 9th but families were not separated – a physically fit man whose wife or child were unfit was exempted. No official notice of this deportation was published and as the newspapers were not allowed to make any reference to it, it was impossible this time to organise any scheme in which the general public could join for the relief of the necessities of the exiles. Help was, however, given to those who needed it at the expense of the Bailiff's Fund. No official explanation was given as to the principle on which this third batch of exiles was selected but it was generally understood that those taken were Freemasons, ex-officers and non-commissioned officers, and people who had recently served a term of imprisonment. Possibly the underlying idea was that if a conspiracy against the Germans were hatched it would be members of a secret society who would do the necessary plotting and ex-officers who would carry out the executive work, while desperate deeds necessary to the plot – such as assassination, sabotage or the theft of weapons – would be more readily undertaken by people of a criminal tendency than by those who had always led blameless lives. No women, whether born in the Channel Islands or elsewhere, had been sent away in the two former batches of exiles except in the company of their husbands but this batch included some unmarried women who had been in prison for offences against the Germans.

Deportation orders caused two tragedies. Rather than obey them a husband and wife carried out a suicide pact, and a man killed himself rather than subject his wife – who if he died would escape deportation – to the hardships that he feared for her.

From time to time letters reached the Island from exiles, who expressed contentment with the treatment they were receiving. These were received with some scepticism as the letters were liable to censorship and would not have been forwarded if they had given accounts of German ill-treatment. Later, however, some exiles were invalided back to Guernsey and gave us verbal accounts that were to be trusted. From these we learned that living conditions in the internment camps were somewhat squalid and that the food issued was both bad in quality and insufficient in quantity, but that, thanks to the parcels of food received from England through the agency of the Red Cross, the exiles were on the whole better fed than were we in Guernsey. Monotony and lack of exercise were the greatest hardships that they had to bear. Those who, to escape these, volunteered to work on neighbouring farms found the Bavarians very friendly. They were allowed to listen to British broadcasts and were thus able to take authentic war news back to the internment camps.

On many nights throughout 1942 heavy anti-aircraft fire told us that British planes were passing over the Island on their way to St Malo, Rennes, St Nazaire or La Palice, but, apart from the attack on shipping in the harbour mentioned earlier in this chapter there were few notable raids on the Island itself. Sometimes bombs were dropped on guns at Jerbourg, Pleinmont or Cobo, and sometimes a plane appeared out of the blue, skimmed over part of the Island, machine-gunning a few troops, and was off again before the anti-aircraft gunners had time to get into action. On one occasion a small scale air-battle developed over the Island. A German plane appeared from seaward and flew towards the airport closely pursued by two British planes, all three just above the housetops. The German plane reached the airport, but in a damaged condition. The British planes then flew off unscathed.

On November 10th the Australian pilot of a crippled Spitfire on its way back to its base baled out and landed near the cliffs. Some men of the Organisation Todt were first on the scene and began to manhandle him but some German military officers interfered, took him into custody and treated him with courtesy. His plane had received its injuries elsewhere, not from local anti-aircraft guns. Throughout the whole period of the occupation local anti-aircraft gunners never once succeeded in bringing down an Allied plane. They did on one occasion shoot down two planes but that was in error. They were German planes. This was in the evening of August 24th, 1943. On that occasion, it appeared, they were especially on the alert as a warning had been telephoned from Jersey that British planes were in the vicinity. At about 6.30pm (sun time) they sighted some planes, said to be of an unfamiliar type, approaching the Island from the south-east, dropping some objects which they supposed to be mines into the sea as they came. Gunners at Jerbourg opened fire and hit one of the planes. It came down near Calais above Fermain Bay. The other plane made off eastwards. As they passed near the Brehon Tower anti-aircraft gunners there opened fire and hit one which came down in flames over Herm. Not until next morning was it generally known that the planes that had been brought down were German. It seems that the German planes had met the British planes, of which warning had been given, and had fled towards Guernsey, jettisoning their loads of bombs as they came, in order to get under the protection of the very anti-aircraft guns that brought down two of their number. A court-martial was held as a result of the tragedy and it was said – the statement could not, of course, be verified – that thirteen Germans were sentenced to be shot.

CHAPTER XIII

SIEGE CONDITIONS 1941-1943

In retrospection the first half of the German occupation seemed a period of comparative plenty. In the next three years we were to experience many hardships from lack of sufficient clothing, food and fuel, and at times real starvation seemed on the horizon, yet it never quite reached us.

Sometimes we narrowly escaped temporary loss of essential services through the depletion of stocks of the fuel required to maintain them. The public were urged – and so far as was possible compelled – to exercise rigid economy in the use of electricity, gas and water. The use of electric light was forbidden between the hours of 11pm and 7am – a prohibition almost impossible to enforce in houses where blacking-out regulations were carefully observed. The sale of electric irons and similar appliances and the use of electric fires was prohibited, though after the timely arrival of a cargo of diesel oil a concession was made by which invalids were allowed to use electric fires and electric kettles. In October, 1943, however, this concession was withdrawn and at the same time the electricity ration was cut down to four units per household per week.

The use of gas during certain hours was forbidden and this prohibition could be, and was, enforced by cutting off the supply at the main twice daily. The lighting allowance was withdrawn during the summer months. Extra allowances were granted to invalids. The use of gas fires was forbidden and the prohibition was enforced by turning off the gas and sealing the tap. Consumers who broke the seals were prosecuted. Those who exceeded their gas rations and disregarded warnings were deprived of their gas altogether, thus being put to the inconvenience of getting their food cooked as best they could and going to bed in the dark. Their gas was restored to them when the amount of gas to which they would have been entitled if they had not been deprived of it was equal to the amount that they had previously consumed in excess of their ration.

In the summer of 1943 the drawing of water between 10pm and 5.30am was forbidden. The Water Board had power to enforce this prohibition in parts of the Island by cutting off supplies at the main. In other parts it had to rely on the submissiveness of the consumer – perhaps too optimistically, as by this time the average man, unable to foretell the future, felt sure that in their own interests the Germans would see that our essential services, on which their comfort as well as ours depended, did not fail so long as they remained in the Island.

A grower who neglected to cultivate his land adequately was fined £50. Restrictions on cattle-breeding enacted in 1940 were continued. In addition all piglets farrowed had to be reported to the Farm Produce Board on reaching the age of six weeks, might not be removed from their place of birth without the knowledge of the Board, and might not be slaughtered until they exceeded 180 pounds in weight. When the owner of a pig wished to slaughter it he had to obtain a permit from the Essential Commodities Committee and state the name of the butcher to whom he intended to sell the meat. He was allowed to retain for his own use a part of the carcase proportionate to the size of his household but was required to satisfy the Committee that he had sufficient salt to preserve the meat.

As the black market price of meat rose to £1 a pound and sometimes more, large illicit profits were to be made by evading the regulations. It was difficult for the police to obtain proof of such evasions as it was to the interest of all parties to a black market transaction to preserve secrecy about it, but sometimes culprits were discovered. A man who killed a pig of his own and sold the meat to private individuals was fined £65. Another who bought a pig for £60, slaughtered it and sold the meat was sentenced to a fine of £15 and imprisonment for three months.

As time went on the Island had to depend more and more on imports from France for its meat supplies. These were somewhat precarious. In 1941 the weekly meat ration varied between 8 oz and 4 oz and at one time was 7 oz with an extra 4 oz for heavy workers. Such opulence did not last. Early in 1943 the ration was permanently reduced to 4 oz a head and was issued irregularly.

We had meat three times in March, four times in April, twice in May and thereafter we had to be content with 4 oz of meat once a fortnight.

Fortunately our weekly bread ration was both more generous and more reliable. In March, 1941, it was fixed at 6 lb 2½ oz for male heavy workers, one pound less for female heavy workers, 4 lb 10 oz for other adults and 3 lb 1½ oz for children and youths under 21 years of age. It stayed at those figures until May, 1943, when it was reduced by German orders because a vessel bound for Guernsey with supplies for the German troops was bombed and sunk by British planes.[3]

The new bread ration was 4 lb 12 oz a week for male manual workers over 21 years of age, 4 lb 4 oz for female manual workers, and 3 lb 12 oz for other adults. For those under 21 years of age the ration remained as before. The original bread ration was resumed on July 31st on the ground that 'there had been no interference recently with the importation of supplies by enemy action'. Our bread was made partly of flour made from locally grown wheat and partly from flour imported from France. Occasionally it was somewhat gritty so that one experienced a

---

3   The official explanation was published in the local papers:

NOTICE

On the CHANNEL ISLANDS, as well as in the territories occupied by German troops, the German Army has secured the current supply of foodstuffs and all necessities of life for the civil population.

The British Military Command, however, disregarding the fact that the population of the Channel Islands are their OWN COUNTRYMEN are attempting in every way to jeopardise the continuous supply to the Islands by incessant NUISANCE RAIDS.

If in consequence of these raids the RATIONS of the ISLAND POPULATION have now to be decreased, the population can thank for this their countrymen ON THE OTHER SIDE OF THE CHANNEL. Churchill and his supporters will not achieve any military success from such nuisance raids. But it characterises the necessary lack of scruples that they do not refrain from exposing their own fellow-countrymen to sufferings that could be avoided.

THE POPULATION OF THE ISLANDS, HOWEVER, MAY AT LEAST KNOW THE CULPRITS.

Den 30 April, 1943. DER OBERBEFEHLSHABER DER ARMEE.

tickling sensation in the throat when swallowing it. Sometimes the crust was very hard. At its worst it was quite palatable even after a deterioration of quality was officially announced in March, 1942, when we were told to expect 'a certain stickiness and apparent lack of cooking'.

The limitation of the bulk of the population to a daily half pint of separated milk per head, first imposed in September, 1940, was continued throughout the whole period of the German occupation. In February, 1941, a concession was made to necessitous invalids, expectant and nursing mothers and children under school age who were allowed to have half their milk ration without payment. In May, 1943, because of a marked decline in health noted among children who, having attained two years of age, ceased to receive two pints of whole milk a day, it was decided to allow the children to have the infants' milk ration until they were six years old. From time to time farmers were fined for disposing of milk to private individuals instead of sending it to the milk depots. The most flagrant case was that of a member of the Dairy Committee and formerly a States Deputy, who was fined £75 for not delivering to the Milk Depot the amount of milk that he should have delivered. This man's wife conducted a boarding house that was a sort of unofficial nursing-home for convalescents and those in need of rest, to all of whom she gave ample quantities of whole milk. In Court the farmer's defence was that he was legally entitled to retain whole milk for members of his household and that his wife's boarders were included in the household.

As was only natural some mistakes were made. Too many early potatoes were at first grown under glass with the result that part of the crop rotted before it was consumed, but it is probable that there would have been far more waste if there had been no control of either prices or production, for potato-growers would have been tempted to concentrate on the forcing of early crops in the hope of getting large profits. An acute shortage of potatoes in November, 1941, may have been partly due to growers who retained control of their land making false returns and withholding potatoes from the depots in order to sell them on the black market, but was principally due to Germans requisitioning 1,700 tons (738 tons for their own use and 962 for export) with a promise to replace them at some unspecified date. The shortage developed into a potato famine which lasted from the beginning of 1941 until April 22nd on which day a meagre ration of 1 lb a head for the week was issued. During the potato famine, however, potatoes could be bought on the black market in limited quantities for 1s 2d a pound. Throughout the years 1940 to 1943 the weekly ration of potatoes – except when none were obtainable – varied from one pound to seven pounds a head each week at prices that ranged from 1d to 4½d a pound.

Restrictions on fishing imposed by the German authorities varied from time to time; sometimes they were so onerous that many fishermen would not go fishing at all. They had to pay deposits – £10 for a boat equipped with a motor, £5 for one having sails and oars only – which were liable to be forfeited. Only professional fishermen were licensed; they were forbidden to put to sea with any unlicensed persons on board and licences were liable to be withdrawn from fishermen who did not bring in satisfactory catches. They were forbidden to sell fish to private individuals but were allowed to retain a reasonable amount for their own consumption. Before they took their share, however, twenty per cent of each catch was set aside for German use.

Until the issue of fish-ration cards conditions in the fish-market were chaotic. These came into use in May, 1941. Thereafter, in the fish-market queues, those whose cards showed that they had made the most recent purchase had to allow people who had been longer without fish to go before them. The amount of fish purchasable at anyone time varied from half a pound to a pound a head according to the quantity on the market at the time. The authorised maximum price was about four times the normal price.

Spider crabs were unrationed during this period because of the small amount of meat they afforded in proportion to their shells. In normal times they were almost unsaleable even at the price of 2d apiece because of the amount of labour involved in extracting the meat from the shell, but they now came on the market in large quantities at the price of 1s a pound.

Owing to the restrictions imposed on fishing, fish was always very scarce. Often none of any kind could be bought except the normally despised limpet which now found a ready market, and even limpets were unobtainable when the Germans forbade access to the beaches. Twice a few salted herrings and dried sandeels imported from France came on the market and were bought eagerly, though the sandeels cost 6d a dozen, which worked out approximately at a penny a mouthful, and the herrings 10d each. An idea of the relative scarcity of fish may be gathered from the author's own experience. Though he bought fish whenever he could, his ration card for 1942 showed that he was able to buy it only seven times in the whole year. Occasionally a small blue shark came on the market and afforded coarse but wholesome food for forty or fifty people, but the red letter day was when some fishermen brought in a porpoise. It had been entangled in their net and was drowned when they found it. At first they thought it hardly worth the labour involved in getting so cumbrous a carcase to the market – it weighed between four and five hundredweight – but decided to do so in the hope that it could be sold as cat's meat. Fortunately it was seen by a few people who knew that porpoise was wholesome food. Either they knew that in England as recently as the reign of William III and Mary II porpoise had an honoured place at royal banquets, or they had seen it in Italian fish markets or had read Frank Bullen's The Cruise of the Cachalot. These bought it eagerly and advised their friends to follow their example, with the happy result that it afforded a square meal of unrationed meat to three or four hundred people courageous enough to make the experiment of eating it. One thing about it may have puzzled those who had read The Cruise of the Cachalot. In Chapter II Bullen wrote 'porpoise beef improves by keeping, getting tenderer every day the longer it lasts, until at last it becomes as tasty a viand as anyone could wish to dine upon'. The flesh of this porpoise, however, went bad on the third day after it had been caught. Again, one expected the flesh to be as pale as pork whereas it was darker even than horse flesh. The explanation in both cases was that as the porpoise is a warm-blooded animal it should be bled when killed. This could not be done as it was already dead when caught. None of those who ate the meat realised this, so no one minded. In flavour it somewhat resembled venison. It was not so good as prime beef, but was much better than the very inferior beef that we usually got at that time. Because local stocks of cod-liver oil and halibut oil were very low it occurred to the Health Services Officer that oil of medicinal value might be obtained from large locally-caught fish such as ray and dogfish. Fishermen were asked to bring in the livers of these fish and experiments were carried out by Mr S.H. Arnold, to whom the Island was already indebted for obtaining salt from sea-water, and Mr M.N. Angell, M.P.S. They succeeded in extracting oil which experiments on guinea-pigs proved to contain vitamins A and D in satisfactory quantities. The Health Services Officer considered it to be more valuable than such cod-liver oil as still remained in the Island because it was fresher, and doctors found that its effect on their patients was very satisfactory. The quantity of oil obtained was too small to allow of its being put on the open market: it was sold only to those who obtained medical certificates signed by their doctors and countersigned by the Health Services Officers.

The plant devised by Mr Arnold in the summer of 1940 at the Model Yacht Pond to obtain salt by the sun-evaporation of sea water was used again in the summers of 1941 and 1942. Then the Germans destroyed the pond to make room for a dump, though there was ample room nearby that would have served. Thereafter the only locally produced salt was made at the States Chemical Department established by Mr Arnold at the Piette Saw Mills. The amount produced was limited by the capacity of the plant and the amount of fuel obtainable and was reserved for butter-making as the salt imported from France was too coarse for that purpose. As by-products magnesium carbonate and magnesium sulphate (Epsom Salts) were also obtained from the sea water.

Shortage of fuel was almost as serious as food shortage. Early in 1941 household coal was temporarily unobtainable and the public had to make the best use they could of anthracite and wood fuel. On several occasions cargoes of gas-coal and diesel-oil arrived only just in time to save the cutting off of gas, on which many people depended entirely for cooking, and of electricity, which was directly concerned in food production, as it was needed for the cold-storage plant and for pumping water for greenhouse crops. Those housewives who depended on gas for cooking were urged to have as much of their food as possible cooked by their bakers. Towards the end of the year some ingenious people converted biscuit tins into stoves capable of burning sawdust. They were said to give very satisfactory results but they did not come into general use. Perhaps the supply of biscuit tins or of sawdust was inadequate, or perhaps they needed more attention to maintain the necessary draught than busy people could give them.

At the approach of winter in 1941 wood from trees felled by States-employed workmen became available, but this came to an end in December when the German authorities announced that no more trees were to be felled except under permit – difficult to obtain – because, it was said, of the value of standing trees in giving cover from raiding British aircraft.

In January, 1942, a very limited quantity of peat, dug at Vazon the previous year, became available, at a cost of 1s 6d a bag, to all who could fetch it for themselves from depots established at the Vrangue brickworks and at St Sampson's. The quality was poor because at the time it was dug only very unskilled workmen were available and those qualified to supervise the digging were more usefully employed elsewhere. In spite of its poor quality and although only those living near enough to the depots to make transport by wheelbarrow or perambulator practicable could avail themselves of it, the demand was so great that the supply was exhausted within a few days.

From the end of March, 1942, until the beginning of October no coal or coke could be bought except by those who had no means of cooking by either gas or electricity, but those who were able to make use of anthracite dust were granted permits to buy it at a cost of 3s 4½d per cwt. When the sale of coal for heating purposes was again permitted the ration for October for one person was 28 lbs a month. A household of from two to four persons was allowed ½ cwt and one of five or more persons ¾ cwt. This allowance was doubled in November and the double allowance remained in force until early in the spring of 1943. In the winter of 1943-1944 the ration was rather more generous. In both winters a small additional ration was allowed to a household in which there were invalid or people over 75 years of age.

So many greenhouses had been badly damaged by shrapnel that it paid speculators to buy some of the most damaged, pull them down and saw the timber into blocks for fuel. Such blocks were at first offered at £12 a ton but the demand was so great that the price quickly leapt to £28 a ton or 30s a cwt. and stayed there until the Controlling Committee fixed the maximum price at 25s 8d per cwt for blocks cut from greenhouse timber and 28s or 3d a pound for kindling wood. These prices were scarcely within the reach of people of moderate means and quite out of reach of the poor. They searched byeways and hedges for fallen branches which became increasingly difficult to find, or stole sawn timber from the German contractors who were digging tunnels and constructing bomb-proof shelters. News of steamers unloading coal brought women from anywhere up to three miles away to gather small bits of coal dropped on the quayside in the course of unloading and carry it away in perambulators. Some even went down on to the harbour mud at low tide to scrape up the coal dust from where the coal ships had berthed. Even people of moderate means could not afford to have fires every day and all day throughout the winter. They had to choose between having fires in the evenings or reserving their fuel for exceptionally cold days. Inevitably cold, combined with lack of proper nourishment resulted in many people suffering severely from chilblains, which in the case of some unfortunates developed into gangrene, necessitating the amputation of fingers and toes.

Some slight alleviation of the fuel problem was obtained by those who could arrange to have mid-day meals at one or other of the town's restaurants which served somewhat cheerless meals of boiled vegetables to customers who brought their own bread and potatoes, or made soup for customers to carry away in their own containers. A number of communal kitchens were established with the approval of the Controlling Committee, which contributed bones for soup-making when these were available. By the autumn of 1941 there were five in the Island serving on the average 3,539 meals a week. They were intended primarily for the use of bachelors of the working-class but did not refuse to serve others. They provided meals of soup, vegetable cutlets, baked potatoes and boiled roots, three, four or in some cases five times a week. The price charged was 6d or 9d a meal, but those who could afford to do so were invited to pay more. The meals at both restaurants and communal kitchens would have been more attractive if it had been possible for caterers occasionally to supply puddings of some kind. This would have been possible only if those to whom meals were served had surrendered part at least of their weekly ration of groceries and cooking-fat into a common pool with a sporting chance of drawing in return more or less than their proper share.

The grocery ration varied from week to week and information at the end of each week was always a news item of real interest. We could always expect 4 ozs of butter, 2 ozs of cooking fat, 4 ozs of sugar and 3 ozs of salt, though occasionally both sugar and salt were temporarily unobtainable, and during one period of several weeks the imported salt was so impure that housewives had to dissolve it in water to precipitate the impurities, strain off the water and use it as brine. We generally had from 4 to 6 ozs of wheat-flour, barley meal or oatmeal or some form of farinaceous food such as macaroni or vermicelli, and sometimes tapioca or dried beans. For a long time we received each week 2 ozs of coffee substitute made of barley and ground acorns with a slight admixture of real coffee. This varied in quality. When barley predominated it was better than when acorn was the main ingredient, but it was always pleasant to drink and we missed it sadly when the issue was reduced from once a week to once a fortnight. Occasionally we had cocoa substitute, nourishing but rather uninteresting, made of ground cocoa pods, and on a very few occasions we had excellent real cocoa. Bovril and marmite, so long as stocks lasted, were reserved for invalids.

Cheese was occasionally issued, at first fairly frequently but more and more seldom as time went on. The cheese that was made locally when milk was abundant sufficed for one issue only. It was of good quality and somewhat resembled Cheshire.

There were red letter days when we were able to buy sardines, tunny, chocolate, fruit paste, dried bananas, sweets or some other treat by surrendering spare coupons from our ration cards. Sometimes the amount of such delicacies was not large enough to allow of distribution to everyone. In such cases their issue was restricted to women and children or to children only. On several occasions the Island received from the International Red Cross Committee or the French Society *Secours Nationale* gifts of vitamin concentrates, condensed milk, cheese, medical supplies, patent food or biscuits. The medical supplies and vitamin concentrates were of course appropriated by the Health Services Officer. The biscuits were distributed to schoolchildren. The patent food and cheese were issued to expectant and nursing mothers who were put on their honour to eat it themselves.

Stocks of imported jam gave out very soon. Thereafter we had occasional issues of jam made locally from imported fruit pulp or from locally grown tomatoes, apples and blackberries. It was not always possible to tell from the flavour what the jam was made of but we were always glad to get it. Stocks did not allow of its being issued more than about once a month. Although most kinds of fruit were practically unobtainable many housewives made jam for immediate use from rhubarb, melon, or grape-thinnings which for a short season could be bought for sixpence a pound or obtained for nothing by those who cared to go to vineries and ask for them. As saccharine had to be used instead of sugar the jam would not keep.

Saccharine was seldom obtainable through lawful channels. Its sale, to any but diabetic patients, was prohibited except when it was issued as a ration. Such occasions were rare, During a period of two years it (or saccharine solution) was issued only six times and a single ration never exceeded two shillings worth, that is one packet containing 200 pastilles – sometimes it was less. It was, however, generally possible to buy saccharine in the black market at prices varying from as little as 5/- to as much as 25/- a packet of 100 pastilles, according to the honesty or rapacity of the boot-legger who sold it. In August, 1941, a French seaman was fined £1 for attempting to smuggle into the Island 60 packets of saccharine. Members of the general public were inclined to regard him as a public benefactor rather than a public enemy and wondered why the local authorities hampered the importation of a commodity that was so badly needed. It was all the more puzzling because some barter shops openly advertised that they would exchange saccharine for second-hand clothes or other barterable commodities. The authorities could hardly have failed to see their advertisements and must have guessed that the saccharine offered had been smuggled for it was wildly improbable that any barter-shop proprietor could do any extensive trading with the very small amount of saccharine allowed him as a ration. The official explanation of the prosecution was not that the saccharine was dutiable but because nothing might be imported into the Island except under licence from the Controlling Committee. Perhaps the unofficial explanation was that the attempt to smuggle had been detected by the German police and the unofficial explanation of the neglect of the local authorities to interfere with the bartering of saccharine was that they realised that there is a time when one should use one's eyes and a time when it is wiser and more charitable to use one's eyelids.

Soap was rationed but was generally of very poor quality and was so seldom obtainable that one had to get accustomed to doing without it. Matches were sold by grocers with other rations at the rate of one box a month to each registered customer. At still rarer intervals smokers were able to buy a box of matches with their tobacco ration.

Before leaving the subject of rations it may be of interest to record the scantiest weekly grocery ration issued during the period in which we were still able to import from France. It was issued in the last week of September, 1943, and consisted of three ozs of sugar, one of salt (the last issued for some time), one of cocoa (real cocoa and of very good quality), four of butter, two of margarine and one box of matches – no flour of any kind (not even soya bean flour which we sometimes had), no macaroni, no coffee substitute and no soap.

Siege conditions taught us to eat some things which we should formerly have disdained to eat – such as limpet, shark, porpoise and spider crab – and other things which it would never have occurred to us to eat – such as seaweed. In September, 1941, the Health Services Officer, Dr Symons, published a letter advising the use of carrageen, the seaweed popularly known as Irish Moss or scientifically chondrus crispus. which he stated to be a valuable food, especially for children, and a lady who had had experience of its use in Eire gave information as to the places on our coasts where it could be found and the best method of preparing it for the table. For the benefit of those who would not have recognised carrageen if they had seen it growing on the rocks the Gas Company exhibited specimens of it in its natural condition as well as samples of prepared carrageen and a jelly made from it. Two days later a lady published recipes for making it into milk jelly or blancmange. At first all who wished to eat this seaweed had to fetch it for themselves from the shore but it became so popular as a food that the collection and drying of it became a profitable industry and it was put on the market ready for cooking at 1/0½ an ounce. Eventually a chemist, Mr J. H. Carre, sold a powder made by pulverising dried carrageen which, he claimed, would keep indefinitely.

Another valuable food was obtained from a variety of mangel-wurzel, known in France as *demi-sucré* and in the Island commonly but erroneously as sugarbeet. It is an exceptionally sugary root, the average sugar content being as high as 15 per cent. In September, 1941, *The Star* gave advice on the production of sugar from this mangel. Part of a somewhat complicated process involved blowing into the juice through an indiarubber tube, thus supplying human lungs the carbon dioxide necessary to precipitate the lime needed for purifying it. If anyone made sugar from the mangel by this process they greedily kept it to themselves but it was discovered that when dessicated it resembled in appearance the patent cereal food called grape-nuts and could be eaten as porridge with milk or could be used as a valuable ingredient in puddings. In October, 1943, a jam substitute resembling molasses made from this mangel-wurzel came on the market under the name of sugar beet syrup. Its chief merit was that it was sweet, its chief defect that it cost three and a half marks (seven shillings and fivepence) a pound. Twenty pounds of the root made four and a half pounds of grape-nuts at a cost of eleven shillings, six of which went to the baker for shredding and dessicating it.

Tea substitutes were made from pea pods, from dessicated carrots (the use of which was condemned by the Health Services Officer on the ground that it was wasteful, as carrot tea had no food value) and especially from dried bramble leaves. Bramble tea substitute became so popular that it was sold by most grocers. They paid 2/6 for seven pounds of the green leaf and sold it in its dried state at 5/4 per pound. In order to get a beverage equal in strength to real tea it was necessary to use twice the weight of the substitute. However, the price compared favourably with the 8/- a pound charged by some grocers for a very inferior coffee-substitute, the ingredients of which were not disclosed. The flavour of 'bramble leaf tea' can best be described by saying that if one could contrive to think of something else while drinking it, one might forget that one was not drinking the genuine article.

When in the autumn of 1940 there was a glut of grapes the Guernsey Brewery Company obtained grape-juice from the Glasshouse Utilisation Board and made from it wine which under the title of 'Sarnia Wine' came on the market in 1941. *The Star*'s reporter described it as of the port type and the *Evening Press* reporter considered that it tasted of both port and claret. Neither Portugal nor France had, perhaps, much to fear from Guernsey's rivalry as a wine-producing country but it was a pleasant drink and it was regrettable that no more than a thousand gallons could be made of it.

The beer made by the Guernsey brewers inevitably

deteriorated as stocks of the essential ingredients dwindled till the supply came to an end altogether, but as late as the end of 1945 the Guernsey Brewery Company made a beverage, of which the alcoholic content was very low, from hops, saccharine, barley, sugar, yeast and carbon dioxide gas. It was sometimes possible to obtain French table wine at a rather high price. More often it was not possible. Whisky and brandy could be bought only by those whose doctors certified that they needed them and eventually whisky became unobtainable. The supply of brandy became sporadic but in 1943 it was occasionally possible to buy crème de menthe or benedictine.

During the first few months of the German Occupation the Island was well off for clothing, as much had been left behind by those who evacuated. Of this, that which was new or nearly new was at first sent to shops for re-sale on behalf of the absent owners and old clothing that was still serviceable was given to the Procureur of the Poor for free distribution. When, on the initiative of Mrs Winifred Heggs and Mrs Van der Sluys, the Children's Emergency Bureau, staffed principally by voluntary workers, came into being, all salvaged clothing was sent to it and was there sorted into four grades – saleable, mendable, convertible and rubbish. The readily saleable was sent to shops. The rubbish, after the removal of useful by-products such as buttons, was disposed of for use as cleaning rags. The remainder, after mending or adaptation – such as the conversion of stiff-fronted men's shirts into summer jumpers for boys – was sold at prices within reach of the poorest. Unfortunately it is impossible to make any form of philanthropy rogue-proof. Many German soldiers eagerly bought clothing from the clothiers' shops to send to their families in Germany and would have liked to buy from the Children's Emergency Bureau but the German authorities very properly forbade them to do so. This gave an opportunity to conscienceless Guernsey people to make large illicit profits by buying children's clothing from the Bureau, under pretence of needing it for their own children, and selling it at a greatly increased price to Germans.

The Germans would have exhausted the stocks in the

clothiers' shops if the German authorities, to whom credit for the step is due, had not forbidden except under permit[4] the sale to them of any but the less essential articles such as hats, neckties, shoe laces and the like. Many Germans evaded the order by commissioning Guernsey people of the Quisling type to buy for them. Decent shopkeepers, of course, tried to prevent this. But it was not easy. One shop-assistant, having good reason to believe that a woman customer was acting on behalf of a German, refused to serve her. The woman, in revenge, went to the German authorities and accused the shop assistant of having applied to Germans in general epithets – which she specified – such as none but the foul-mouthed use. The unfortunate shopman was arrested and imprisoned for a fortnight before being tried by a German court. He was then acquitted on the testimony of a Wesleyan Methodist minister who declared him to be incapable of using the foul language attributed to him.

It was not until May, 1941, that Germans were forbidden to buy essential clothes. By that time stocks were seriously depleted. The Controller of Clothing and Footwear had by that time taken steps both to husband what still remained and to ascertain what it was advisable to endeavour to buy from France. He used powers conferred on him to forbid sales to the general public of articles specially needed by certain classes; for example he forbade the sale, except for the use of children under two years of age, of materials especially suitable for infants. Incidentally, because children outgrow their clothes more quickly than they wear them out, he arranged a scheme by which part-worn boots and shoes might be exchanged for others of larger or smaller size. At all too rare intervals he was able to announce good news such as that a limited quantity of dress material or ladies' stockings or some other form of clothing had arrived in the Island and would be on sale at specified prices. Usually such stocks were sold out within a few hours and people who had been unable to buy them relieved their feelings by writing anonoymous letters to the newspapers in which they accused shopkeepers of giving preference to favoured customers and the Clothing Controller

---

4   But permits were easily obtained and still more easily altered.

of mismanaging his job. Many women were compelled to leave off wearing stockings altogether.

Scarcity of footwear affected all classes, especially heavy workers and children. In its report for 1942 the Education Council stated that unsatisfactory school attendance was principally due to children's lack of boots and shoes. All schools kept rope-soled canvas shoes for the use of children arriving at school with wet feet. Wellington rubber boots, when available, were reserved for fishermen and cowmen. In January, 1941, the Labour Officer appealed to owners of unwanted workmen's boots to give them to him for distribution and in the following month the States subsidised a factory to make heavy boots with leather soles and canvas uppers. When made they were sold to bona-fide land-workers only who had to obtain from the Labour Officer permission to buy them. An advertisement that a boot-and-shoe shop had obtained some leather, and would therefore be able to undertake repairs, caused a queue of seventy-two people to form outside the shop before it was opened. Disused motor tyres were extensively used for the re-soling of boots. A pound of knitting-wool, if anyone had been allowed to buy so much, would have cost as much as a complete suit of clothes before the war. It was sold in small quantities at from 4/4 to 5/10 per oz and purchasers, before being allowed to buy it, had to satisfy the Clothing Controller as to the reality of their need. Grievous as these prices were they were low in comparison with some. Elastic of a quality that before the war had cost a penny a yard now, for example, cost 5/3 a yard – sixty-three times its original price.

The Red Cross Committee would doubtless have found a way of sending surgical appliances if asked to do so. This, however, would have involved delays. Fortunately local enterprise supplied the need when necessary. Messrs Lovell & Co made an artificial limb to replace an amputated leg and Mr Stonelake, the chemist, made a spinal jacket under medical direction. He had to appeal to the good nature of the public to supply him with the hooks and buckles that he needed as he found it impossible to obtain these through the usual trade channels.

In August, 1941, the tobacco ration was stabilised at an ounce of pipe tobacco and 20 cigarettes each fortnight. This continued as long as tobacco was obtainable. At rare intervals the Controlling Committee was able to allow a small addition to the ration.

The price of rationed pipe tobacco was 1/9½ per ounce if made of Continental, or 2/6 per ounce if made of Virginian tobacco. The price of unrationed tobacco obtainable only by private treaty reached very high figures – forty shillings for twenty locally made cigarettes was perhaps the highest paid until the last year of the occupation. In March, 1943, locally grown tobacco, dried and cut ready for smoking but inferior in quality to the tobacco locally made from imported leaf, was put on the market at 4½ marks (9/6½) an ounce. Six months later, owing to the healthy effect of competition, the price was reduced to 21 marks (5/3½) an ounce, but whether it was worth buying even at the lower price was a matter of individual opinion.[5]

It was to be expected that, when the shortage of imported tobacco became acute, those who had hitherto grown the plant as a garden ornament would make experiments in growing, drying and curing the leaf for smoking. Results varied. Some of the dried leaf would not burn. Some proved too strong to be smoked unless blended. Some by a happy accident resembled the best South African 'Boer' tobacco. Someone with the necessary experience published detailed information as to how the leaf should be cured but most of those who read it were discouraged to learn that the maturing process should be spread over several years!

The tobacco shortage led to experiments in the use of substitutes. Dried coltsfoot leaf was the most popular at first, probably because coltsfoot could be found and gathered so easily, but a rumour spread that it was deleterious to health. Thereafter dried vine-leaves and dried rose-petals had a vogue. Eventually dried bramble leaf was most used, not because it

---

[5] After we were cut off from France the price went up to 100 marks an ounce, at which price it was bought by Germans, who had little else on which they could spend their pay.

was a better substitute than others, but because it was in such demand as a tea substitute that it could be bought without difficulty from any grocer. By itself it could not be described as a satisfactory substitute for tobacco but blended with the real article, especially if a little snuff were sprinkled over it, it helped to eke out the meagre ration. As it burned readily it was useful to blend with local grown leaf that did not burn freely. Most smokers were not too proud to save the dottels from their pipes and the stubs of their cigarettes. These also helped to make the tobacco ration go further.

The difficulties of the time are well illustrated in advertisements that appeared in the local papers. One offered an evening frock in exchange for a warm skirt; another cord breeches for shoes; a third candles or dried beans for shoes. The owner of a 'frock coat suit complete with top-hat and leather hat-box valued at £10' advertised that he would exchange it for the best offer of flour, tea, sugar, jam or eggs. 'I want a gas-mantle – what do you want?', 'What do you want in exchange for paraffin?', 'Soap! Soap! Soap! Would clean chimneys for the above or for cash', 'I have a few pounds of good tobacco. What would you like to part with?' 'Can someone spare fruit or walnuts for wedding cake?', 'Keep yourself warm. Bring us your spare blankets and sheets and we will make you trousers, shirts, vests and underpants', are a few examples of many hundreds of advertisements, and during the salt famine an advertiser announced that he was prepared to deliver purified sea water at customers' doors.

The Price Determination Committee's efforts to keep the prices of vegetables and fruit within reasonable limits were not wholly successful. A flagrant instance of its failure in this respect was in regard to cauliflowers. When the Committee fixed the maximum retail price at 7d a pound they were marketed with not only all their outer leaves but all their stalks as well so that the purchaser was compelled to buy with each pound of edible cauliflower two pounds or more of useless vegetation that he carried home and threw into his dustbin. Similarly whoever bought leeks at 9d a pound spent half that amount on worthless green leaves. The situation from the purchasers' point of view was only partially improved by an enactment that vegetables sent to market must be 'reasonably trimmed'.

The Committee failed still more signally in attempting to control the price of soft fruit. In 1943 it fixed the maximum price of strawberries at 2/6 a pound, of black currants at 1/-, of red currants at 1/9 and of gooseberries at 10d. In consequence none of these came on the market at all throughout the year. (Sybarites had been paying 13/- a pound for strawberries.) They were obtainable only by private arrangement with the grower. Apples and pears at 1/- and figs at 2/6 a pound occasionally came on the market in small quantities and could be bought only by those who had leisure to stand in queues for the purpose. On the other hand melons at 1/- a pound, rhubarb at 10d. and grapes at prices varying from 10d. to 1/9 according to variety and quality could be bought without difficulty and the supply of tomatoes was so large that for the greater part of the season they could be bought for less than the controlled price of 7d a pound.

Prices paid for articles and commodities that were neither produced locally nor imported by the Controlling Committee reached a fantastic height. At auctions held in 1942 seventeen shillings was paid for a pound of rice, £2 for a tin of curry powder, 15/- for a small tin of Bird's custard powder, £1 11s 0d for a tin of salmon, £1 10s 0d for a large tin of sardines, £1 3s 0d for a tin of peaches, £60 for a 5 lb chest of tea and £4 for a half-pint bottle of olive oil. But housewives were not concerned only with their larders. A scrubbing brush was sold for 15/-, a large tin of Brasso for £1 6s 0d, a packet of Lux for 12/-and a tablet of Sunlight soap for £1 5s 0d – fifty times its pre-occupation price. That the real value of an article is the price that people are prepared to pay for it is a fact not always clear to the official mind. In May, 1942, the police officially valued 200 pounds of soap – the proceeds of a burglary – at £8. It would have been nearer the truth to have valued it at £200.

At an auction held shortly before Christmas 1941, twenty-five shillings was paid for a duck, £2 17s 6d for a turkey and £4 18s 0d for a goose. These prices were very moderate compared with those paid when Christmas 1942 was drawing near. Then, according to popular reports, £25 was paid for a turkey, £17 for a goose and £2 15s 0d for a quarter of a pound of chocolate. It is impossible to verify these figures because they were black market prices. In December, 1942, a Price Restriction Ordinance (too long to quote or even to summarise; it filled five columns of *The Star*) came into force at the instigation of the German authorities, who had told the King's Procureur that they were 'shocked and horrified' at some of the prices prevailing. It enacted that nothing, except a few exempted articles – such as antiques and works of art – should be sold except at a price authorised by a Price Determination Committee. The ordinance entirely failed to have the intended effect. Its only practical result was to make many saleable commodities unobtainable except by unlawful methods. The highest recorded price lawfully paid before the Committee was established was £7 10s 0d for half a pound of tea.

CHAPTER XIV

SIEGE CONDITIONS 1941-1943 (CONTINUED)

Freedom to abuse those who govern us is one of the most highly cherished privileges of the British people. The German authorities did nothing to curtail ours so long as we uttered no word of complaint against them and confined ourselves to criticism of the Controlling Committee, and its offshoots, the Essential Commodities Committee and others. These bodies were subjected to a good deal of criticism. It usually took the form of anonymous letters to the newspapers written by people who seem to have imagined that the Essential Commodities Committee, through the States' buyers in France, could obtain anything it wished as freely as in happier days any of us could buy in unlimited quantities from one or another of our local shops. An announcement that men were to have an additional tobacco ration generally produced a letter demanding that in common justice women should have more chocolate. One such letter urged that the Committee should reserve cereal foods, such as macaroni, for the use of children with the comment that the Committee had 'an exceedingly dim view of how a large section of the Island lives'. Probably the writer had a still dimmer view of the difficulties under which the Committee laboured. Probably few of the Committee's critics appreciated the significance of the fact that every announcement of a forthcoming issue of an extra ration concluded with the words '*Genehmigt* (approved) *Jersey. Der Feldkommandant. gez. Knackfuss Oberst*' with the date on which the Commandant had given his approval. Had they realised that our Controlling Committee was controlled in its turn by the German authorities they might have realised that the Committee had often to bear the blame for faults for which the German authorities were responsible.

Whatever the faults of the Controlling Committee we should have fared badly without it. The high prices quoted in the previous chapter as having been paid for luxuries give an idea of the horrible scramble for necessities that might have occurred if no control over their sale had been exercised. To keep necessities within reach of the poor man's pocket the price for them was based not on what the States had to pay for them but on what the poor man could reasonably be expected to pay. The States bought meat, coal and other vital necessities in a market that was constantly fluctuating but sold them at fixed prices and, when it was unavoidable, sold at a loss. The price of bread, for example, was stabilised at 2d. a pound. This was so much below cost prices that by the autumn of 1943 the subsidy was costing the States (at the rate of) £30,000 a year.

In May, 1942, an anonymous correspondent wrote to *The Star* pointing out that there were 'hundreds of Island children, who, owing to the fact that their parents cannot afford it, are not getting their fair share of the little extras (chocolate, oranges, etc) that have been purchased for their especial benefit' and suggested that *The Star* should open a fund for the purpose. This was done and during the next four months subscriptions amounted to £1,284. In August, 1943, the States voted £6,000 to provide for the relief of working-class families whose earnings were insufficient to provide their children with necessities.

No doubt the poorest paid members of the working classes suffered most from the hardships of siege conditions but there can have been few members of the community who did not suffer to some extent. The winter of 1941-1942 – a bitterly cold one – was, perhaps, the worst of this three-year period, although there was at that time some improvement in part of our ration. Vegetables were scarce and our most important food, next to bread, was potatoes. As early as November, 1941, these were so scarce[6] that they could not be bought without a permit from the Market Keeper and to secure a permit it was advisable to be in the market place at a very early hour. The Market Keeper's office was opened at 8.30am but long before that time queues began to form outside it and those who had not risen early enough to get foremost places were lucky if they did not have to wait for a full hour before they got their permits for their day's supply. After securing a permit it was necessary to join another

6   The Germans had requisitioned 690 tons of Guernsey-grown potatoes.

SIEGE CONDITIONS 1941-1943 (CONTINUED)

queue at one or other of the few market stalls where potatoes were obtainable. There the delays incidental to scrutinising permits, to weighing potatoes, to receiving payment and giving change occupied so much time that the buyer might have to wait another hour before obtaining his day's supply. It might happen that just before his turn came to be served the stock of potatoes available at the stall he had selected was exhausted so that he had to go to the tail of another queue on the chance of having better luck there. It might be that after all his trouble he got no potatoes at all and in any case he was lucky if he received his allowance in less than two hours from the time when he reached the market. Throughout the winter of 1941-1942 Germany kept central European summer time, which was two hours ahead of Greenwich time, and as we had to synchronise our clocks with German clocks those who did not live fairly near the market had to leave home two hours or more before sunrise – a dreary prelude to a winter day. In Christmas week a ration of 2 lbs of potatoes was issued to all, but after Christmas the potato supply failed altogether. We had no more until the last week of the following April.

Until potatoes were again obtainable their place as a staple food had to be filled by roots – parsnips, swedes and cattle carrots – often rotting. People who had hitherto regarded parsnips as scarcely fit to eat learned to prefer them to other roots, not for the sake of their flavour but because of their food value, rabbit-owners having discovered that their rabbits fattened more quickly on parsnips than on any other roots. In the middle of April we were promised a half ration of new, greenhouse-grown potatoes, but the promise was not fulfilled. The potatoes had been dug and delivered at the depots but before they could be distributed the Germans requisitioned them. By the end of April the meat ration which had dwindled since Christmas became irregular but the release for sale as food of a small quantity of beans that had hitherto been reserved for seed afforded some compensation. Throughout the whole month we had no sugar but in the last week of April we had a potato ration, the first of the year, of one pound per head. In the second week of May we had again one pound of potatoes but no meat. By this time the stock of winter roots – of which we had become heartily weary – was exhausted but their place was taken by scanty supplies of young greenhouse-grown carrots, turnips, cabbage, spinach-beet, and especially green peas which sold readily at prices from one shilling to eighteenpence a pound. We had a meat ration that week and the grocery ration was augmented with issues of cheese, pea-flour and the first sugar ration we had had for seven weeks.

The worst of the hunger period was past. In the third week of May we had three ounces of meat, green peas were plentiful at a shilling a pound and broad beans had come on the market. To get all possible food value from the broad beans many housewives cooked the pods with the beans. In the following week the sugar ration was continued, a double allowance of cheese was issued and the weekly potato ration rose to two and a half pounds a head. At the end of the month it rose again to five pounds a head and strawberries came on the market at twelve shillings a pound. No one worried about the price of strawberries. What mattered was that the hunger period that had lasted for nearly six weary months was definitely over.

Throughout that hunger period most people had risen from every meal with regret, prepared, if such a thing had been possible, to sit down at once to another meal of the same size. During that period recipes published in the newspapers for the making of 'limpet pie' and 'parsnip honey' had been of real practical value. A matter of curious psychological interest is worth mentioning. It might have been expected that advertisements in grocers' shop windows of Stork margarine with coloured pictures of jam tarts and still more of suet puddings thickly studded with sultanas, would, if they aroused any emotion at all, annoy by tantalising. Instead such pictures of food gave a curious thrill of pleasure such as one feels in looking at a picture of a fine sunset.

That such experiences had a physical cause may be gathered from quotations from the report for 1941 of the Medical Officer of Health who noted 'a general lowering of health, especially marked in the poorer inhabitants of the town and in the older

SIEGE CONDITIONS 1941-1943 (CONTINUED)

people; also the widespread occurrence of certain deficiency diseases'.

> There has been a widespread and continued outbreak of diarrhoea, sometimes accompanied by vomiting, in which no infective agent could be discovered and which in most cases was probably due to the composition of the present diet and possibly in some cases to a deficiency in vitamins...
>
> As the year progressed so our diet became more and more restricted. The standard rationed diet is only a subsistence diet, i.e., of 1,500-1,600 calorific value only, which is just sufficient for a man resting in bed, but for a man doing moderate work another 1,500 calories are required and for a heavy worker at least 4,000 calories or a further 1,000 calories daily are required. To sum up the present diet is insufficient for most of the population in calories (quantity) and in proteins and fats (quality); there is also evidence of vitamin deficiency. In adults a deficiency of fats caused the appearance of such symptoms as great sensibility to cold, fatigue after exertion and a 'dried-up' feeling ...

We suffered less from food shortage in the milder winter of 1942-1943, although we got less flour and such cereals as macaroni with our grocery ration and although our meat ration had dwindled to four ounces a head and was issued only once a fortnight instead of once a week. We had learned to rely less on imported food and more on food grown in the Island. More people had taken advantage of permission to glean in the cornfields after the harvesters. They had the wheat they thus obtained ground at the local mills into flour which they used at home or disposed of at the barter shops. Maize was far more grown than in previous years. Much of it was eaten in its green state in the autumn but much also was dried and ground into meal for winter consumption. Dried beans were issued as a ration until April and – most important of all – our potato ration, except for one week, continued throughout the winter.

Whereas in the previous winter we had suffered mostly from hunger, now, though the winter was milder, cold was our chief hardship. The statement that a household of from two to six people was allowed no more than one and a half hundredweight of coal a month does not perhaps convey much impression to anyone but an experienced housekeeper, but when it is realised that this represented five and three-fifths pounds of coal a day – and it was very inferior coal – it will be understood that the coal ration was meagre indeed, and it could not be supplemented with wood except at an exorbitant price. Since the German authorities did not allow the felling of trees, except with the express permission of a German official appointed for the purpose, only those who could afford to buy logs at 23/- the hundredweight could afford to have fires all day and every day. Happy was he near whose house a tree was blown down by a winter gale! Only the youngest and healthiest escaped chilblains severe enough to be called frostbite.

It is difficult to give an account of food conditions in 1943 without unduly stressing hardships or, on the other hand, exaggerating alleviations. The reader may be helped to form a correct impression if detailed accounts are given of one special meal, a festal dinner in honour of a child's birthday, and of the meals consumed in one week by a family able to live within its income without serious difficulty but not affluent enough – or too conscientious – to deal in the black market, except under special temptation; it bought salt in the black market for instance during the salt famine and saccharine whenever opportunity occurred.

The birthday dinner was held in May when the food supply was about at its worst. It consisted of boiled new potatoes flavoured with a sauce made from a small tin of Heinz tomato soup, followed by a tin of California peaches. The new potatoes were bought in the black market for 1/2 a pound, a violation of the law that the occasion was held to justify. The tomato soup came from a tin that was the very last of the tins bought for storage at the time before the outbreak of war when we were

SIEGE CONDITIONS 1941-1943 (CONTINUED)

officially advised to lay in ample stocks of non-perishable food. The tin of California peaches – pre-war price 1/5 – had been bought at an auction in anticipation of the event for £2 10s 0d. Roots, which had formed everyone's staple food for many weeks previous, were deliberately excluded as unsuitable for a meal that it was intended to make as festal as possible.

Sunday's breakfast in the week selected for illustration consisted of stewed potatoes and peas – the peas were fresh picked, the potatoes old, flavourless and discoloured – dry bread, because the previous week's butter ration was exhausted, and coffee substitute. Sunday's dinner consisted of spider-crab, potatoes and peas, and cider (the last bottle; no more was obtainable for several months). There was no pudding because of shortage of both bread and milk. The five o'clock meal, normally called 'afternoon tea', consisted of coffee substitute and bread and jam – 3½ oz of bread allowed for each person – and for supper the family again had stewed potatoes and peas, preceded by vegetable soup.

On every other day of the week except Saturday, when their place was taken by fried potatoes, breakfast consisted of grape-nuts, mentioned in the previous chapter as made from mangel-wurzel, moistened with milk, and on one occasion enriched with buttermilk cream, and 'bramble leaf tea'. At Monday's breakfast bread had again to be eaten dry, but the week's rations, bought later in the day, included cocoa-substitute so that on the other days of the week the breakfast bread was moistened with 'chocolate spread' made of milk thickened with flour or some farinaceous substance such as sago, tapioca or ground macaroni and flavoured with this cocoa substitute. Later in the year 'spread' was flavoured with stewed rhubarb, tomato or melon.

No meat was issued in the week selected for illustration but on the Thursday it had been possible – the only occasion in more than a month – to obtain some fish. On the other days, except Saturday, dinner consisted of boiled potatoes, green peas, swedes and cabbage with onion sauce followed by a pudding made of baked breadcrumbs and milk thickened with maize meal. On Saturday it was possible to have food cooked in the baker's oven, so baked potatoes replaced boiled. The afternoon meal each day consisted of two thick slices of bread and butter and two moistened with 'chocolate spread', accompanied by 'bramble leaf tea'. Coffee-substitute would have been preferred but the amount of the ration did not allow of its being drunk more than one day in each week, whereas bramble leaf tea could be bought without restriction. The week's ration had included a small amount of cheese. This was eaten at supper on Monday accompanied by a salad of lettuce, radishes and spring onions. On the other days supper consisted of vegetable soup followed by stewed potatoes and peas, with on each day what remained of the bread ration. The buttermilk cream used on one occasion to enrich the grape-nuts was obtained by straining boiled buttermilk through muslin. Buttermilk at a cost of twopence a pint was available to those who had the strength and energy to fetch it from the States Dairy at St Martin's – a six mile round journey for dwellers in the town – and the leisure to wait for a long time in a queue. Residents of St Martin's parish, by living near the States Dairy, had a great advantage over town-dwellers. This provoked some of the latter to urge, through the medium of letters to the papers, that the buttermilk should be brought into town for distribution. St Martin's residents retorted that it was only fair that they should retain their advantage as they themselves were frequently disappointed when they walked into town to get fish, and residents of the remoter parishes, who could not obtain buttermilk at all without sacrificing a whole day for the purpose, contended that it should be distributed in each parish in turn. This was found to be impracticable and eventually a plan came into operation by which all who cared to register their names were served in rotation, an arrangement by which each registered customer obtained buttermilk about once a month, those who lived in St Martin's continuing to enjoy much of the advantage of living near the dairy.

Some other people derived an advantage from living in certain localities. Those who lived near enough to the gas-works could buy tar which, mixed with coal dust or sawdust, supplemented their fuel ration. Those who lived near the Piette saw-mills

SIEGE CONDITIONS 1941-1943 (CONTINUED)

could obtain from them hot water for nothing and brine, with which to supplement their salt ration, on payment of a penny a quart. Bullock's blood for the making of black puddings, an unattractive but very nourishing form of food, could be bought at the slaughter house in the weeks when meat was issued and sometimes those who lived near potato depots could buy small potatoes, such as in normal times were regarded as not worth the trouble of cooking and therefore useful only as pig food.

To complete the picture of life during this part of the German occupation, two factors should be mentioned: the closing of public laundries and the difficulty of obtaining domestic service. Because the laundries were closed it was necessary for each household to do its own washing, handicapped by lack of soap and the difficulty, owing to the fuel shortage, of obtaining sufficient hot water. White handkerchiefs and white collars went out of use to a great extent because even after a washing their colour was a dingy grey. The difficulty of obtaining domestic service was a far greater hardship. It was due to the fact that from an early stage of the occupation most domestic servants sought employment by German officers – partly on account of the high wages that the Germans paid – and could afford to pay because the money came from the States Treasury – but principally because the Germans gave them food in addition to the rations they were entitled to buy. Many households that had formerly employed two or more servants living on the premises had to rely on the services of a single charwoman for one, two or three hours a day on six days in the week. For a young housewife in good health it was no great hardship to have to learn how to cook and to lay and light a fire but it bore heavily on elderly ladies of the class that had been trained in childhood to consider unladylike any domestic occupation more useful than fancy needlework and embroidery. Such ladies suffered from the hardships of siege conditions more than any other members of the community. Inability to cook their food properly bore more hardly on them than did the food shortage and the health of some of them was so seriously affected that their doctors arranged for their reception at Blanchelande, where invalids, irrespective of social status or religious denomination, received equal care from the Sisters of the Sacred Heart.

CHAPTER XV

WHERE THE FETTERS CHAFED

From the entirely selfish point of view of one interested solely in his own safety we in Guernsey were more fortunate than the people of Great Britain. Though we suffered more hardship from shortage of food and essential commodities we were, of course, safe from German air raids and – except for the slight danger from falling anti-aircraft shell fired at Allied planes and the still smaller danger of being hit when British planes dropped bombs on guns and other military targets in the Island – our lives, except for the danger of diseases arising from malnutrition, were as safe as if no war had been in progress.

But it irked those of us who valued a Briton's hardly won liberties to have to obey decrees in the making of which we had no part and the wisdom of which – many of them were impracticable and some of them extraordinarily silly – we might not criticise, but so long as we did not too flagrantly disregard the many official orders that were from time to time promulgated we were free to live our lives almost as we chose. Circumspection was, however, constantly necessary. If two or more people stood talking in the streets or market-place they were liable – though it seldom happened – to be summarily fined one mark each, presumably on the ground that street-gatherings were forbidden. If what the offenders were discussing was war news they might be taken to the Kommandantur and possibly sentenced to a few weeks' imprisonment for 'dissemination of anti-German news'. The discussion of war-news became still more risky after the confiscation of wireless sets had been ordered, for it was liable to give the German police a clue to the whereabouts of a hidden radio, the discovery of which involved imprisonment for the owner. We dared not forget that we were no longer free men living in a free country. But football matches continued – except when the Germans wanted the necessary ground for their own games or for drilling troops. Concerts and dramatic performances were permitted so long as producers took care that nothing was said that might hurt the Germans' very touchy feelings and that no music composed by Mendelssohn or any other Jewish composer was played. We could buy what we liked of what little was available in the shops or on market stalls if no Germans wanted what we wished to buy. Germans and Guernseymen mingled in barbers' shops without any friction so long as no Guernseyman protested when a German demanded to be served before his proper turn.

To many what was harder to bear than any physical suffering was the mental distress caused by the difficulty – for the first few months of the occupation even the impossibility – of communicating with relatives and friends in England. The evacuation of nearly half the population of the Island had severed parent from child, husband from wife, sister from brother, and during the brief period of time that elapsed between the evacuation and the German occupation the mail services were so severely disorganised that few letters from those who had evacuated reached the Island. Consequently many of those who stayed behind knew nothing for several months as to the whereabouts or even the safety of those who had gone.

A week after the occupation began anxiety as to the welfare of those who had evacuated was to some extent mitigated by the announcement made by the British Broadcasting Corporation that a committee had been formed in London to relieve distress among our refugees; seventeen days later we learned that of a gift of £7,500 from the Maharajah of Gondal, £1,000 had been allocated to children from the Channel Islands; and on August 29th the Headmaster of St Andrew's Schools broadcast the information that schoolchildren evacuated from Guernsey were still under the care of teachers who had gone with them and were well and happy.

It was known that it was the practice of the International Red Cross Committee at Geneva during times of war to arrange facilities for correspondence between private individuals in opposing belligerent countries, but we in Guernsey had no means of getting into touch with that Committee so we had to wait patiently for it to get into touch with us. Through its receipt and despatch of messages. In theory each family was allowed to send one message each month but only one person in each family. If a wife wished to write to one of her relatives her husband could not write to any of his relations; only near relatives might be written to; and in practice messages could not be sent as often as every month. Messages had to be written on special forms printed in Paris. When the supply of these ran out no more messages might be sent until a fresh supply arrived. The forms could perfectly well have been printed in Guernsey but this the Commandant would not allow.

It was good to get family news from England but the relief from anxiety that the messages brought us was gravely discounted by the inordinate time that they took to reach us. A few – very few – took less than seven weeks to reach us. Most took four or five months. In the meanwhile their senders naturally fretted with anxiety, not understanding the apparent dilatoriness of their correspondents. It was exasperating to receive from a correspondent, to all of whose frequent messages prompt replies had been sent, such questions as 'Can you not answer? I have heard nothing from you.' Messages passed through a number of offices and were perhaps in danger of getting entangled in red tape at anyone of them. One, which may be typical, was handed in at the Guernsey office of the Red Cross Committee on 7th May, 1941; the reply reached the sender on 2nd March, 1942; it bore four date-stamps – 24 June 1941 – 4 July 1941 – 14 Sept 1941, and 19 Dec 1941, apparently placed on it by offices through which it had passed. In one isolated case, which probably established a record, a message reached the person to whom it was addressed only 15 days after it had been written. Some took more than a year to make the one-way journey.

In normal times few people realise how greatly the publication in the newspapers of police-court reports safeguards the citizens from injustice. If a magistrate were to impose an unreasonably harsh sentence on an offender or were to pronounce a flagrantly unjust decision the newspapers would publish it, the public would know about it and public opinion would bring the magistrate to book. Those of us who had the misfortune to come into conflict with the German police were denied this safeguard. All cases in which a German brought a charge against a local inhabitant were tried by a German court in private. No reports of such cases were allowed to appear in the newspapers. As in Spain or Venice when the Inquisition had power, a man was at liberty on one day, on the next he was not to be found. It was a reasonable inference on the part of those who missed him that he had been imprisoned but nothing certain was known either as to the nature of his alleged offence or the length of his prison sentence until he was seen in his accustomed haunts once more and was able to give his own account of what had happened to him.

The first case of the kind was typical of many others. A maid-servant employed at an hotel occupied by Germans was so imprudent as to remark within a German's hearing that it was unfair that the Germans should be better fed than our own people. The Guernsey police were sent for and instructed to imprison the girl in the local civil prison. A week later they were told that a German court had sentenced her to a fortnight's imprisonment and that she was therefore to be released after another week had elapsed. The trial can have been nothing but a formal farce. The girl was not represented at it nor was she present to defend herself and it may be presumed that the only evidence heard was that of the prosecution.

A woman employed at the same hotel was offered some milk pudding on condition that she would say 'Heil, Hitler'. She replied that she would rather say 'Heil, Churchill'. On being pressed by the chief cook she declared that she would see him damned before she would say 'Heil, Hitler'. The incident then seemed to close for nothing further happened till three months had elapsed. Then without warning the woman was arrested. It was generally believed that she had been sent to France, but no two rumours agreed as to the punishment inflicted on her until one day the Dean of Guernsey, visiting prisoners sentenced to imprisonment by the Guernsey Court, chanced to see her in the exercising yard and learned from her that she had been sentenced to six months' imprisonment. More fortunate was a man who, in collaboration with French seamen employed on the vessels that brought our supplies from Granville and St Malo and with the connivance of some members of the German police, did a brisk black market trade in Normandy butter, flour, sugar and other smuggled goods. He was betrayed and sentenced to a term of imprisonment, which he duly served, but his German accomplices contrived to arrange that he should occasionally be released from prison for a few hours at a time. He profited by these short periods of liberty to visit his clients and take orders for further supplies to be delivered as opportunity offered after he had served his sentence.

If all the Germans had behaved with consideration and decency it would be unreasonable to emphasise the hardship caused by German demands on our housing accommodation, since it was a burden that we could not expect to escape. Although the conduct of many of the soldiers billeted in private houses was exemplary, that of some others was bestial and few even of the decent ones hesitated to turn elderly ladies out of the most comfortable bedrooms or to requisition the sunniest of the sitting-rooms. In any case the lot of householders compelled to receive soldiers in their houses was better than that of those who were turned out of their homes to make room for Germans. The former were able to some extent to protect their property from theft or damage; the latter were powerless to do so. Many German officers living in houses from which the owners had been evicted behaved as if the furniture belonged to them. If a German found that the house he occupied contained more armchairs or other articles of furniture than he needed, he, as many did, allowed less fortunate compatriots to take them away; or, if he packed Buhl cabinets, Sheraton bookcases, or K'ang-hsi porcelain into cases and shipped them to Germany, the real owner had little chance of discovering his loss in time to make an effective complaint to the German police. At one time a rumour spread through the Island that a vessel had left St Peter Port loaded with stolen furniture. Soon afterwards it was rumoured that she had been captured and taken to a British port. The latter rumour was probably based on no better foundation than a hope that she would be captured, but it was nevertheless very cheering.

It is the manifest duty of a civilised government not only to take measures to safeguard from theft the property of the governed but also – since no government is all powerful to allow the governed opportunity to protect their property from thieves. In this respect the German administration in Guernsey failed lamentably. When a Guernseyman, in obedience to curfew restrictions, retired into his house at night he left unprotected all the property that he could not take indoors with him. The fruit in his greenhouses, the potatoes and cabbages in his garden, his fowls, his rabbits, even his pigs were at the mercy of any thief reckless enough to disregard the curfew or – as were the German troops – exempt from its restrictions.

Only in a few cases was anyone who had been robbed able to find evidence by which the thieves could be traced and convicted and Germans often robbed with impunity even in daylight. A Guernsey grower exasperated by many losses went to the Commandant's office and complained that he had actually seen a German soldier in uniform stealing from his greenhouse. Asked if he would recognise the man if he saw him again he said that he could not do so with certainty as his greenhouse was a large one and the thief escaped by one door as he entered at the other. Far from getting any satisfaction the grower was fined five marks for making an accusation that he could not substantiate. The Guernsey police were almost powerless. Their instructions from the Commandant's office were that they must not arrest or in any way interfere with a German but, if they had sufficient grounds for bringing a charge against one, might follow him to his billet in order to ascertain his name and regimental number. If the policeman did so the German, after passing through the barbed-wire barrier that surrounded the billet, called on his comrades to block the passage way and if the Guernsey policeman summoned German police to the billet the culprit had disappeared by the time they arrived and all the soldiers in the billet would flatly deny all knowledge of the affair.

That a few of the thefts of foodstuffs were committed by

Guernseymen is probable. The nationality of the thieves, however, did not affect the duty of the German administration to protect the property of people to whom they denied the means of protecting it for themselves.

The hardship caused by German demands on our locally-produced food, if not the most grievous, was the one that affected the greatest number of people. At an early date shops were forbidden to sell eggs to the general public until the number available exceeded German requirements – assessed at 700 a week. In theory every Islander was entitled to a definite daily ration of separated milk; in practice the milk that was shared out each day by the appointed milk-distributors was what was left over after German demands had been satisfied. When fish-rationing was introduced it was announced that a quarter of each day's catch was to be reserved for Germans before the remainder was put on the market. In practice whenever – as was usually the case – there was a scarcity of fish the Germans took all of it. Often a German officer, accompanied by two or three privates carrying empty sacks, would go to the head of a queue in the vegetable market and buy everything that was on a stall.

Saddle-horses are of little use in Guernsey. The cultivable land is so thickly covered with greenhouses and so closely intersected with stone-walls that riding across country is practicably impossible except for short distances. As a means of quick transport from point to point, therefore, the saddle-horse is of little value compared with the infinitely less expensive bicycle. Yet the Germans imported a considerable number of saddle-horses, perhaps because the German High Command had issued an order that all officers whose rank entitled them to wear spurs must learn to ride. Naturally the officers who used the horses, whether for pleasure or under compulsion, preferred soft ground to the hard high road and made use of it where they could find it with no regard for hay or standing crops. The damage they did to farm land was however insignificant in comparison with the damage done to it by the engineers of the Organisation Todt. They drove roads across plough-land or pasture whenever they wished, dug huge underground shelters and threw the excavated debris on the top of growing crops, and stripped valuable turf to cover their gun emplacements. Wholesale damage was done to growing crops in the spring of 1944 by the erection on fields and all open level ground of poles designed to prevent invading British planes and gliders from landing. Wherever a pole was erected a circle of earth with a radius of six or seven feet was trampled down. The erection on cultivated land of each pole therefore involved the destruction of more than a hundred square feet of growing corn, potatoes, roots or pasture. As the number of poles erected must have run into thousands the loss to farmers from this cause alone was considerable.

It seems questionable whether International Law gave the Commandant the right to attend meetings of the States and sit in the seat of the Lieutenant Governor, as he did on several occasions, causing His Majesty's Sheriff to summon him in the traditional manner. The question, however, is not of great importance, and it probably gave him a delicious sense of importance, though it must have been galling to any member of the States who had any sense of civic pride.

What is of far more importance is that on at least one occasion the German authorities interfered with the Royal Court (which was still the Royal Court owing allegiance to His Britannic Majesty, not a Nazi German Court) in a way that must have been bitterly humiliating to all but the most obsequious of its members. On 23rd October, 1940, at a special sitting convened at short notice His Majesty's Comptroller addressed the Court, which on that occasion consisted of the Bailiff and nine jurats, asking for the registration in the Court records at the Greffe of an order cited as 'relating to measures against the Jews, dated September 27th, 1940, for application in French territory occupied by the German army and adapted for application to Guernsey'. According to the newspaper report of the sitting 'after consideration the Court agreed that the order be registered as indicated'.

There was nothing particularly oppressive in the order itself which merely required that all Jews were to be registered on a special register, that every Jewish-owned business was to be indicated by a special notice as a Jewish undertaking, that Jews who had fled from an occupied zone were not to be allowed to return and that directors of Israelite communities should co-operate with the authorities in the application of the order. But it is difficult to believe that any member of the Royal Court who gave his vote for its registration was so anti-Semite in feeling as to consider fit for inclusion in the archives of the Island an order that, though harmless enough in itself, made possible in Guernsey barbarous persecutions such as those in Germany which had made the Nazi regime abhorrent to all decent people – including many Germans. It seems more probable that each member of the Royal Court present at the special sitting considered that to refuse his vote for the registration of the order, however much it offended his conscience and judgment, would be futile, that such refusal would probably involve himself and possibly others in unpleasant consequences and, that the order would do little harm to the few who would be affected by it.[7]

A member of the Guernsey bar said that it was necessary for the Royal Court to direct the Greffier to register the order because if it were not so registered people who were affected by it might remain ignorant of it and suffer penalties for ignoring it. He was speaking of course as a lawyer. To a simple layman his explanation seemed absolute rubbish. All German orders were published in the newspapers so that there was no need for anyone to go to the Greffe to read them. Again the order might have been registered at the Greffe without the Royal Court's authority for its registration, for many of the orders decreed by the German authorities were sent to the Bailiff and transmitted by him direct to the Greffe without the Royal Court being concerned with them at all. For a layman unversed in the intricacies of legal procedure it is difficult to understand why the German authorities, if they wished their orders to be registered at the Greffe, did not send them direct to the Greffier.

---

7   As a matter of fact less than half a dozen people were affected by the 'Measures against Jews', and most of these were Christians, three-quarter Gentile but with a Jewish grandparent.

Such a course would have offended no one's conscience, for it is a Greffier's duty simply to register any order sent to him for registration without expressing any opinion as to its wisdom or justice. It is the duty of a jurat, on the other hand, to vote against the registration of any order of which he does not approve. Since it seems incredible that the jurats concerned approved the 'Measures against the Jews' Order it surely follows that they voted for its registration because they had no choice in the matter. In other words the German authorities imposed their will on the Royal Court in a matter that constitutionally should have been left to the judgment of the jurats, thus degrading the Royal Court to the ignominious status of a puppet tribunal.

Whether it was the deliberate intention of the German authorities to humiliate the members of the Royal Court is perhaps questionable. The insult, if one was intended, was more subtle than one would expect from a German. Lack of psychological insight is notoriously a German weakness. Accustomed as most Germans are to obey without question anyone in authority over them it is possible that it never occurred to the German authorities in Guernsey that there was anything offensive in demanding sheep-like acquiescence with their policy from people accustomed to a higher standard of liberty than theirs. Yet, although the German authorities may perhaps be acquitted of any deliberate attempt to degrade the Royal Court the fact that they did so will be remembered with shame for many years to come.

CHAPTER XVI

ALDERNEY, HERM, AND SARK

Alderney was the only island in the Bailiwick of Guernsey to be totally evacuated. On Saturday, June 22nd, 1940, Judge French, the President of the Alderney Royal Court, who had been in direct communication with the Home Government, announced that the British Government advised the total evacuation of the island, that it was not compulsory on any individual but was highly advisable, that he himself intended to go and that steamers to take the people to England might arrive at any moment.

Schoolchildren had already left. They had been brought to Guernsey and sent on to England with the Guernsey schoolchildren. Twelve hundred people remained to be evacuated. Steamers began to arrive at 6am on Sunday, June 23rd, and the last left five hours later. The evacuation was therefore even more hurried than it was in Guernsey, and as they were not warned to prepare for it until after the banks had closed on the previous day the evacuees could take only such money as they happened to have by them. According to a radio broadcast on July 24th, most of the Alderney evacuees were sent to Scotland. Nineteen people – one at least of whom did not hear of the proposed evacuation until it was over – still remained in the island. Two of these, both invalids, were brought to Guernsey on June 24th by the lifeboat sent at the request of the Bailiff to bring away as many stragglers as could be induced to leave, but others still remained.

On the following day, June 25th, the local steamer *Courier* was sent to Alderney with a number of farmers and farm-labourers, charged with the duty of rounding up and bringing away livestock, and nine members of St John's Ambulance Brigade, whose errand was partly to salvage medical stores and equipment from the Mignot Hospital, but principally to search the island for any inhabitants who for one reason or another had until then stayed in Alderney and to persuade

201

them to come away. They experienced considerable difficulty in discharging this errand. One man said he could not leave until he had finished packing his portable property which he valued at several thousand pounds. Another – an old fellow whom they found philosophically eating his dinner – saw no reason why he should leave the home in which he had lived for more than ninety years. The ambulance men's uniforms, especially their steel helmets, instead of giving them prestige, increased their difficulties; a woman at sight of them locked herself and her children in her house under the impression that they were Germans, and at another house they were actually threatened with a shot-gun. They did not accomplish their task without exercising much tact and patience.

The salvage party of farmers and farm-labourers could not bring away all the livestock as some pigs would not allow themselves to be caught, and some cows that had gone mad with milk fever had to be shot. During four days, however, they shipped four hundred head of cattle, twenty-one horses and ponies and an unspecified number of pigs on to the three salvaging vessels *Courier*, *New Fawn* and *Isle of Alderney*. Some of the pigs were lost to us as the *Courier*, on which they had been shipped, left for England under Admiralty orders before they could be landed in Guernsey.

Alderney's still unreaped harvest was a potential asset too valuable to neglect, and the stocks of the abandoned shops were worth collecting. The Labour Department therefore called for volunteers prepared to stay in Alderney for long enough to complete this salvage work and a party of twenty men went to the island on July 20th under guard of a detachment of German soldiers. Two days later they were joined by another ten men.

Their first task was the disposal of the putrefying carcases of animals that the first salving party had been obliged to shoot and the cleaning up of mess made by the pigs that it had failed to catch: some of these had taken up their quarters in the sitting-rooms of unlocked houses and a sow had farrowed in the Post Office. After cleaning up the worst of the mess the salvagers rounded up some pigs, which they sent to Guernsey, one or two cows that supplied them with milk, and some horses that they used for general purposes. They then collected the contents of abandoned shops and shipped to Guernsey about twenty-five tons of flour, and a quantity of miscellaneous articles, including some to which Guernsey's needs had given exceptional value such as boots and agricultural seeds. They then harvested the hay, the corn, and lastly the potatoes.

The original party of salvagers returned to Guernsey in November but their place was taken by another party sent to repair damaged houses and to lift and stack root-crops. Thenceforward Alderney, besides being a German garrison, was for a long while inhabited by men from Guernsey and Sark who were employed to till the land under the direction of an Agricultural Organiser, and to keep houses in repair on behalf of absentee owners. Individuals came and went as need arose, but there were always some Channel Islanders and many Germans there. As early as August, 1940, the Germans brought over a party of French navvies to lengthen the runways of Alderney's airport and in the autumn of 1942 a large number of Russian prisoners were imported to work on the fortifications which the German authorities considered necessary.

The relations between British and Germans, according to our local newspapers, were very friendly. It was reported, for example, that on Christmas Day, 1940, the British serenaded the Germans 'with drums, bells and anything else that would make a noise' and received in return a Christmas present of champagne and cigarettes. The testimony of our local newspapers on such a subject was not however wholly reliable. As shown in another chapter, they published everything that they were told to publish and nothing that the German Pressestelle did not wish them to publish. For instance, they told us nothing as to the truth or falsehoods of reports, brought to Guernsey by men returning from Alderney on leave, of visits paid to Alderney by British aircraft and British light naval forces. It was said that the Royal Air Force must have watched with interest the work of improving Alderney's airport, for they dropped bombs on the runway as soon as the lengthening was completed and the work was not renewed. In July, 1940, from a similar credible but unverifiable source, we in Guernsey learned that Royal Air Force planes machine-gunned German troops there, and that some German hospital-nurses sent to Alderney to nurse the wounded fell victims to a land-mine buried there. Confirmation of this report seems to be afforded by a local report that immediately afterwards thirty coffins were sent to Alderney by order of the German authorities. Again in the following October a report reached Guernsey that a party of British had landed in Alderney, killed some Germans and gone away again taking with them a number of German prisoners. It was practically impossible to verify these reports, for the men who brought them were liable to get into trouble with the Germans for doing so and might tell a story to an intimate friend of which they would deny all knowledge to a stranger.

Our local newspapers, on the other hand, gave us a very full account of a matter discreditable to our own people. When the second salvage party went to Alderney charged with the duty of salvaging stocks from the abandoned shops they found that many premises had already been broken into and looted. As by this time German soldiers had been in the island for nearly three weeks suspicion not unnaturally fell upon them. The German authorities begun to investigate, but at so leisurely a pace that they did not put the matter into the hands of the Guernsey police until May of the following year. The Guernsey police in their turn were dilatory and eventually the German authorities took the matter into their own hands again. On October 28th, 1941, thirteen men were brought before a German military tribunal and charged with theft from abandoned shops and houses in Alderney. Of these one was sentenced to one year's imprisonment and five to terms of imprisonment ranging between three weeks and two months. The others were acquitted.

The case was brought because in the words of *The Star*'s report[8] 'the honour of the German army was affected to a high degree as, through this action, it had to be ascertained whether,

---

8   The accounts of the trial printed in *The Star* and the *Evening Press*

and if so to what extent, German soldiers had taken a part in the plundering'.

It is difficult to believe that with the ample opportunities they had the German soldiers did no looting whatever, but the trial did show that some looting was done before any Germans set foot in Alderney, and from July 20th onward. According to unconvincing evidence given by an Alderney woman, who seemed anxious to curry favour by exonerating the Germans from all suspicion, 'some of the Red Cross men had trunks in which may have been linen clothes and other goods appropriated while pilfering'. It is more reasonable to suppose that the contents of the trunks were what they had been sent to fetch. Another witness declared that Red Cross men had been seen breaking open the door of a shop with a pickaxe. This may be true, but if the shop contained anything likely to be of use in a hospital they were perfectly justified in doing so. The Germans, at any rate, brought no member of St John's Ambulance Brigade to trial. Evidence was also offered that, while the men who had been sent to bring away livestock were at work, members of the steamers *Courier* and *New Fawn*, that had brought them, indulged in looting. This is more probable, but in the circumstances one can hardly regard the offence with pious horror. Whatever they took had been abandoned by its lawful owners: the island was being evacuated: 'better to take the stuff', they might have pleaded, 'than leave it to moulder away'. Again it was said that fishermen, who had escaped in a lifeboat from France and had spent the night in Alderney on their way to England, had broken into a shop and stolen tobacco. Very likely they did, and who will blame them? So much for the looting that took place before the arrival of the Germans.

Although, after their arrival on July 20th, 1940, the Germans stationed guards in the streets to prevent pilfering, looting on a small scale seems to have been a comparatively easy matter. At any rate the five men who were sentenced to short terms

---

respectively were not identical, but had in common peculiarities which seemed to indicate that they were taken from a report written in exceptionally good English by a German.

of imprisonment for theft or plundering were Guernseymen who were not in Alderney after July 20th. When judgment was passed by the Tribunal on these men it was taken into consideration as mitigation that the thefts of which they were guilty were of small and relatively unimportant articles and that there was 'great provocation for the accused'. No such excuse was suggested on behalf of the man who was sentenced to a year's imprisonment. He had lived in Alderney for some time before the German occupation, and though he left when others evacuated he returned at the end of July, 1940. He appears to have robbed quite openly, leaving the wheelbarrow in which he carried away his loot outside shops and houses while he ransacked indoors[9]. When the German police searched a house in Guernsey occupied by the thief's wife they found it so full that in some parts it was impossible to move without obstruction, and the list of the articles he was accused of stealing included, besides a quantity of tobacco and foodstuffs, 69 shirts, 13 clocks, 76 curtains, 77 carpets and one tailor's dummy.

The trial by the German tribunal seems to have been a perfectly fair one, but the report of it might with advantage have said less about 'the honour of the German army' being impugned by the suspicion that members of it may have been guilty of pilfering because in Guernsey Germans robbed wholesale. The reference to German honour is therefore just a little bit nauseating, but it is redeemed by another passage. Referring to the man who was sentenced to a year's imprisonment the report says that he had made himself suspect on his return from Guernsey at the end of July, 1940, by seeking the friendship of the German Army of Occupation in an effusive manner, claiming German ancestry and professing violent antipathy to the English – this although he was in receipt of a British pension. It must be set down to German credit that this man and others who tried to buy German favour by unpatriotic conduct got little good by it.

---

[9] The report of the case gives no explanation as to why the German sentries posted to prevent pilfering allowed this. That they did so affords support to a belief held by many people in Guernsey that the average German private soldier will yield to anyone who bluffs with sufficient self-confidence.

After giving very full accounts of that trial our newspapers gave us no information whatever about happenings in Alderney. Of subsequent events there we learned only by chance. On one occasion, after local undertakers had had orders to make thirty coffins for shipment to Alderney, two small vessels were towed to Guernsey for repair, bringing some Guernseymen as well as some German soldiers, all wounded by machine-gun fire from Allied planes. On another occasion, when Guernsey florists had orders to send a number of wreaths to Alderney, it was reported that a British commando party had landed there, killing some Germans and taking others prisoner.

After the Allies invaded Normandy watchers in Guernsey could sometimes see the smoke of explosions above Alderney. At one time communication between Guernsey and the Northern island was interrupted for three weeks. About a fortnight after the invasion began it was rumoured that Allied headquarters had informed the local German authorities that, if they wished to evacuate Alderney, the evacuating ships would not be attacked, and on June 25th a large number of Russian, French and Algerian prisoners of war were brought to Guernsey for trans-shipment to France. With them came a number of Frenchwomen, who had been taken to Alderney to serve the German troops as prostitutes, and a large party – probably at least a thousand – of Germans in convict garb, probably political prisoners who had protested against Nazi practices. The latter were kept under guard at Blanc Bois but the Frenchwomen were left at liberty and paraded the Town in small parties singing the *Marseillaise* and waving tricolour flags.

When, on May 17th, 1945, British forces occupied Alderney they found about 2,500 Germans still there. Newspaper correspondents who landed with the forces reported that less damage to buildings had been done than in Guernsey, but that many houses in the little town of St Anne had been completely gutted, all the houses at the bottom of Braye Hill and on Crabbé and Platte Saline had been demolished to make way for a road, the Parish Church had been used as a food store after the removal of pews and other fittings, and the Roman Catholic church had been badly damaged. The island was found to be intensively fortified; ringed with gun batteries of very heavy calibre, honeycombed with underground galleries topped with solid concrete and bristling with anti-aircraft guns. The military authorities at once appointed a commission to investigate allegations that between 800 and 1,000 foreign labourers had been shot, beaten to death or had died from malnutrition.

During the early period of the occupation, while Germany still had hopes of invading England, Herm's sandy beaches were used for the training of men in landing from barges; German officers amused themselves by shooting rabbits on the sand dunes; a film photograph of German soldiers performing the ceremony of guard-mounting on the Herm pier was taken for propaganda purposes: but nothing else of any interest at all seems to have happened on that small island during the whole period of the occupation.

The few people who lived on Brecqhou were evicted in April, 1941, without, of course, any reason being assigned.

A propaganda photographer who visited Sark had an experience less pleasant to himself than to the Sark people who were with him. After landing at Creux Harbour he was walking through the tunnel that connects it with the interior of the island when men at work on the new breakwater exploded a charge of dynamite. At the sound of the explosion the German flung himself to the ground, squirmed on his stomach to such cover as an overturned boat could afford him, drew his revolver and prepared to sell his life dearly. It was some time before he could be persuaded that his fears were groundless.

As in Guernsey so in Sark the severance of communication from England greatly affected economic conditions. For the previous fifty years or so Sark's principal wealth in an ever increasing degree had been drawn from the pockets of English holiday-makers. The loss of this income together with the cutting off of supplies of foodstuffs from England forced on the island conditions resembling those of a century ago when it produced practically all the food it consumed. Sark's adversity had one compensation; fuel shortage and the need for more land to cultivate resulted in extensive clearing of gorse from cliff and common land.

The war gave Sark its share of sensational events. Once a German officer was murdered in his bed. As soon as it was known, everyone was compelled to remain indoors while each house in turn was minutely searched for a watch and a hammer that had belonged to him, and cigarettes of a particular brand that he smoked. The people were told that if the murderer were not discovered the whole male population between the ages of fourteen and sixty would be sent to concentration camps and the women deported to Jersey. For a while no fisherman was allowed to put to sea and no civilian was allowed to enter or leave the island. In the meanwhile the dead man's batman was arrested. He escaped from custody and a proclamation was made ordering anyone who saw him to report. Soon afterwards the body of the batman was found drowned in a well. Probably he had committed suicide but it was possible that he, too, had been murdered. Sark people therefore were still kept under strict supervision, everyone except children and aged people being required to report daily to the German police.

But one event transcended all others, partly by its intrinsic importance but far more by the far-reaching results that followed it. On October 4th, 1942, at an early hour in the morning a small party of British raided Sark. The date and the fact of the landing are the only two points on which there is full agreement.

The official British account as broadcast by radio stated that the raiders killed ten Germans with bombs and took five prisoners but four of the five tried to escape and had to be shot. Of the local accounts that reached Guernsey none are official and none are based on the reports of eye-witnesses. One stated that ten men landed and went to the Bel Air Hotel, where they killed four men and took one man prisoner. Another, emanating from a German in sympathy with the British stated that twenty Germans were killed or wounded and that one of the raiders was left a prisoner in German hands. The German account published in the page of *The Star* of October 8th reserved by the German Press Officer for his propaganda stated that:

In the early morning hours sixteen British soldiers attacked a German working party consisting of an NCO and four men. The German men, clad only in their shirts, were bound with a strong cord, prevented from putting on any further garments, and taken to the shore. When the German soldiers offered resistance against this unheard of treatment, the NCO and one man were killed by rifle-shots and bayonet thrusts, while a further man was wounded. This fact is confirmed by the statement of a German sapper who succeeded in escaping in the scuffle. The cross-examination has brought to light that the binding had been planned by the British beforehand ...

The German Supreme Command has therefore been compelled to issue the following orders: From noon on October 8th all British officers and men taken prisoner at Dieppe will be bound.

On October 13th *The Star*'s propaganda page had more than a column on the subject. It began by quoting a statement attributed to the British War Ministry:

The raid on Sark was carried out by a party of ten officers and men. Seven men of the party took five German soldiers as prisoners. The hands of the German soldiers were bound that the men who actually executed the taking of the prisoners were able to interlink their arms and lead them away. There was no written order or any other instructions. On their way to the boat the prisoners had to pass by barracks occupied by German troops, and precautionary measures had therefore to be taken. In spite of these precautions four of the prisoners broke away and had therefore to be shot to prevent them from raising an alarm.

This was followed by German comment too long and verbose to be quoted verbatim. It argued that the British statement afforded proof that a British military order for the 'chaining' (sic) of German prisoners actually existed; it scored a point by remarking that the shooting of the prisoners must have made a greater noise than could be made by escaping men trying to raise an alarm; and it denied that the prisoners on their way to the boat had to pass barracks occupied by German troops.

With regard to this last point we know that the raiders landed in Dixcart Bay, for a lady who lived in a cottage in Dixcart Valley, Mrs Pittard, was imprisoned on a charge of helping the raiders by telling them the way, If, as we were told, the raiders went to the Bel Air Hotel they, on their return to their boat, must have passed two of the largest buildings in Sark, Stock's Hotel and Dixcart Hotel, which the raiders may reasonably have assumed to hold German troops. It is true that the rifle shots would have made more actual noise than could be made by an escaping prisoner but they might have escaped notice before daybreak in an island patrolled by nervous German sentries, whereas an escaped prisoner who dashed into quarters occupied by Germans clad only in his shirt and shouting for help could hardly fail to attract attention.

It will be remembered that the German Supreme Command carried out its threat to fetter all British officers and men made prisoners of war at Dieppe, and kept them bound until the British War Cabinet retaliated by fettering an equal number of German prisoners of war.

For a while after the Sark raid troops in Guernsey exercised even more vigilance than was usual. Soldiers were on the alert all night patrolling the main roads and the sea front and many roads were barricaded until so late an hour that some working people did not reach the scene of their daily work until as late as ten o'clock in the morning. During this period of abnormal vigilance some islanders on whom Germans were billeted learned that a search was being made for ten soldiers who had mysteriously disappeared, and that the official theory was that the missing men had deserted and were being hidden and fed by islanders. Enquiries for the missing men were not abandoned until so much time had elapsed that, as a German officer is said to have remarked, no Islanders could have fed them for so long a time. It is worth noting that the night post of the missing men was on the coast road at Belgrave Bay. This justifies the idea that a British raiding party may have landed in Belgrave Bay and managed to take them prisoner without attracting the attention of anyone else.[10]

Another precautionary measure that the Germans adopted as a result of the Sark raid was the regrouping of their troops in Guernsey into easily defensible areas. Many people who had hitherto escaped eviction were thus turned out of their homes, even bed-ridden invalids being sent adrift to find quarters where they could.

It is believed that the Sark raiding party carried away with them from the Bel Air Hotel or elsewhere a copy of a Guernsey newspaper from which it became known in England that a number of people had been taken from Guernsey to internment camps in Germany. That the Germans feared this to be the case seemed probable when in February, 1943, a second party was warned to prepare to be deported. On this occasion no official notice was published and no mention of it was allowed to appear in the newspapers. In consequence it was impossible adequately to organise means of supplying those who were to be deported with clothing and other necessaries of which they might have stood in need. Thirty-five Sark people, including Mrs Pittard, who was released from prison for the purpose, were sent to Germany with this party. Some of these had even more need of assistance than the Guernsey exiles because, not knowing why they had been made to leave Sark and supposing that they would be allowed to return within a few days, they brought with them, when they came to Guernsey for trans-shipment to France, no more than necessities for a few nights and were ill-equipped for absence from home for a prolonged period.

---

10   After our liberation we learned that on a number of occasions they landed in Guernsey and took away German prisoners for interrogation.

CHAPTER XVII

OUR MARIONETTE PRESS

Among other hardships inflicted on us by the German occupation was loss of the freedom of the Press. Our newspapers were allowed to print nothing that the German authorities, represented by a Press Officer, did not wish them to print and were compelled to print whatever they were told to print. Opposition to the Press Officer's decrees would have entailed the suppression of the newspaper in which it appeared. An editor, Mr Gartell, was dismissed from his post by order of the German authorities. His offence was that he had 'insulted' the Press Officer by saying that the news value of a censored paragraph was so small that its omission from his paper was immaterial.

One of the functions of the Press is to guide public opinion and no doubt the German High Command, by putting a Press Officer in control of our newspapers, hoped to persuade some of us to become disciples of Nazi doctrine. At first he went to work with a certain amount of cunning. If from the very earliest days of the German occupation the tone of our newspapers had been as blatantly pro-Nazi as it eventually became even the dullest intellect would have detected the hand that moved the marionettes. To be convincing the process had to be gradual. On the day after the German occupation the only sign of German influence over our newspapers was that they published no British war news and made no reference to the German air raid of three days before – they published the names of the victims but without mentioning how they came by their deaths. For a week they published no war news of any sort and then began to make a daily feature of the official German communiqué – to the great distress of those who were so foolish as to believe it.

Happily we had on a number of occasions the evidence of our own eyes to prove to us that news from a German source was quite unreliable. For example, in the early hours of October 11th, 1940, many people whose houses overlooked the Little

Russell were awakened by the rattling of their windows. Those who looked out saw in the sky in the direction of Cherbourg a fiery glow that extended to several degrees above the horizon. It increased in intensity till it was lost in the sunrise and gave place to a heavy pall of smoke that hung over the French coast for several hours. The natural conclusion, verified later by the BBC's news-bulletin, was that Cherbourg had been very heavily raided. Three days later the official German account of the affair given to us was that a small unit of the British Navy had attempted to shell Cherbourg, but had been driven off by the fire of the coastal batteries after an action lasting no more than three minutes.

Some months elapsed before the newspapers were compelled to publish German propaganda to any extent. Until then lack of British news made it difficult for the editors to find matter with which to fill their columns.

For lack of British news both newspapers devoted much space to so-called 'war-time recipes'. For a long while these had very little relation to our actual war-time conditions. We were told how to souse mackerel at a time when, as all fishing was prohibited, mackerel were unprocurable; when none but Germans could buy eggs it was suggested that curried eggs made an excellent war-time dinner; and in case any of us wished to hoard our meagre meat ration and could spare the necessary salt from a weekly three-ounce ration we were given full directions for the salting of beef. It was not until 1941 that the cookery experts faced realities and gave us recipes for limpet-soup, sorrel soup, stewed dandelion in leaves and seaweed-jelly.

It was not to be expected that either newspaper would publish anything the least likely to annoy the Germans, but chauvinistic members of the general public considered that at least they should have abstained from paying the Germans compliments. On July 5th, less than a week after the Germans landed in the Island, one paper gave a prominent position to a paragraph headed 'GERMAN OFFICER'S KINDLY DEED' in which it stated that an officer had stopped his car to offer a lift to a cripple. Three days later the same newspaper told us that a German soldier had given a child some chocolate and on August 30th it was recorded that two members of the German forces had attended a church service.

The inference that any instance of decent behaviour on the part of a German was remarkable enough to be worth recording was perhaps hardly complimentary to the Germans as a whole and if the creditor's object was to allay the fears of the timid the publication of these trivial news-items was justifiable and even commendable. But it is difficult to find any excuse for an appeal to owners of tennis racquets and tennis balls to give them to the troops. That attempt to lick German boots met with a snub from the Commandant who published an announcement that the appeal had been made without his authority and that the troops did not require sports gear. That paper's next attempt to earn a pat on the back from the German authorities had unfortunate results for the Islanders. Usurping the functions of the Controlling Committee one of its representatives asked the Commandant to make the curfew regulations more explicit. Hitherto the police had been allowed to use their commonsense in enforcing these regulations. Now this was taken from them. The Commandant replied that the regulations must be rigidly obeyed; that a householder might not even go into his own garden during curfew hours; that a cyclist prevented by a punctured tyre from reaching his home before dark should demand shelter at the nearest house and stay there till daylight; and that a farmer expecting a cow to calve must spend the whole night in the stable with it. This last very unreasonable and oppressive interpretation of the curfew regulations was modified later on when, perhaps, the Commandant was in a better temper.

A series of articles on pages devoted to German propaganda over the signature 'Sarnian' which told us that 'Germany, like Switzerland, fills one's heart with happy calm'; another advocating the teaching of German in the Island on the ground 'that there is no doubt that after the war German will be the premier European language'; and one published on the second anniversary of the German Occupation of Guernsey which, after referring to the admittedly lenient treatment by the Germans of Symes and Nicolle, the two young army officers who were landed on the Island for espionage purposes, and the light sentences passed on the police who had been convicted of the theft of German stores, said that 'these two examples will suffice to show how much credence can be given to the British propaganda stories of German atrocities in occupied territories' may conceivably have expressed the genuine opinions of one or more local people anxious to be fair to the Germans. It is more likely that the writer or writers obtained – or hoped to obtain – some advantage by cringing to the Germans. It is still more likely that they were the work of the German Press Officer himself.

The Press Officer did not begin propaganda work on a large scale until some four months after the landing of the Germans. Both newspapers were made to publish paragraphs calculated to give the impression that their editors had misgivings as to the British military power. These were followed by articles which appeared to indicate that the editors were beginning to have honest doubts as to the justice of Britain's cause, and were strongly impressed by the social benefits of Nazi rule. Finally the tone of the papers was such that anyone so simple as not to recognise German propaganda would have supposed that the editors had become wholehearted and enthusiastic admirers of Nazism.

As a general rule the paragraphs and articles sent by the Press Officer to the newspapers were not in the form of editorials but had the outward appearance of having been culled by the editors from independent sources. Speeches recorded in the British newspapers were occasionally quoted. When the First Lord of the Admiralty ended a stirringly optimistic speech with a warning against complacency we were given the warning but not the optimistic part of the speech. We were told that a Canadian statesman had said that the help that Canada would give to Britain would be limited whereas what he had actually said, as listeners to British broadcasts knew, was that Canada's help would be limited only by Canada's power to help. Because we knew that these speeches had been misquoted we were better able to read with equanimity scathing criticisms of the War Cabinet which were attributed to newspapers of such standing as *The Star* and *The Manchester Guardian*. And no one was greatly distressed by jeremiads frequently quoted from a South American journal, *Razon*, attributed to Mr Hore-Belisha, MP, especially as they were seldom published until they had lost their sting.

Unidentified journals such as 'a newspaper published in Shanghai' or foreign newspapers, the names of most of which were till then unknown to the average newspaper reader, were quoted in support of statements to the effect that the British working classes were definitely opposed to the war, that the natives of Britain's African colonies were seething with unrest and that the South African Dutch, with the solitary exception of Field-Marshal Smuts, were looking forward to the time when the Germans would free them from the British yoke.

One device for concealing the strings that controlled our marionette Press was the insertion of paragraphs of an entirely harmless character. Thus some headed 'Enormous accusations against Lord Beaverbrook', '100,000 inhabitants of London sleep in tunnels of Underground Railway' and one that asserted that the Egyptian Prime Minister had been murdered by an agent of the British Secret Service, were interspersed with news items that had no relation to the war, such as 'Tornado in Havana' and 'Snowstorm in California' or snippets apparently taken from some popular magazine such as 'Of what tree is vegetable ivory the product?' 'How is soda-water made?' and 'What is the number of stars visible to the naked eye?' This device, however, was robbed of whatever effect it might otherwise have had by the carelessness or stupidity of the Press Officer in sending the same articles to both newspapers thus disclosing that both were under the same control and that the pro-German or anti-British matter that they published came from the same source. It sometimes happened – and this surely must have been due to sheer laziness on the part of the Press Officer – that some paragraphs were reprinted again and again until they were almost as familiar as standing advertisements. As a rule the paragraphs were written in good English but one, which seemed an honest attempt to give a fair summary of a speech broadcast by the BBC was somewhat difficult to understand:- 'The British Colonial Minister told about the difficulties of his work in the London wireless. In future England will be obliged to use people of the British Colonies. The youth in the colonies is educated in the same spirit as the British youth. England may have confidence to its negroes.'

The purpose of these paragraphs – except the few that had no relation to the war – was presumably to make us believe that Britain could not hope for victory. It is to be supposed that the propagandist who chose them, with the ignorance of psychology which has always been a German characteristic, judged our mentality by that of the average German and thought that desire to be on the winning-side would influence us more than love of country. In November, 1940, he tried to shake our faith in British justice by causing the publication in our newspapers of a violently anti-British article entitled 'To remind you – Blockade 1919 – when Germany was starved in peace time'. With a view perhaps to giving the impression that the article was an honest expression of editorial opinion it did not appear in both papers on the same day and the editors were told that they must not reveal the source from which they had obtained it. This was followed by a series of articles designed to show how pleasant and prosperous was the life of the individual citizen under Nazi government. We were told that the National Socialist People's Organisation was the greatest welfare organisation in the world, that the Four-Year Plan was a triumphant success, that Germany had become independent of raw materials, that her labouring classes had become so prosperous that all German workmen could afford motor-cars of their own and that under the enlightened direction of their Fuehrer the German people had become so devout that churches were filled to overflowing, ecclesiastical institutions were growing in number, religious publications were increasing their circulations and that 'on special occasions' German soldiers attended religious services.

It had long been the custom of our newspapers to insert in their news columns paragraphs calling attention to advertisements, especially official advertisements, that had a news value. This was of service to the general reader because he might fail to read the advertisement and because official advertisements are often so worded that they are not readily understood unless paraphrased in ordinary English. On one occasion the following official notice appeared in both papers:

> All observations made by civilians in the coastal area, such as drifting boats, departures from the Island, landings, etc., must be reported without delay verbally to the nearest German sentry-guard or by telephone to the Inselkommandantur.

As landings on the Island at any place except a harbour were not likely to be made except by someone – such as a British Secret Service agent – who did not wish the Germans to know of his arrival and departure from any point other than a harbour would almost certainly be attempts by Guernseymen to escape from the Island, this notice – except the part of it which referred to drifting boats was an order to Guernseymen to betray their fellow countrymen. Yet both papers printed a comment expressing warm approval of it.

> We wish to draw the particular attention of our readers to a Notice of the Feldkommandantur which appears in to-day's issue.
> The war demands of every individual an increased sense of duty. Often a human life may be saved by swift action. Many a shipwrecked man, already in sight of land, has perished only because help could not be brought to him in time.
> The Island of Guernsey is in the War Zone, and it may be that daily and hourly human beings are in distress and are trying to reach the coast by exerting their last ounce of strength. No matter to what nationality they may belong, whether they be friend

or foe, everything possible must be done in order to save them.

This is the meaning of the Notice, which requests every individual inhabitant to report without delay all observations in the Coastal area, and to report them to the right quarters, in order that no precious time – often it may be a matter of minutes – may be lost.

Please note. – Inselkommandantur, Mount Durand, Guernsey – Telephone No. 1450.

Note. – In this connection, we have just learned that a reward will be granted to those through whose timely intervention the rescue of human lives has been rendered possible.

The use of the editorial 'we' was cunning. It was obviously designed to give the impression that the comment was the work of some journalist on the staff of the paper in which it appeared, although anyone who read it would probably consider the writer to be singularly muddle-headed if he thought that any lives could be saved by reporting the safe arrival of a boat or the intentional departure of one from the Island. As, however, the comment appeared in both papers in identical words it was obviously the work of the Press Officer. If he had taken the trouble to draft two pseudo-editorials on the subject of the notice the fraud might not have been detected. By his laziness and carelessness in causing the publication in both papers of identically worded appeals he tore the screen from behind his marionettes and showed us the strings that moved them.

On the whole the propaganda was more stupid than cunning. Because there was nothing that the Press Officer desired less than to cheer us up it was stupid of him to give us a news item entitled 'Demonstrations in Johannesburg' that told us of the breaking up of an anti-British meeting and the wrecking of the offices of an anti-British newspaper, for it contradicted his frequent assertions that South Africans were almost unanimous in their desire for a German victory. Another very cheering news item, given us before the United States had entered the war, was that four thousand Americans who had the same surname as the British Prime Minister had formed themselves into an association, members of which were pledged to make financial sacrifices in favour of Britain. Apparently the Press Officer published this paragraph because it gave him the opportunity to entitle it 'One fool makes many'. For no better reason he gave us the good news that the Abyssinian emperor had offered the services of his native troops to the British Government under the heading 'The King of Kings – the Clown of the Troupe'.

The German propaganda was only occasionally vulgar but it was often very funny. When Rudolf Hess flew to England we were given the following explanation of his action:-

> He knew the peace proposals of the Fuehrer better than anyone else in Germany. Evidently he realised in his own conscience that the continuation of war would lead to the complete destruction of the British Empire and therefore wanted to stop this disastrous development by personal sacrifice. The Nationalist Socialist Party regrets that this idealist of the highest ability should become the victim of such a curious misconception.

An article entitled 'Colonies – a vital question' told us that 'the coloured natives of the German protectorates have asked for twenty years 'why do not our good German masters come back to us?''. A long article written to mark the anniversary of Italy's entry into the war ended with the statement that 'Mussolini's soldiers have already begun to drive England out of her position in the middle and Eastern part of the Mediterranean' and another told us that Mussolini did not know when Italy would reconquer her East African Empire but she certainly would reconquer it and avenge her dead.

British methods of warfare were frequently denounced, although a German officer stationed in the Island testified to the care that our bombers had taken to avoid damaging Cologne cathedral and another who, when on leave, had witnessed a

British air raid, said that our airmen had evidently endeavoured, as far as possible, to do no harm to civilians. In a description, from the German point of view, of a Commando raid on Sark in December, 1943, we were told that:

> the dead who were left behind had their faces blackened and carried very sharp daggers and incendiary grenades, they were therefore not armed like truthful and respectful fighting soldiers, but like murderers. Characteristic of the mentality of the participants in these Commando raids is the finding of a cross and an English prayer-book on one of the dead.
>
> This is characteristic of the methods of the English: in one hand they hold a prayer-book, and in the other weapons of death.

We were frequently told also that Germany would do something terrible at some future date to be selected by her Fuehrer. These threats were generally in extracts from speeches broadcast from Bremen and elsewhere in the English language. For example, extracts for one single speech, published in the *Evening Press* of December 1st, 1943 warned us that 'Germany will pay back in full measure for the terrorist raids now being made on Germany ... Reich Minister Goebbels did not say when, where or how the blows would fall, but he did ask Britain to note that retaliation was being prepared ... Roosevelt and Churchill are responsible for what is coming ... The bombing of German cities would bring catastrophe to the British people. This is no threat – it is a statement of fact and as such it will be proved'.

Attacks on the competence of both Mr Churchill and Mr Roosevelt were frequent. The latter began before the United States' entry into the war but after it had become apparent that Britain would receive moral and material help from America. After we had been assured that American help to Britain would be small and would come too late to be of any use or would even fail to materialise, and that ninety per cent of Americans were opposed to Roosevelt's policy, we were given a spate of paragraphs with such titles as 'Roosevelt loses public confidence', 'Panic and hysteria in the USA', and, at a time when the President took a short holiday under medical advice, 'President Roosevelt in a convalescent home. Ill or insane?'

We heard less about Mr Roosevelt after 1941 when Germany carried the war into Russia, with the quixotic intention, so we were told, of saving Europe, including Great Britain, from the horrors of Bolshevism. Limelight had been turned on Russia earlier in the year when we were told that Molotoff was on his way to Berlin for a conference with Hitler and that the result of that conference would create consternation in Britain. Naturally we read the German propaganda eagerly during the next few days in order to learn what sort of bombshell was about to explode to Britain's hurt. The German propaganda often announced in advance successes that Germany intended to achieve and as day after day passed without any further reference to the conference or the consternation it was to create we realised that yet another German firework had proved to be damp.

In September, 1941, we were told that the annihilation of the Soviets, 'which of course is only a question of time', would pave the way for the final settlement with Britain, because there would remain no land power which could seriously threaten Germany and that Germany, strengthened by the granaries and raw materials captured from Russia, would be able to build more warships and merchant vessels than England and the United States together.

There were occasions when the propagandist found it necessary to explain in what way Germany had gained a victory in a battle in which the uninstructed might have supposed that she had been defeated. The battle for Rostov at the end of November, 1941, affords an excellent illustration of this. On December 3rd we were told that 'in clever recognition of the situation and for the purpose of carrying out necessary retaliation against the partisans in Rostov, the German Command had evacuated the town'. Six days later the situation was explained more fully:

> Whilst the attacks of the German troops against

Moscow proceed the Soviets have massed their troops at Rostov and in the Donetz district in order to drive them inconsiderately to counter-attacks. Here they follow their principle that the sacrifices of masses of men have not to be considered if there is any success or even a fancied success to be reached.

They even incited the population at Rostov against the international law to fight at the back of the German troops. This criminal method of fighting has led to the order of the troops of occupation to evacuate the district of the town of Rostov. By this evacuation the opportunity is given to treat the population according to the international law.

An ingenious explanation but perhaps somewhat unconvincing! A paragraph on the same page, after referring to the 'great credit' that German news bulletins had in the world, told us that 'the Bolshevists have almost made a profession of the political lie. They turn facts upside down, and do not even take care to give to their reports a semblance of probability'. This statement somehow recalls what the pot called the kettle.

The retreat of the Germans in 1943 from the Volga to the Dnieper was represented, in an article entitled 'Germany has every advantage with winter defence line', as a masterly achievement. The terrain on the latter river was said to present 'insuperable and natural obstacles to the Soviets, the nature of which could be of decisive importance in the greatest battle of the age'. The Dnieper River itself was said to be one of the most formidable of these natural hazards because of its great width and depth and because the western bank of the river is higher than the eastern. It was unfortunate for the author of the article that Russians had crossed the Dnieper in several places before it was in print in our newspapers.

It often happened that the prophecies of the propaganda department were proved by the swift march of events to be baseless even before they were printed. This was generally due to the carelessness of the Press Officer who seems to have taken no trouble to consider whether the propaganda material supplied to him from Germany was still suitable when it reached his hands. On May 30th, 1941, we were told that British mechanised units operating in Iraq had been repulsed with heavy losses by Raschid Ali's troops, but by then we had already heard of Raschid Ali's flight to Iran and on the day when the news item was printed we heard that his troops had asked for an armistice. On another occasion we were told that the Grand Mufti of Jerusalem was organising the Mohammedan world against us but we were not told of it until the Grand Mufti had followed Raschid Ali's example. We were told that Rommel had consolidated his position by establishing his forces on the Mareth Line in Tunisia from which he would strike back when the time was ripe. This information was not published until after the German-Italian forces had retreated from the Mareth Line to beyond Gabes. On a later occasion the Press Officer caused the publication of a paragraph which stated that British and American 'terror-raids' on Turin, Milan, Genoa and Naples were stiffening the determination of the Italians to resist us. This paragraph did not appear in a Guernsey newspaper until five weeks after the Italians had sued for peace!

Much of the propaganda was directed towards creating ill-feeling between Britain and the United States or alternatively between Britain and the United States on the one hand and Soviet Russia on the other. Both Churchill and Roosevelt were sometimes represented as Stalin's dupes unwittingly furthering Soviet aims and on one occasion we were even told that the war had been brought about by Stalin for his own ends. When he signed the German-Soviet Pact of August, 1939, we were told, he knew that Germany, with her back stiffened by a pact with the Soviet Union, would not hesitate to attack Poland which inevitably would bring France and England into a war that would bring about the complete destruction of Western Europe. If this theory is accepted Hitler also must be numbered amongst those whom Stalin had duped. At other times Germans were represented as chivalrous knights sacrificing their lives to save Europe, including Britain, from the horrors of Bolshevism. 'It would one day be recognised', Dr Goebbels was reported to have said, 'as the greatest scandal of the century that the world should have left the fight against Bolshevism to Germany alone, supported by a few allies'.

In other articles Stalin, Roosevelt, Churchill and the nations of which they were the heads were represented as all under the secret domination of the Jews. One such article seemed to prove that at least some members of the staff of Germany's propaganda bureau actually believed that what they wrote was really true. The article was entitled 'Englishman imprisoned for plain-speaking on the Jewish Question' and the writer of it solemnly told us that an Englishman, who had lived for some time in Germany as a prisoner-of-war, had told him that in 1938 a London court had sentenced him to two months' imprisonment, 'which he had really served', for making an anti-Jewish remark before English people, and that not only he but also 'many others, among them also leaders of political organisations, experienced the same fate'. It may be recalled that some of the disciples of Sir Oswald Moseley who had made inflammatory speeches in the East End of London received sentences of imprisonment, not for making anti-Jewish remarks but for inciting their audience to smash the windows of Jewish shopkeepers.

If the Press Officer who passed that article for publication had sufficient knowledge of contemporary history to be qualified for his post he must have known that an open-air orator in England is allowed, so long as he does not incite his audience to riot, to make any anti-Jewish, anti-Christian, anti-capitalist, anti-Communist, anti-British, anti-German or any other kind of offensive remark without fear of arrest. The conclusion, therefore, to be drawn is that either the Press Officer was incompetent or that he carelessly sent the article to be printed without taking the trouble to read it.

One sometimes wondered what was the object of the German authorities in making our newspapers publish their propaganda. So far as it was aimed at inspiring us with doubts as to the justice of Britain's cause and with approval of the Nazi form of government the purpose underlying its publication was intelligible. But what purpose did they hope to serve by inflicting on us matter calculated to sow dissension among the allies, or to create misgivings as to the competence of our leaders? Cut off as we were from England we could not have helped their plans, even if we had wished to do so, by writing letters to English newspapers, by inspiring questions in the House of Commons or by any other of the methods by which private individuals in England seek to influence the British Government.

In the early days of the German occupation the propaganda showed the use of intelligence on the part of the Press Officer because it was of a kind that might have perverted the ignorant or those whose mental balance was unsteady. At a later date attempts to win us by subtlety were abandoned and, so far as one could perceive any purpose in it at all, it sought only to depress us. It was entirely futile and – even from the German point of view – not worth the ink consumed in printing it.

CHAPTER XVIII

PROBLEMS SOLVED – OR SHELVED

Many difficulties may be found to have a humorous side if examined from the right angle. The local prison was too small to accommodate all who were sentenced to terms of imprisonment even although several empty houses were converted into use as temporary prisons. In December, 1942, the Royal Court, therefore, ordained that at the discretion of the Court terms of imprisonment might be postponed until room in the prison was available, or served in part and part postponed, or remitted altogether if the offender gave bail to be of good behaviour for a specified time. Consequently those guilty of minor offences either escaped punishment altogether or had leisure before they were incarcerated to arrange for their businesses to be carried on during their absence. On one occasion the question which of two offenders should go to prison was settled by tossing a coin.

Few, however, could see a humorous side to the Island's labour problem which, because it seriously affected our food supply, directly or indirectly affected all of us. A German boast, frequently repeated in the German propaganda columns of our newspapers, was that under Nazi management unemployment had been abolished both in Germany itself and in all countries occupied by Germany. Unlike most statements made in the propaganda columns this boast was justified at least so far as Guernsey was concerned. By employing, largely at the Island's expense, a great number of both male and female workers – many at work of no importance whatever[11] – the Germans abolished unemployment in Guernsey and created in its place a shortage of labour problem so grave that in 1941 the States passed a 'Compulsory Civil Duties Law' which gave the President of the States, or anyone authorised by him for the purpose, to conscript

---

11   A working-man, applying for permission to borrow books from the Priaulx Library, remarked that he had much time on his hands as he was working for the Germans.

men over eighteen years of age to do any work assigned to them. That law was enforced, yet the shortage of labour for work on the land was in 1943 so acute that in April of that year an appeal was made to all women, without regard to position or rank, who were not fully engaged in essential work, to offer their services for work on the land. A month later all women between the ages of 15 and 45 were required to register their names stating, if they were housewives, the number of persons in their households and whether they would be able to do part-time work either on the land or in the care of invalids, or, if they were domestic servants, charwomen or shop-assistants, the number of hours they were engaged each day and week. In June 200 women were working whole or part-time on the land but the labour shortage was still so acute that the Labour Office predicted the conscription of women for food production.

The problem would have been less acute if the Germans had allowed the Controlling Committee to manage the Island's internal affairs without interference. As it was no longer possible to export tomatoes to England the Committee wished the large area under that fruit to be devoted instead to the production of foodstuffs for local consumption. But immediately after their arrival the German authorities ordered that 50 per cent of the area was to be kept under tomatoes. This absorbed a great deal of labour – and incidentally much water that the States Waterworks could ill spare. The German intention was that the tomatoes should be exported to Germany, but as the German authorities were frequently unable to provide adequate transport they often rotted before they were shipped.

Throughout the occupation the efforts of the Controlling Committee to ensure the local production of as much food as possible were hampered by the tendency of growers to use their land for purposes that would be financially more profitable than food production. The local cultivation of tobacco proved very profitable, so much so that the dried and more-or-less cured leaf was practically unobtainable at the controlled price; on the black market as much as 8/6 an ounce was asked and paid for it. The cultivation of the particular variety of mangel-wurzel locally misnamed 'sugar beet' – from which syrup was made was also very profitable, the syrup selling readily at nearly 15/- a pound. The Controlling Committee therefore restricted the cultivation of tobacco and 'sugar beet', and in 1944 it tightened up already existing regulations. A proposal to discourage flower cultivation by controlling the sale price was dropped on the ground of the hardship such an order would entail on small growers whose plots were too small to plough up but existing regulations restricting the area that might be used for their cultivation were more strictly enforced. A grower who grew tobacco without permission was fined £25. A subsidy of 3/- a pound for outdoor grown beans and 4/- a pound for beans grown under glass, both to be dried for winter consumption, was promised, but when they were ready for the market the German authorities demanded the whole crop.

Our salt ration, always meagre, often failed altogether. The lack of it was partially, but very inadequately, remedied in 1944 by the distribution of sea water. Depots were established in various parts of the Island and were visited weekly or fortnightly by a water-cart from which sea water was sold at the rate of five pfennigs – a penny farthing – a half gallon. It would have been more in keeping with the patriotic spirit of the Controlling Committee to have charged a British penny rather than a German five-pfennig piece, but as British copper coins were by then exceedingly scarce this would have been highly inconvenient to the purchaser.

For a variety of reasons, some easy and some difficult to understand, British money was gradually superseded by German money. First British notes and then British silver coins ceased to circulate and even English and Guernsey copper coins, though they never entirely ceased to circulate, became so rare as to cause great inconvenience to the banks, the shops and the public in general. The issue of States of Guernsey notes for 2/6, 1/3 and 6d partially and only temporarily relieved the situation. They, too, eventually became rare.

Efforts were made to get English coins back into circulation. Many people supposed that the shortage of coins was due to the Guernsey countryman's tendency to hoard money. With this theory in view banks displayed placards entreating their customers to bank their coins, the States Supervisor backed this appeal with an offer to make arrangements for their collection if desired, and Mr Leale, speaking with authority both as President of the Finance Committee and President of the Controlling Committee published a statement that an English half-crown contained no more than sixpence worth of silver. The appeal had no perceptible result. Between £300,000 and £400,000 worth of Guernsey currency ceased to circulate and the German authorities would not permit a new issue of States of Guernsey notes.

It is possible that the official theory as to the cause of the disappearance of British silver was partly correct, but perhaps a large proportion of it, after passing into German hands, left the Island altogether. Guernsey pennies and halfpennies may have been taken as souvenirs or to add to coin-collections and it is not impossible that there were speculators in Guernsey who bought English silver with an eye to future profit in case after the war the value of the mark should fall to the depths it reached after the war of 1914-1918 when German million-mark notes were sold at a considerable profit for sixpence apiece by London street hawkers. An English half-crown may be intrinsically worth no more than sixpence but even so it is worth far more than a tubful of worthless paper money.

The reason for the disappearance of British Treasury notes can easily be explained. Black market agents who dealt in commodities imported from France demanded payment in English paper-money and were ready to buy it at a premium, paying 18 marks – locally worth £1 18s 5½d – for a £1 note. The notes they obtained went to France where it is to be supposed they passed into the possession of speculators who did not share the official German belief in the certainty of a German victory. English gold was even more eagerly sought. Barter shops were willing to pay marks to the local value of £14 for an English sovereign and it is creditably reported that before the end a German offered forty pounds worth. Even Guernsey notes were at a premium, barter-shops and black market agents being prepared to pay twenty-one shillings' worth of marks for a States of Guernsey pound note.

The almost complete disappearance of English shillings caused especial inconvenience to householders whose gas passed through slot meters. For a while the Guernsey Gas Light Company met the difficulty by retaining all the shillings that came into its possession and issuing them in restricted quantities in exchange for German paper money to gas-consumers who needed them. Later, when shillings became still scarcer, a new procedure had to be adopted. Collectors, each supplied with a shilling, called periodically on consumers and, in return for paper money, dropped the coin again and again into their meters until they registered as much gas, within the limits of their gas rations, as consumers wished.

Though it would have been humiliating to our national pride it would have saved the community a great deal of inconvenience if, when British currency had practically disappeared, German money had been officially recognised as our medium of exchange. If the Price Controlling Committee had expressed maximum prices in marks and pfennigs instead of shillings and pence shops could have followed suit and both buyers and sellers would have been spared much mental arithmetic in calculating exact amounts payable or due as change.

During the first two months of the occupation German paper money was officially valued at 7 marks to the pound sterling. In September, 1942, the rate of exchange was fixed at 9 marks 36 pfennigs to the pound. The officially recognised 'ready-reckoners' that were published told us that 10 marks were worth £1 1s 4d, but as we did not use a decimal coinage one mark had to be valued at 2/1½ and half a mark at 1/0½. Consequently ten separate marks tendered in one payment were worth £1 1s 4d but spent at one time had the purchasing value of £1 1s 3d. A 10 pfennig coin was recognised as worth 2½d but a 5 pfennig coin was, for all practical purposes – since few English farthings or Guernsey doubles were in circulation – worth only 1d. Consequently banks and accountants had to be content with the striking of approximate, rather than exact balances, and employers of labour on a large scale found that the wages lists of amounts paid to each employee each week would not agree with the total of wages worked out by the bank, with the result that their suspense accounts had to be debited each week with the discrepancy as 'loss on the rate of exchange'.

When in September, 1940, the value of the mark fell from 7 to 9.60 to the pound many traders suffered loss. The States regarded this loss as war-damage and made it good to them. When two years later the mark moved in the other direction many traders thereby received unearned increment. At the request of the President of the Controlling Committee the States Accountant very reasonably wrote to the firms that had been reimbursed when the value of the mark fell and suggested that they should repay the States from their unexpected profits. Some conscientious firms did so but on the whole the response was not gratifying.

The continuation of children's education presented difficulties. Many children remained in the Island, but of the teachers normally employed by the Education Council only twelve remained, the others having left, in charge of the children who were evacuated. The difficulty was eventually met by securing the services, on a whole – or part-time basis – of competent people, some of whom gave their services gratuitously. Some of the school buildings were no longer available, either because the Germans had requisitioned them or because the adjoining playgrounds were used for the drilling of troops who afforded a tempting target for the machine-guns of raiding British planes. It was, therefore, found necessary to hold some of the schools in privately owned buildings, the owners of which in some cases generously lent them rent-free. Forty-eight selected children were given the opportunity of learning German and German was included among the subjects taught in the continuation classes when these were resumed.

Everything possible was done to maintain the health of the children. In 1942 midday meals were served to those attending the Intermediate schools, all were given a daily half pint of milk at the expense of the States, besides which those who needed it were given tonics and body-building medicines. When the children's shoes began to wear out stocks of rope-soled shoes were kept at the schools for the use of children who in bad weather arrived at schools with wet feet.

Inadequate means of transport affected school-children and everybody else. A few days after the occupation the Guernsey Railway Company applied for permission to run a service of horse-drawn buses but the Controlling Committee refused the application on the ground that horses were more urgently needed for agricultural work. Eventually in 1942 the Civil Transport Service imported a Brandt gasogene which proved satisfactory and by degrees all indispensable vehicles, the Company's motor-buses included, were adapted to be driven by gas generated from charcoal. Then four limited and somewhat expensive bi-weekly bus-services were inaugurated, but in June, 1944, they had to be discontinued because stocks of charcoal had fallen very low and could not be replenished.

Housewives and others had to carry home their purchases from shop or market. Their problem was largely alleviated by some ingenious pupil of Mr Heath Robinson who invented a hand-drawn vehicle – a garden-basket on perambulator wheels attached to a walking stick with which the contrivance could be dragged uphill with comparative ease and pushed on the level. Necessity demanded and ingenuity responded. Rat and mouse traps were made with springs taken from the seats of derelict motor cars, and shaving brushes with bunches of small feathers tightly bound to handles. Ovens that could be heated on gas-jets were made from biscuit tins and tinsmiths made tin hot-water bottles for customers who could supply stoppers from perished rubber hot-water bottles.

As time went on crockery and cutlery became very scarce. (After we were liberated a restaurant advertised 'We don't ask you to bring your own cup, but we do ask to be allowed to purchase any odd cups you can spare. We cannot open otherwise.') The hospitals' urgent need of these was supplied by public contribution at the request of Doctor Symons, the Health

Officer, who also appealed, not in vain, for such sheets and towels as housewives could spare. But private stocks of bed linen dwindled and when early in 1944 hospital supplies of dressings were exhausted a further appeal to the public might have met with a poor response, so the Controlling Committee decided to requisition sheets and other linen, belonging to people who had left the Island, which since the evacuation had been in States' custody.

Least pressing – because it had to a great extent to be shelved until after the occupation – but far the most serious and difficult problem was that of States finance. Expenditure mounted and liabilities piled up while revenue dwindled. Revenue from import duties practically ceased because so little that was taxable was imported. As only privileged people – such as doctors – were allowed to keep and use their cars, revenue from the automobile tax was negligible. Because there was less transfer of property there was less revenue from stamp duties. The sales tax dwindled as stocks in the shops were depleted. Because it was difficult to devise new taxes existing ones were increased. Income tax was raised to 5/- in the pound. The entertainment tax was doubled. So were the import duties on tobacco, wines and spirits; that on cordials was trebled. Siege conditions had created a new war industry – tobacco-growing – and that was not allowed to escape its share of the burden. A tax of 10/8 a pound was imposed on the finished product.

But no feasible taxation could bring the Island's revenue into reasonable relation with its expenditure. The States had to pay the rent of German billets, the wages of the servants who worked for German officers, and the cost of running a cinema for the German troops. These items, by the end of the occupation, had cost approximately £1,000,000. Heavy subsidies were paid to keep the price of bread and other vital necessities within reach of all. Claims for compensation for war damage of a score of different kinds were constantly being filed; compensation for the value of standing crops destroyed by the Germans, of valuable land covered with gravel or subsoil from their deep excavations, for houses damaged by concussion when long-range guns were fired, or by falling shrapnel, for greenhouses wrecked or demolished under German orders. For all such damage the Germans were directly responsible, but it seemed idle to hope that Germany, bankrupt as she must inevitably be after her defeat, could ever be made to pay for it.

There were other kinds of damage for which the Germans were less directly responsible. Immediately after the evacuation the States undertook the custody of furniture left in houses whose occupants had left the Island. This was stored in depots where, however, it proved impossible adequately to safeguard it. The lawlessness of the German troops, which the German authorities could not or would not restrain, combined with difficulties created by curfew restrictions, made burglary a comparatively safe enterprise and the States' furniture depots were frequently broken into, much was stolen, much broken and the remainder was so inextricably mixed that it became impossible to distinguish the property of one absentee owner from that of another. Again many houses, vacated by their owners, of which the States had become custodian tended to become uninhabitable because people in search of fuel frequently broke into them and removed stairs, flooring boards and anything else that was combustible.

Responsibility for some of the overdraft granted by local banks to those whose incomes were derived from property or investments outside the Island was another States liability. As time went on these overdrafts and the States' debts to the banks became so large that the local bank managers became nervous and asked the Controlling Committee to pledge, not merely the credit of the Island, but also its assets – such as its essential services and future revenue. The Controlling Committee, however, did not feel justified in taking such a step and the matter was allowed to drop.

The States had also another heavy liability, the undertaking made by the Controlling Committee, on behalf of the States Treasury, to relieve the banks of all German paper money which they were obliged to accept. This paper money was in the form of *reichskreditkassen* issued solely in German occupied countries and not negotiable in Germany itself.[12] It was paid into the banks by shopkeepers and others who sold goods to Germans and imported foreign labourers and later, as British and Guernsey currency ceased to circulate, by the general public.

If the States had not undertaken to relieve the banks of *reichskreditkassen* the banks would have been obliged to pass the liability on to their customers. They would have done this by changing their system of book-keeping. When a customer paid into his account *reichskreditkassen* to the nominal value of a pound sterling, instead of crediting him with having actually paid in a pound sterling, as they did and continued to do, they would, under the new system, have had to credit him with having paid in exactly what he did pay in. This would not have greatly affected holders of current accounts who in an average week or month drew out as much money as they deposited – when British and States of Guernsey notes had practically ceased to circulate some medium of exchange was needed in its place and *reichskreditkassen* served the purpose as well as any other – but it would have been disastrous to depositors who wished to save money. When the Island was again free they would have found that the sums standing to their credit in the bank's book would be, not pounds, shillings and pence but German paper money which, though for all practical purposes worth its nominal value when it was paid in, had in all probability become of no value whatever.

The financial situation became very grave. The *reichskreditkassen* which, although they were actually worthless, the States had to buy at their nominal value, accumulated at an alarming rate. The accumulation was very largely due to the eagerness with which Germans bought gold and jewels. Both barter-shops and regular jewellers were prepared to pay, for re-sale to Germans, £14 worth of German paper money for

12   One of Guernsey's bank clerks noticed the date 1935 on a wrapper enclosing this paper money. From this it is to be inferred that it was printed during or before that year and that Germany was preparing to invade neighbouring countries at least four years before the invasion began. This is interesting in view of frequent German assertions that the war was forced on her.

an English sovereign (the price offered for a sovereign is said to have been as much as £40 worth before the end came) and they inserted prominent advertisements in the newspapers promising high prices for diamonds, set or unset, gold watches and jewellery in general; and many people who had these to dispose of were glad to sell them in order to obtain money with which to supplement their meagre rations by buying foodstuffs, such as maize and millet which, not being controlled or rationed, were very expensive.

Probably few of the people who sold their trinkets realised that by so doing they were both helping the enemy and laying a heavy burden on the States Treasury and any propaganda that would have explained this to them would have been suppressed by the German authorities, who would not have tolerated interference with a traffic which enabled Germany to obtain valuables with which to bolster up her foreign exchange in return for paper money which cost her nothing. One thing the Controlling Committee did do. In April, 1943, it prohibited the publication of advertisements offering to purchase jewellery, but by that time the harm was done.

In July, 1944, a man was fined £2 merely for attempting to buy a pound of butter and on the same day a farmer who succeeded in selling a pound of butter was fined £20. But the infliction of heavy fines on offenders, though it may have checked black marketing, failed to stamp it out, and scarcely a week passed without the prosecution of one or more farmers or growers for the illicit sale of produce. The traffic was so profitable that detected offenders could afford to pay heavy fines and the prisons were so congested that it was hardly practicable to punish with imprisonment instead of fines. Pork, which it was said cost 10/- a pound to produce on account of the high cost of pig-feed and the great difficulty of getting fuel with which to cook it, was sold for 20/- a pound, butter for as much as 60/- a pound and other foods at proportionately high prices.

The fact that such extravagantly high prices were paid by people who were as unscrupulous as they were greedy does not prove that the Controlling Committee was negligent or inefficient, but it does most emphatically show how great was the need of control such as the Committee exercised. Without such control the price of bread would have risen to a height that the average wage-earner could not have paid and he would have had difficulty even in buying potatoes and roots to take its place, for growers would have found it more profitable to keep these for the fattening of pigs than to sell them to greengrocers. Wage-earners employed in food production would have successfully demanded extravagantly high wages while others, except those engaged in absolutely essential work, and all people with fixed incomes would have been reduced to penury. Many infants and children, deprived of milk and sugar, would, even if they had survived, have been injured in health for life. It seems no exaggeration to say that, without such control as the Controlling Committee exercised, while farmers and a few of the richest members of the community would have been able to live in almost pre-war comfort, the remainder would have suffered severe privation and many would have died from cold and lack of nourishment. Thanks to the Committee we were spared this tragedy. Under its autocratic control the burden we had to share was more evenly divided. A certain degree of hardship fell on all of us but, until the last few months of the occupation, few suffered actual privation and very few if any of our children were handicapped for life by lack of proper nourishment in infancy.

In attempting to judge the work of the Controlling Committee one question insistently arises – were its members too docile in their relations to the German authorities or would they have served the people of the Island better if they had more stoutly resisted unreasonable German demands and German interference? They did protest – very frequently – but as the general public did not know this hostile critics had an unfair advantage. In some cases their protests were effective. In others they were compelled to yield. On one occasion – when in December, 1943, the German authorities ordered the Committee to reduce the butter ration – submission went so sorely against the grain that they contemplated resigning in a body and were deterred only by the belief that if they did so they would be doing ill service to the Island. Had they resigned the Germans would almost certainly have taken over complete control of the Island's internal affairs and the Committee had had sufficient experience of German mismanagement to know that that could not have been to our advantage. But they did feel that they could not continue to hold office unless they knew that they had the confidence of the States of Deliberation. The Bailiff was therefore asked to put the question to the States when next they met. This was done and the States not only approved the Committee's action but also 'by acclamation bore testimony to the confidence which they had reposed in the Committee since its inception'.

CHAPTER XIX

THE GERMANS

It would be unjust not to admit that the German rule to which we were subjected was on the whole mild and that the behaviour of most individual Germans was good. This may have been because we had the good fortune to be ruled by Germans of a good class or perhaps it was the policy of the High Command that we should be treated leniently, either because it was hoped that in the event of a German victory we should more readily become loyal German subjects or because Great Britain held a number of German prisoners of war on whom reprisals for harsh treatment of us might be made, or because in the event of a German defeat, their mild treatment of us while in power over us would be set to their credit when the time came for the settlement of accounts.

In one or two cases local officials showed lenience in spite of, rather than in obedience to, Higher Authority.

Among the British soldiers who were on leave in the Island at the time of the German occupation was one who would have returned to England two days before if it had not been for the German bombing raid of June 29th, 1940. He had gone to the White Rock to embark that evening but his two daughters who had gone there to see him off were both killed and he stayed ashore to bury them. Before this was done the Germans had occupied the Island and his chance of returning to England was gone. The German Chief of Staff, in pity for the man's misfortune, exempted him from deportation with the other service men, employed him as a personal chauffeur and, on leaving the Island, asked his successor to allow the man to remain at liberty. His successor thought it necessary to obtain approval for this act of clemency from his superiors in France. It was refused and eventually the bereaved father was sent away to a prison camp.

On one occasion a German soldier was tried by a German court on a charge of raping a Guernsey woman. The woman who accused him was spared the terrible ordeal of giving evidence in open court and was allowed to sit in a room apart where the questions the judges wished to ask were put to her by a sympathetic woman-interpreter. The verdict of the court was not made known but it is believed that the soldier was convicted and sentenced to death.

When by the order of the High German Command Mrs Michael and Mrs Le Masurier were deported to France (as recorded in Chapter IX) for having harboured Lieutenants Mulholland and Martel the Commandant himself effected their arrest, told them that they might take as much luggage as they liked, stressed the advisability of their providing themselves with sufficient warm clothing, and in every way treated them with as much consideration as was consistent with his duty.

When the inhabitants of a defined area in St Martin's parish were ordered to surrender their radios as a (illegal) communal punishment for the writing of 'V"s on walls and notice-boards the Commandant exempted from the order a blind man who pleaded that neither he nor his aged mother could have been guilty of the offence and that their radio was their chief source of amusement.

British airmen who landed on the Island after the loss of their planes and other military prisoners were on the whole treated well and no vindictiveness was shown to Guemseymen imprisoned for retaining radios or cameras, after the surrender of these had been ordered, or otherwise disobeying German orders. Sometimes, when sentencing a man to a term of imprisonment, they allowed him to remain at liberty for a few days before entering prison, so that he might arrange for the carrying on of his business during his absence. It is to the credit, too, of the German officials that they accorded no preferential treatment to people who toadied to them; the two most notorious sycophants were included in the first batch of Islanders deported to Germany.

Although on the whole they treated us with consideration rather than harshness the conduct of the German officials was not always correct. Occasionally they violated International Law on the treatment of the inhabitants of an enemy occupied country, as when they inflicted communal punishments on the population,[13] when, as recorded in Chapter XVI, they degraded the Royal Court by forcing its members, against their judgment and consciences, to register anti-Jewish enactments,[14] and when they gutted the Masonic Temple in Le Marchant Street, shipping off to Germany the regalia, jewels, documents and even the furniture, a robbery which they could hardly justify as imperatively demanded by the necessities of war.[15] But the blame for violating International Law should probably be laid on the Higher German Command whose orders the local officials had to carry out.

Less than two months after the occupation began the head of the Guernsey branch of the Feldkommandantur told a representative of the *Evening Press* the arrangements that had been made for the German management of the Island's affairs. The Feldkommandant himself, a Doctor of Law in private life, was to deal with agriculture and provisioning; a Doctor of Jurisprudence was to control general administration, police matters, newspapers and cinemas; while commercial and industrial matters, fishing, traffic, coal, petrol, electricity, social problems and the control of prices were to be the affair of an official described as a specialist in commercial matters.

Here, apparently, was the framework on which a model Nazi administration was to be built. It was possible that the German authorities believed that they could manage our internal affairs better than we could manage them ourselves, but like the bandar-log in Kipling's *Jungle Book* they were apt to forget what they had intended to do, though some of their ideas might have proved excellent if they had materialised. At one time, for example, they conceived the idea of establishing a combined pig-farm and sausage factory, which might have proved of great value to the Island. They appropriated a field belonging to the Country Hospital, stripped off the turf and started to build pig-

---

13 *Manual of Military Law* 1914, Chapter XIV, Section VIII, paragraph 385.
14 *Manual of Military Law* 1914, Chapter XIV, Section VIII, paragraph 364.
15 *Manual of Military Law* 1914, Chapter XIV, Section VIII, paragraphs 406 and 407.

sties that were apparently to be of the most up-to-date hygienic kind. These were beginning to take shape when the project was abandoned. The net result was the complete destruction of some valuable pasture and no gain to the Germans or anyone else.

Either the Feldkommandant who had taken agriculture under his wing or the specialist in commercial matters to whom industrial matters were entrusted had, perhaps, memories of prosperous small holdings in Germany where the children milked the cows and the mother drove the plough while the father pruned the vines. An article entitled 'Intensive Vegetable Culture: New measures to meet changed conditions', which was published in both our newspapers, declared that the Island's vegetable gardens and greenhouses were insufficiently cultivated, and continued:-

> The prevailing small concerns existing in Guernsey must change over to working with their own personnel, i.e., with members of their family ... Control measures which have been planned will contribute to the aforementioned production-directions being observed. He, however, who believes that he can continue in the old lackadaisical way, must – by non-observance of the orders issued – expect to be stigmatised as a saboteur, and liable to severe punishment.

It is to be supposed that after the publication of this article the mind of whoever was responsible for it was distracted to some other project for the threat to compel growers' families to be more industrious did not materialise. If the specialist in commercial matters was the author of this project, this failure to materialise was probably fortunate, for the fishing regulations which he made were such as to deprive us almost entirely of fish. German interference with the glasshouse industry was disastrous. The authorities insisted that tomatoes should be grown on a scale that would allow for a large exportation of the crop but failed to secure profitable markets for them, whereas, if the Controlling Committee had been allowed to do what it thought best, it would have used the greenhouses to grow crops – such as beans – that circumstances had made of far more value to us than tomatoes.

The Germans were responsible for very little purely domestic legislation. An order forbidding cyclists to ride abreast was very sensible, if not very important. An order that all dogs out of doors must be leashed was to a great extent ignored. One eminently sensible German practice was introduced into Guernsey – that of allowing police to deal summarily with minor infractions of bye-laws. If an insufficiently screened light was seen by German military-police on patrol they knocked up the householder concerned, called his attention to the light, fined him two marks, gave him a receipt for the money and troubled him no further. In less than five minutes the incident was closed. If on the other hand the light was seen by one of the Guernsey civil police the offender was obliged, a day or so later, to neglect his other business while he attended the Police Court and perhaps wait an hour or more before being allowed to pay his fine and go.

That many individual Germans wished to be regarded as friendly was obvious from the fact that they generally offered to shake hands with any Guernseyman with whom they came in contact and looked puzzled rather than annoyed if the proffered hand was ignored. That they even expected to be received socially is obvious from the fact that on the day after their landing in the Island the officer commanding the occupying troops paid a formal call on the Bailiff at his private house and that the German Chief of Staff proposed to give a dinner-party followed by a dance to leading Islanders at which the German officers might make the acquaintance of local ladies. How the project was received is recorded in Chapter XX.

The central German authority in the Island was either weak or unwilling to enforce its orders. On one occasion the Security Officer complained that heavy artillery had engaged in target practice without giving him warning with the result that he had had no opportunity of warning people who lived near the guns to take precautions against concussion. The Commandant apologised, saying that notice should have been given but that the artillery were a law unto themselves. The Chief Air Raid Precautions Officer once protested against the seizure by Germans, looking for billets, of a room that he had fitted up as an emergency dressing-station. He was told that the seizure was 'unfortunate' but was advised to submit to it. At the same time he was to furnish a list of his other dressing-stations so that they might be protected. He did so but the promised protection proved worthless. When a gentleman complained that his radio had been seized for an officers' mess in a house near his own he was told that its seizure was unjustified but that it would be 'impolitic' to order its return. When the Guernsey Commandant authorised the collection of gulls' eggs on Burhou, an islet near Alderney, the authorities in Alderney, though subordinate to the Guernsey commandant, interfered, with the result that the men of the egg collecting party were detained for several weeks and did not get to Burhou until after the eggs were hatched. A boy was once fatally injured by a motor car driven by a German. The driver and his German passengers were asked to attend the inquest but neglected to do so and apparently the German authorities were either unwilling or unable to compel their attendance.

In many respects the German authorities were like well-meaning but incompetent schoolmasters who try to enforce their authority by alternate severity, cajolery, threats and the encouragement of tale-bearers. An incompetent schoolmaster is inclined to be especially severe when punishing offences against his own dignity; the Germans inflicted a sentence of two years and three months imprisonment on a woman for composing and privately circulating a song in derision of the Germans. Cajolery and threats appear in the following proclamation which emanated from the Military Commander in France in April, 1941, but impartial minds may perhaps see in it evidence of goodwill as well:-

Certain incidents have occurred in which, on the

part of the inhabitants of the Island, acts have been committed which were against the safety of the Army of Occupation. Those who were guilty have been, or will be punished according to the degree of martial law by sentence of death.

In their own interest I warn the public most solemnly against perpetrating any further acts of this kind. Any person involved in such an act, either as perpetrator, participant or instigator will, upon conviction by court martial without power of appeal, be condemned to suffer the death penalty.

People of the Island! Your destiny and your welfare is in your own hands. Your home interests demand that you should refrain from, and to the best of your power prevent, all such actions which must inevitably be followed by such disastrous consequences.

The Military Commander in France,
(Signed) V. STULPNAGEL.

It should be noted that no Guernseyman was sentenced to death either before or after the proclamation, and none of the offences against the Germans for which any Guemseymen were punished seriously endangered German safety. The above proclamation was, however, less objectionable than many others in that it did not tell us that it was our duty to betray our fellow countrymen.

In July, 1942, all orders relating to the confiscation of cameras contained the words 'any person having knowledge of the presence of objects liable to be surrendered is bound to report same'. In the following month an order forbidding the sheltering of aircraft crews or parachutists who might land on the Island offered a reward for their betrayal. Two days later this was followed by a proclamation which stated that any Channel Islander held in custody by Germans might be used as a hostage and shot in reprisal for acts of sabotage and that the Commandant reserved to himself the right to nominate certain members of any parish who would be liable to the death penalty in reprisal for sabotage, if perpetrated with the assistance or knowledge of inhabitants of the parish concerned and concluded with the words:-

> In their own interest I call upon the population for an increased activity and watchfulness in combating all suspicious elements and to co-operate in the discovery of the guilty persons.

It would have been difficult to evade some orders – such as that which requisitioned motor vehicles – but demands for the surrender of small articles such as motor tools, tyres, cameras, air-guns, revolvers and other small weapons were in many cases ignored.[16] Sometimes, when such orders were repeated, it was promised that those who obeyed promptly would not be punished for not having obeyed before, and an order published on September 1st, 1943, besides promising immunity from punishment to persons in possession of weapons if they surrendered within fifteen days, also promised to pardon anyone who had neglected to denounce possessors of war material if they did so before September 15th, 1943.

Though the general intention of the German authorities may have been benevolent the behaviour of some individual Germans was certainly outrageous. A certain householder, when ordered to evacuate his house for the use of German officers, asked and was granted leave to retain the use of one room. In this he stored his household silver and such wine and groceries as remained from the stocks he had laid in at the time when we were officially urged to store reserves of non-perishable food. Later the German officers who were occupying his house invited him to what they called a cocoa party. Under strong pressure he reluctantly accepted the invitation and found that the room he had been given leave to reserve had been broken into, for the German officers were feasting on his own food and using his

---

16 Incidentally it is worth mentioning that it was fairly safe to traverse roads conspicuously marked as 'Forbidden to civilians'. If one encountered a German he would not interfere unless specifically detailed to guard the road.

own silver. With offensive humour they offered him a cup of his own cocoa while they themselves drank his wine. Had this householder complained to the Commandant he might have had some redress but it is more probable that he would have been told that although the behaviour of the German officers was incorrect it would be 'impolitic' to do anything in the matter.

German bullies did not always get their own way. A naval officer made a practice of threatening with deportation to Germany anyone who resisted his demands, until a tradesman called his bluff. He had demanded some articles and when told that that particular article was out of stock had made his usual threat. The tradesman said he would go at once to the Commandant and explain to him that the desired article was not procurable from anywhere in the Island. The naval officer then changed his tone and even followed the tradesman up High Street entreating him not to go to the Commandant. The tradesman refused to be put off his errand. Soon afterwards that particular German left the Island. It was of course impossible to know whether he had been posted to other duties or whether he was sent away for misconduct.

Occasionally Germans who were fully authorised to make demands could be put off by a display of firmness. A German sergeant, detailed to examine houses and report on their suitability for billeting troops, called at the house of a retired Brigadier-General who refused to admit him, saying that he would have no German below field rank in his house and that he would not discuss the matter with a non-commissioned rank. The sergeant stood to attention on learning that he was speaking to a general and went meekly away. The Brigadier-General was left unmolested for more than a year thereafter.

Islanders were compelled to exercise the most rigid economy in the use of electricity, gas and water, because of the difficulty, due to fuel shortage, of maintaining these essential services. Germans on the other hand were allowed to be as extravagant as they pleased. Soldiers billeted in houses fitted with slot meters broke open the boxes into which the money dropped and used the same coins over and over again. In offices used by Germans gas-fires – the use of which was denied to Islanders – were kept burning continuously even in rooms that were seldom used. At an inquiry into the death of a German soldier by gas poisoning it was learned that he had been in the habit of warming his bedroom by keeping a gas jet burning all night. During the first eleven months of 1943 more water was consumed in the Island than ever before – though the population, including Germans, was less than in normal years. This excessive consumption was attributable to German extravagance which the officials of the Water Board were powerless to check. Though they demanded no economy from their own people the German authorities enforced it on the foreign labourers they imported. Printed notices posted up in the billets inhabited by these unfortunates warned them that owing to shortage of diesel oil and gas coal no gas was to be used for heating or cooking and all electric lights were to be switched off at 9pm

The Germans allowed no consideration for our welfare to affect their own comfort. As stocks of cattle-food diminished the milk yield became smaller and it became necessary for the medical officers comprising the Milk Board to reduce the allowance of whole milk granted to invalids. But the German consumption of whole milk did not diminish. In December, 1943, the shortage was so acute that it became necessary altogether to deny whole milk to invalids, yet the German consumption of whole milk was then as great as it had been twelve months earlier when there had been twice as many Germans in the Island.

Whenever the Germans found that the welfare of the Islanders conflicted with their own convenience it was the Islanders who had to suffer. They turned bed-ridden invalids out of houses desired for officers' quarters even when there were vacant houses nearby that could have been used instead without causing hardship to anyone. They upset the excellent work that was being done at a communal kitchen by requisitioning its cooking utensils, all of which had been contributed by the public spirit of neighbours. When they requisitioned adjoining houses they knocked holes in the party walls and fences to facilitate passage from one house to the other. Evicted householders were compelled to leave behind them all carpets, curtains, furniture and even bed linen and crockery, but when it suited Germans to move from one house to another they took with them any furniture they chose without taking steps to enable the rightful owner eventually to recover his property. Sometimes they evicted all the householders in a street and then changed their plans and left the houses empty. No householder had any security of tenure and, even after the number of troops in the Island had considerably diminished, evictions continued. Many houses temporarily occupied by Germans were found to be unfit for habitation after they had gone; baths, water-pipes, mantelpieces and other permanent fittings were missing, bannisters torn down and holes made in floors and ceilings.

As the German authorities showed such disregard of the welfare of evicted householders it was not to be expected that individual Germans would show more consideration. Some German tenants respected the houses they were in and the furniture in them and in one case an evicted householder, when able to examine his property, found it cleaner and in better repair than when he left it, with nothing missing except two-thirds of a store of highly cherished soap, but in many cases temporary German occupants behaved like hooligans. Mahogany sideboards were converted into rabbit-hutches, other furniture was broken up for firewood and locks were forced. A house in Candie Road was occupied three times. During the first occupation no damage was done except that a valuable Indian rug was stolen. During the second much furniture was wantonly broken. The third set of occupants before leaving turned on all gas-taps and, after plugging the waste-pipes of sinks and baths, left all water taps running. As they locked all doors before leaving and left without notifying the Custodian of Unoccupied Houses of their departure much irreparable damage was done before the house was again entered.

One lady, turned out of her house at three hours' notice, was invited to put such of her personal belongings as she could not take with her at the moment into a spare-room, take the key of the room with her, and return for her belongings at her leisure.

When she returned she found that the lock of her spare-room had been forced and all her winter clothing stolen. No property at all was safe and cases of downright robbery reported to the German police were seldom redressed. At the Grange Club, occupied for a time as German offices, some silver spoons were stolen and an alms-box belonging to the Local Blind Association that stood in the smoking-room was emptied. Vigorous representations resulted in the recovery of the spoons, but the contents of the alms-box were not refunded on the ground that it was impossible to know how much it had contained.

Thefts ranging in degree from petty larceny to wholesale robbery with violence were rampant. All sorts of useful and almost irreplaceable articles, such as gas-mantles and cooking utensils, were pillaged openly from poor people unlikely to have the nerve to denounce the robbers. A number of farmers lost pigs – the smell of chloroform lingering in their empty sties indicated why the pigs had not given audible warning of the robbery. A grape-grower lost all the grapes in a greenhouse span and a householder half his crop of potatoes in one night. As none but Germans could be out of doors with impunity during curfew hours the thieves must almost certainly have been Germans. But protest was generally useless. It was the custom of the German police, when a complaint of theft was made to them, to ask the name and regimental number of the thief and few could obtain redress unless they could not only prove the theft but also provide all the evidence needed to enable the thief to be identified. If this was forthcoming they had some chance of redress. A farmer complained to the German police that two of his heifers had been stolen. All the satisfaction he got at the moment was the repetition of a formula, customarily used by the German authorities in such cases, to the effect that German soldiers were too honourable to steal. Later he reported that the stolen heifers were grazing in a field near the airport that was under German control. Asked how he could prove that the heifers were his he produced the sketches officially made of their colour markings when they were calved for record with their pedigrees. He was allowed to take his heifers back to his farm. Another farmer caught a German soldier in his cow-shed at night milking one of his cows. He shut and bolted the door and, though the man's comrades fired shots through it, kept it shut until he had secured the thief's cap, belt and bayonet with which to identify him. Another farmer, who had good reason to believe that his cows were milked at night succeeded in persuading the German police to set a watch for the thieves. At two o'clock in the morning two Germans, an officer and a private, were detected in the act. A struggle ensued in which the farmer was wounded in the hand. The private soldier escaped but the officer was caught. In this case the German authorities promised that the culprits should be punished and it is believed that the officer was degraded to the ranks – but a man who found one morning that his nanny goat had been killed and disembowelled during the night – the slaughter of the goat involved the death of her two newly-born kids – could get no redress, and another who thrashed a thief whom he caught stealing his grapes was punished for the offence of assaulting a German soldier. In justice to the Germans as a body it should be recorded that one officer – not connected with the police – offered compensation out of his own pocket for green peas stolen from a garden. With exemplary conscientiousness the garden-owner refused the compensation when he discovered that the thieves were rats.

Though the German police showed little anxiety to stamp out theft it is to be supposed that this arose as much from inefficiency as from lack of goodwill. That they were inefficient is obvious – otherwise it would not have been possible for so many Islanders to retain possession of their radios. While some of us suffered from the ineptitude of the German police, therefore, others gained.

Amongst the German propaganda that our newspapers were compelled to publish was a statement that among other benefits conferred on the German nation by Hitler's wise rule was a striking improvement in the intelligence of the average German. Scientific investigations, we were told, showed that as a result of the Hitler Youth Movement ninety-seven per cent of young Germans could be classified as 'highly gifted'. If that estimate was correct most of the Germans sent to Guernsey must either have been drawn from the remaining three per cent or were too old to have benefited by the Youth Movement. Efficiency has generally been regarded as an outstanding German characteristic but both the officials and the rank and file here did much to explode that belief.

Perhaps the most striking example of official inefficiency followed the crashing of a German plane near the airport. Apparently it did not occur to anyone in authority that it would be advisable to station a guard over the wreckage and German soldiers of the rank and file, trained to obey orders but not to use their own initiative, put no obstacle in the way of a crowd of souvenir hunters who gaily carried away costly and still quite serviceable gadgets such as compasses, dynamos and gauges. One man even took a balloon-tyred wheel so large that it needed a handcart for its removal. When eventually the German authorities realised that the plane was disappearing piecemeal they stationed a sentry to guard what remained of it and published an order that everything taken from it must be surrendered at the Police Station. Some of the souvenir-hunters obeyed the order; some ignored it.

Some metal canisters were washed up on the beach near Grandes Rocques. The German authorities supposed them to be drifting mines and, instead of having them detonated by machine-gun fire on the spot, which in that lonely place would have involved no danger to anyone, ordered their removal to a yard at the back of the Police Station. This was the last place to which they should have been taken for the yard is just below the windows of the Royal Court building. If they had exploded there and the States had been in session at the time, the lives of many of the leading men in the Island would have been endangered. The German authorities did, however, take steps to avert danger to anyone in the adjacent small public garden by ordering a special constable to be stationed in the vicinity to warn people away. He was relieved from his duty after a police constable had opened one of the canisters and found that it contained nothing more dangerous than spent carbide that had been used to make acetylene gas.

A lady who lived in a house on the cliffs above Petit Bot was made to evacuate it. Later it was burned to the ground, for unspecified 'military reasons'. That she was given no opportunity of removing such of her property as was moveable was due probably to official ineptitude rather than to ill will.

German inefficiency was not confined to the military. Several of the tunnels dug under the supervision of the Organisation Todt caved in with fatal results; in one case as many as forty foreign labourers being killed.

During the early days of the occupation the sight of an unidentified plane in the sky sent all Germans running for cover. That they expected that the Royal Air Force would bomb the Island indiscriminately, regardless of our welfare, was obvious from the precautions that were taken by the German authorities. On the ground that the German forces had 'taken charge' of the protection of the civilian population against the effects of air raids they ordered that all attics were to be cleared, that the local Air Raid Precautions Organisation was to continue, that fire-fighting squads were to be organised in all public buildings, that in localities where no hydrants were established ponds were to be dug and kept full of water, that sign-boards were to be placed in all main streets pointing the way to the nearest air raid shelters and that shelter-trenches were to be dug in residential areas where no air raid shelters were available. They even thought that the RAF might use poison-gas ('gas-alarm' gongs were hung in buildings occupied by any considerable number of Germans) or destroy our crops. In August, 1941, and at the approach of harvest in subsequent years, proclamations entitled 'Protection of crops against aerial attacks' advised reapers to search for incendiary leaves and enacted that any person when called upon by police or parish-constable should 'promptly possess himself of a spade or other implement suitable for the purpose and search for or destroy or assist in the destruction of incendiary leaves'. It was characteristic of the German authorities that they supplied no information that would enable a searcher to identify an incendiary leaf when he saw one.

The order that shelter-trenches were to be dug in residential areas seemed to lay on each individual householder the onus of digging one for his or her household. It caused some consternation among elderly ladies who, because casual labour was unobtainable, did not know how to obey the order unless they dug the trenches themselves. But the bulk of the population, perfectly confident that we were in no danger of indiscriminate bombing by the Royal Air Force, placidly ignored the orders. No ponds were dug. No demolitions squads were organised. The orders were repeated in 1942 with the addition that fire-fighting squads were to be organised in private houses as well as public buildings and that each squad was to provide itself with two shovels and two hatchets, neither of which tools was by that time obtainable from any ironmongers' shop.

'Blacking out' regulations, such as were in force before the occupation, were continued and supplemented by an order forbidding fires in the open for the burning of rubbish or any other purpose except during daylight and then only between 11am and 3pm. These orders could not be ignored with impunity because at night the sky above us was patrolled by a plane – locally named 'Useless Eustace' – that dropped flares to call the attention of military pickets patrolling the roads to any light visible from the air. After some months of active service 'Useless Eustace', it was believed, crashed off Sark, and the patrolling of the sky was discontinued.

As the German authorities obviously thought it possible that British airmen might endeavour to destroy the crops of their own fellow countrymen when they were growing on land temporarily occupied by an enemy, it is reasonable to suppose that German airmen would not have hesitated to set fire to German food if the situation had been reversed. German views on the ethics of warfare were curious. A young German officer who insisted on discussing the war said that it was all England's fault, that Germans liked the English and would have avoided war with England if that had been possible. 'Why', he asked, 'did England declare war on Germany?' He was told that England was compelled to do so by her promise to Poland and was reminded how frequently Germany had broken her promises. 'But it is not always convenient to keep a promise' he protested. The same officer earnestly declared – and seemed honestly to believe – that Germany's methods of warfare were always strictly honourable. He was asked how he could justify the action of the German airman who on June 28th, 1940, machine-gunned the Guernsey lifeboat which he could not possibly have mistaken for any sort of war vessel. He replied that probably the German airman thought that the lifeboat might be engaged on reconnaissance work. To use for espionage purposes a boat of a kind universally recognised as devoted to the welfare of mankind irrespective of nationality would be as morally indefensible as would be the making of a bayonet attack under cover of a white flag. Yet this officer could see nothing dishonourable in it. Though he seemed to be of the very best type of German he would probably have done any foul thing without any qualms of conscience if ordered to do so by a superior officer.

If British people have ethical standards that Germans cannot understand there is, on the other hand, much in German mentality that is quite incomprehensible to the British mind. The Germans in Guernsey did not seem to be able to realise that we could regard any matter from an angle different from their own. When they first arrived in the Island a long series of successes had put them into a festive mood and they saw nothing incongruous in generously proposing to entertain leading Islanders to a dinner followed by a dance. That was in August, 1940, when we had good reason to be melancholy. In October, 1943, when the tide of war had definitely turned in our favour and the severity of our bombing raids on German towns was steadily increasing they thought that we ought to share their gloom; the Commandant, when asked to cancel his prohibition of public dances, said that public amusements were in bad taste at such a time of crisis when so many people were being killed.

The German Press Officer could not appreciate that behaviour that is courteous to a friendly nation becomes servile to an enemy nation. The neglect of some Jersey people to show conventional marks of respect for the German National Anthem

– which they probably did not recognise – inspired him to publish in the *Evening Press* a peevish comment accompanied by a threat under the headline 'International Courtesy'.

> It has long been the established custom of cultured nations to pay the necessary respect during national celebrations of other nations, especially during the singing of the National Anthems. People standing in the vicinity are naturally expected to take off their hats and not show deliberate disrespect by adopting a lazy attitude with hands in both pockets.
>
> Up to the present it has been found unnecessary by any nation to publish special regulations regarding this behaviour. The recent railway-opening celebration in Jersey, however, made it clear that this obvious act of respect is unknown in the Island. The Germans have always understood that all British subjects are well acquainted with these customs, but if the population puts itself outside the realm of the simplest rules of international courtesy, it must expect the consequences.

Occasionally, especially during the first year of the occupation, the Germans officially made overtures that were no doubt intended to be friendly. When German bands played in the Candie Grounds on Sunday afternoons we were invited to attend on payment of sixpence a head which we were told would be devoted to Red Cross funds. Possibly the International Red Cross was meant. If so this was not explained and, as German airmen in the raid on Guernsey which preceded the occupation had machine-gunned our clearly marked ambulance, we could not be expected to contribute gladly towards the funds of the German Red Cross. Whatever the cause attendance at these concerts by Guernsey people was small, though our marionette Press lied lustily about the large crowds that assembled to listen to them. On one other occasion we were invited to listen to a German band on payment of threepence a head, which we were told would be used for the purchase of prizes for schoolchildren who were learning German, and it was hinted that the money might also be used for 'awards for progress and industry in other facets of Island industry'. Even this bait failed to attract large audiences to the concerts.

As a step towards our conversion to Nazism librarians and booksellers were ordered to surrender for confiscation books by certain authors and all books of an anti-German character. At the Priaulx Library, which was visited by an armed party under an officer, the librarian, with a view to getting rid of his visitors as quickly as possible pretended to be eager to comply with the order, surrendered two novels by H.G. Wells, worth, secondhand, about a shilling each, expressed regret that he had nothing else to offer and suggested that, as Heine was a Jew, a set of his works (which would have been easily replaceable) should be confiscated. The officer, who seemed never to have heard of the famous German poet, refused the offer and withdrew his party. The librarian then spent a busy hour removing to a hiding place all books that would have been confiscated if the officer had carried out his orders more intelligently.

Germans are by no means all of one type. At one end of the scale are men who are courteous, scholarly, well-bred, sufficiently sure of their own worth to feel no impulse to swagger, boast or domineer. At the other end are oafish louts, inwardly conscious of inferiority which they seek to hide by truculence, bullying and aggressive manners in general. Both of these types were represented among the Germans who occupied Guernsey and, happily for us, we had perhaps more of the former type than of the latter.

Exemplary courtesy was shown by two Germans who drove up to a house in the Grande Rue, St Martin's, and asked the way to Cobo. It was late in the evening and, when they heard that a complicated cross-country journey was involved, they decided to stay where they were till morning. Germans of the arrogant type would probably have demanded to be furnished with beds, even if it had involved two of the occupants of the house in sitting up all night. These, however, said that they would spend the night in their car and asked if they might borrow rug, and pillows, which were lent them. Very early next morning the owner of the house, hearing a slight noise, looked out of his bedroom window and saw the Germans pushing their car down the drive. They did not start up its engines until they had it out on the road. The pillows they had borrowed and the rugs, neatly folded, were later found on the doorstep of the house.

The majority of Germans, both officers and men, billeted in private houses behaved decently. There is one authenticated case of some German soldiers of the working class who not only insisted on paying for small services rendered them by the woman of the house but even, when her husband was ill, carried water and chopped wood for her. Many Germans, however, seemed to regard courtesy as an effeminacy unworthy of a virile people. Innumerable cases are recorded of Germans entering houses without previously knocking at the doors, either in search of information or because they had been instructed to lay telephone wires across the garden behind. Respect for hygiene, formerly a marked German characteristic, also seemed to have been abandoned as effeminate. The Press Officer kept pigs for some time in the area adjoining the front door of his house in Cambridge Park Terrace and pigs were kept in the basements of some houses such as Old Government House Hotel, which was used as a 'Soldiers' Home'.

Some Germans billeted in private houses behaved swinishly, especially when drunk. Important occasions, such as an Axis victory or a speech by Adolph Hitler, were celebrated by a free issue of brandy to the troops. A broad-minded man of the world can forgive another man, especially if young and inexperienced, if, lacking the sense to stop drinking while sober, he gets drunk inadvertently. Many Germans, however, when sitting down to consume their ration of brandy deliberately set themselves to get drunk as speedily as possible; two German officers, for example, finished a half litre of brandy between them in less than half an hour, with disastrous results to their unwilling host's furniture, over which they vomited copiously. Few, if any, Germans guilty of such offences ever showed any contrition afterwards or apologised to their hosts, but it is to the credit of the German authorities that, when complaints of such occurrences were made to them, they sent German soldiers to clean up the mess. Extreme cases of swinishness, credibly reported, are the painting of pornographic pictures on the walls of houses before vacating them, and the deposit of excrement on their floors.

Sentimentality is a German characteristic. At Christmas time they did not hesitate to loot young coniferous trees from private gardens in order that they might celebrate the season of goodwill to all men in the traditional fashion. When the bodies of British sailors or airmen were washed ashore the German Commandant sent wreaths and ordered German firing parties to attend the funerals. The funeral of nineteen ratings of H.M.S. *Charybdis* was made the occasion of an impressive function. It was attended by the Sea Commandant, the Harbour Commandant and the Field Commandant, each of whom brought wreaths, by a detachment of marines and by a firing party that fired a salute over the graves. The Harbour Commandant who was responsible for the arrangements followed the Continental custom of making a laudatory speech and omitted nothing that tended to make the ceremony pompous, but he told the Dean of Guernsey that it must be compressed within the space of half an hour and was annoyed with the Dean for insisting that the service for such as were Roman Catholics should be read by a priest of their own communion. The Germans showed less respect for our dead when they took tombstones from the old cemetery at the bottom of Cornet Street to place under the wheels of guns on the Mignot plateau, and in order that their own dead might lie together in the military cemetery at Fort George they dug up the coffins of some eighteen British soldiers who had formerly been buried there.

A large proportion of the German soldiers who were quartered in Guernsey were by no means whole-hearted in their allegiance to their Fuehrer. This was especially the case with those who had lived for any length of time in England or the United States of America. One man is even reported to have confided to a barber who attended him that he would gladly give his life for the chance of cutting Hitler's throat. Even the German and Austrian maid-servants employed in the Island before the outbreak of war and released from internment when the Island was demilitarised, showed that residence in a free country had infected them with a spirit of independence. In March, 1941, they were summoned to the Commandant's office and an attempt was made to persuade them to return to their native land of their own free will. According to accounts of the interview given by these women to their Guernsey employers they almost without exception refused to return. Apparently they believed that if they did so they would be conscripted for less congenial work on the land or in factories. When asked for their reasons for not wishing to return to Germany some said that they hoped to marry English husbands because Englishmen were more indulgent to their wives than German husbands and gave them greater liberty. And very soon after being summoned to the Commandant's office several of the women bought themselves engagement rings so that they could pretend to be affianced even if they were not.

Attempts were made by the German authorities to keep the rank and file from hearing any war news except that given them from German official sources. A German private learned of the sinking of the Graf Spee (on which his brother had been serving) from an illustrated paper in a dentist's room. As a result the dentist was visited by two German officers who ordered the paper to be burned in their presence.

When they first arrived in the Island the Germans were very naturally flushed with victory and seemed really to believe that within a few weeks Britain would be sufficiently in German hands to allow of their Fuehrer making one of his famous speeches from the balcony of Buckingham Palace. This general optimism did not last long. Our airport – until it was thoroughly well bombed by the Royal Air Force – was the starting point of some of the German planes employed in the Battle of Britain and observant Germans could not be kept ignorant of the fact that of the planes that left Guernsey a considerable proportion failed to return. Depression set in, especially among men who had been warned that they were to be trained as parachutists, some of whom sought from kindly Islanders the sympathy which perhaps they shrank from seeking among their own comrades. After the German defeat in the Battle of Britain many Germans of all ranks expected that the British would speedily recapture the Island and the rank and file believed that if the British attacked their officers would escape by air, leaving them to their fate. Many, war-weary and disheartened, expressed hopes that the British would retake the Island. Some made enquiries as to the whereabouts of caves, saying that if an order was given to evacuate the Island they would hide till the evacuation was complete.

During the first year of the occupation there was, on several occasions, evidence of disaffection among the troops. In November, 1940, four riots broke out within one week-in the Pollet, in Trinity Square, at Cobo and at L'Ancresse. In these an officer and several others were killed. In January, 1941, when troops paraded on the Quay before embarking, several men tried to break away but were brought back and herded on board at revolver point. In April, 1941, there was a disorderly demonstration of both soldiers and seamen near the White Rock Weighbridge. It was said that they were expressing discontent with their rations. More serious disaffection broke out at the end of July, 1941, and lasted for nearly a week; a riot occurred in Amherst Road at three o'clock in the morning; a detachment of men at La Passée were kept in order by a threat that machine-gun fire would be turned on them; at Beaucamps an officer was stoned and his car overturned; some troops embarking for active service in Russia were marched on board ship at the point of the bayonet after they themselves had been deprived of their side arms. It was reported – but the report could not, of course, be verified – that three officers were shot by their own men during this week.

Apart from disaffection there was at this time marked despondency among the troops. According to reports – not verifiable but made on good authority – one officer and three men of lower rank committed suicide during the period covered by the last week in July and the first week in August, 1941, and throughout the occupation German suicides were frequently reported.

Evidence of unrest and incipient mutiny among the German rank and file raised false hope among the Islanders of an early end to the war. It seemed to show that the German war-machine was cracking. False though our hopes were they were not unreasonable for discontent was by no means confined to the lower ranks. On several occasions German officers told Islanders on whom they were billeted that the troops would lay down their arms by a specified date. The first date mentioned was Christmas, 1941. Later dates were subsequently given but as time wore on the prophecies were not renewed. Such statements were eagerly and widely circulated by members of the Guernsey Underground News Service. Some of them may have been invented. Some were undoubtedly authentic. At any rate it was evident that the German people were by no means unanimous in loyalty to Hitler. The first German victim of German land mines was said to have loudly cursed Hitler before he died. A civilian member of the Organisation Todt who could speak no English let a cobbler to whom he had taken his boots for repair know his feelings by saying 'Hitler' and drawing his finger across his throat. Another who spoke good English said that he would gladly give his life for a chance to kill Hitler. Less bombastic but more convincing was the evidence afforded by an officer who sought an interview with the author of a recently published book, *Guernsey Present and Past*, on the ground that he wished to ask some questions about the history of the Island. When they met, however, he showed no interest whatever in the Island's history. Instead of asking questions he described the principal events in the growth of Nazi power to which he applied the words 'this terrible tragedy'. He said that when first young men paraded the streets of German towns under the Nazi banner sensible Germans regarded the movement as a safety-valve for discontent and were not alive to its danger until it had become too strong to check. At first this officer was listened to somewhat coldly lest he should be in reality an agent provocateur, but there was unmistakably genuine emotion in his voice and face when he spoke of friends driven into exile or incarcerated in concentration camps and it became obvious that he had sought the interview solely in order to unburden his mind to someone whom he hoped would prove sympathetic.

Had it been possible to ascertain the feelings of each individual German amongst us it would probably have been found that only a very small proportion were whole-hearted disciples of Hitler and were eager for Germany to fight to the bitter end.[17] Of the remainder the majority, though they had hoped for and expected a German victory during the early days of the occupation, became apathetic as the chances of victory dwindled and were ready to welcome any end to the war, defeat or victory, that would restore them to their homes and their peace-time occupations. The rest were opposed to the war from its inception and hoped for an Allied victory that would overturn Hitler and give Germans their freedom again rather than a German victory that would perpetuate Nazism.

What was the secret of Hitler's power, backed as he was only by a small proportion of the German nation, to secure obedience from the whole? On November 8th, 1942 – a Sunday – members of the Organisation Todt assembled on the Elizabeth College cricket ground to listen to a speech from a prominent German. After the speech all with uplifted hands renewed their oaths of allegiance to their Fuehrer. Along the hedge that flanked the ground were machine-guns manned by soldiers in battle kit. The presence of those machine-guns at a political meeting seemed to explain much that would otherwise have been obscure.

---

17   It may or may not be significant that the Nazi form of salute with outstretched arm copied from the Italian Fascists was very rarely seen. An observer, interested in the matter, saw it given only on eight occasions during the whole period of the German occupation – once by a non-combatant member of the Organisation Todt, once by a middle-aged officer, six times by very young officers, never by a soldier of lower rank – until the abortive attempt to assassinate Hitler in 1944, after which the Nazi salute was compulsory but was generally very perfunctorily given.

CHAPTER XX

WE OURSELVES

In the darkest days of the war when the German forces were over-running France and it seemed to the faint hearted that Britain's day was done a placard appeared in the window of a shop in the Commercial Arcade kept by Miss Mary Toms. On it was printed the proud announcement 'There is no depression in this shop and we are not interested in the possibilities of defeat'. If this placard had been left in the shop-window after the German occupation had become an accomplished fact it would have invited heavy-footed German reprisals. It was replaced with another on which was printed 'Blessed are the cheerful in heart for they lighten the road for themselves and their fellow-travellers'. It was in this spirit that the majority of the Guernsey people faced the troubles and anxieties caused by the German occupation, both in the early days and when with the passage of years our troubles and anxieties increased. The contribution that any of us could make towards winning the war was now infinitesimally small but there was a general feeling that anyone who kept a stiff upper lip and made light of our misfortunes was doing his or her duty towards the British Empire.

There was, however, a fairly large minority of people who were more concerned with the British Empire's duty towards themselves. When German planes raided the Island a few days before the occupation they blamed the Royal Air Force for failing to intercept them and drive them away and when the German forces occupied the Island they blamed the Home Government for not liberating us immediately and at all costs. 'Britain', they said, 'has let us down'. Such people suffered from what may be diagnosed as fatty degeneration of the spirit. They read the German communiqués and implicitly believed them, foresaw no possible ending to the war better than a stalemate due to exhaustion on both sides, whined because they disliked tea and coffee substitutes and – worst of all – whenever British planes flew over the Island and attacked military targets, wished that the Royal Air Force would leave Guernsey alone because their visits 'annoyed the Germans' and they feared lest Germans should make us suffer for their annoyance.

Some people actually shared the German fear that British planes might bomb our thickly populated Island indiscriminately. A scrap-iron merchant generously offered to lend scrap-iron free of charge to anyone who wished to construct a shelter on his own premises, and church services were transferred from the Castel Methodist Church to the Parish School because of the proximity of the latter to places that could be used as shelters. Few probably feared that the Royal Air Force might drop poison-gas on the Island, but the *Evening Press* in a leading article urged householders to make the members of their households practice gasmask drill at least once a week. That amazing advice was, however, probably given at the instigation of the Press Officer. It is scarcely credible that any, even of the most faint-hearted Guernseymen, believed that the British Government had abandoned us so utterly as to be capable of employing the Royal Air Force to use a method of warfare that would have harmed more Guernsey civilians than German soldiers. The stout-hearted majority welcomed British air raids as evidence of British air power.

Some people not only refused to despond but even contrived to find a humorous side to our troubles. A good example was set by the Publicity Officer who, when the danger that water and gas supplies might cease was being stressed by the Controlling Committee, published in the newspapers such slogans as

   'Don't gas and spread rumours. Save gas'
and
   'Little drops of water running now to waste
   Make the day of shortage come with greater haste'.

A captious critic might regard the humour in these slogans as cheap, but cheap humour is preferable to costly gloom.

Shopping queues are fertile breeding grounds of discontent but even in those jokes were more often heard than grumbles.

On Saturday mornings housewives waiting to buy carrots or parsnips would enliven the tedium of waiting by discussing with gusto the various appetising ways in which they might cook the Sunday joint – the point of the joke being that no Sunday joint was obtainable and that, if no potato ration had been issued, the carrots or parsnips would form the principal item in the Sunday dinner. A sense of humour is a gift that Providence seems to have denied to the average German. A fortnight before the Allied invasion of France began the German propaganda published in the *Evening Press* included an anecdote which we were told was being related in London to the effect that Stalin had telephoned to Churchill asking if the British Government would consider conditions ripe for an invasion of the Continent if the Russian armies advanced as far as Calais. The quoter of the anecdote apparently did not understand that the British love to tell stories against themselves for he commented 'this tale shows what state the people's minds are in England on the subject of the invasion of Europe. Everyone is alarmed at the lack of action by the British Government while the Soviets multiply their offensives and their advances'.

In some respects the circumstances of the occupation gave a novel spice to our lives. It was interesting to make experiments in the discovery of substitutes for tea, tobacco and soap and in the concoction of appetising food from seaweed and other unfamiliar materials. Whenever while searching byways and hedges for fuel one came on some uncompleted work of the Organisation Todt engineers and was able surreptitiously to add to one's faggot some useful length of good sawn timber from an unguarded pile, one experienced a deliciously exciting thrill such as in boyhood's days one felt when robbing a neighbour's orchard. It was exciting, too, to meet a German when trespassing on a road clearly marked as forbidden to civilians. Such thrills were occasional. A daily excitement after our radios had been confiscated was the collection and dissemination, at the risk of a term of imprisonment, of war news broadcast by the BBC. No one of the hundreds who engaged in it could complain that his life was dull and insipid.

WE OURSELVES

Life could have been made far more exciting than it was by indulgence in acts of sabotage, but practically nothing could be done that would have appreciably hindered the German war effort: we had no munition factories to set on fire, no trains to derail except one small one imported by the Germans to transport cement and other materials for the building of fortifications. It would have been difficult to do any damage to shipping, for Guernseymen admitted on to the piers and jetties were closely scrutinised. When, however, the Germans began to fit up the lifeboat with anti-aircraft guns, her coxswain, under pretence of tuning-up her engines, contrived to put them out of action. The job of repairing them was entrusted first to the States Maintenance Engineer, and then, when he failed to get them into working order, to a private engineer, who in his turn succeeded in making the engines quite useless.

A minor act of sabotage was an ingenious trick by which a lorry driver became the richer by a load of precious fuel. A cargo of coal imported by the Germans for their own use was being transported to a depot in lorries requisitioned by the Germans but driven by Guernseymen in their employment. This particular lorry driver had no doubt heard – it was common knowledge – that anyone in need of a bag of cement could get one by arrangement with one of the drivers employed to transport it from the harbour to fortifications that were not within reach of the coast road train. He drove his lorry down to the ship, waited placidly while the foreign labourers employed in discharging the cargo filled it with coal, and drove away. It was no business of the foreign labourers to ask questions and the sentry at the barbed wire barrier that excluded the general public from the White Rock showed no interest in him. Who eventually burned that coal is known only to those who were so fortunate as to be able to obtain some of it. The German authorities made no effort to trace it and it is to be supposed that they never missed it.

The circumstances of the German occupation tended to develop in the community some of the good qualities attributed to the early Christians. Because war news was so precious one sought it cautiously from anyone able to impart it. The search in many cases led to contacts between people, such as shop-assistant and customer, housewife and charwoman, who normally had no interests in common outside their business relations; and because, owing to the danger involved, one imparted news only to those whose fidelity one could trust, such contacts led to many very real friendships and tended to break down estranging social barriers.

Difficulties fostered neighbourliness. Many people who could not keep fowls or rabbits carefully put aside unwanted cabbage leaves to give to their more fortunate neighbours – a small service, certainly, but still a service, as it would have been less trouble to throw their vegetable refuse into their dust-bins.

Social service of a more valuable kind was offered by the Save-the-Children Fund, the Children's Emergency Bureau and the Special Aid Society. The work of the Save-the-Children Fund, organised by *The Star* at the suggestion of the anonymous donor of the first subscription is described in Chapter XIV. The Children's Emergency Bureau, described in Chapter XIII, started its useful career with a loan of £10 from the States but very soon it was able to repay the loan and to supplement the help of voluntary workers with paid assistance. At a later date it was even able to contribute to a fund raised to pay the French philanthropic organisation Secours National for biscuits sent by that society for distribution among Guernsey schoolchildren.

The Special Aid Society owed its genesis to Mrs Owen Fuzzey. Established before the occupation to supply comforts to the troops and afford recreation to soldiers stationed in the Island it found itself at a loose end when it could no longer send parcels out of the Island and there were no longer any British troops here to entertain. Instead of disbanding it found a new outlet for its benevolent activities. The room in High Street that was formerly used as a canteen for soldiers now became a rest room for tired shoppers and a restaurant where they could drink coffee-substitute and even eat modest lunches made of whatever unrationed food was obtainable. It also acted as intermediary agent for people who wanted to exchange something useful that they could spare for something equally useful of which they were in greater need – such as pillow cases or kettles or serviceable shoes for wheat-gleaners. It did a great service, too, to lonely bachelors, grass-widowers and overworked housewives by undertaking for moderate fees any kind of mending from the darning of socks to the patching of clothes.

Islanders were not unanimous in their attitude towards Germans as individuals. Some hated and despised them as the accomplices or at best the docile tools of a band of political adventurers who owed their victories more to breaches of international faith and to acts of unprecedented barbarism than to methods of warfare used by civilised nations. Others, more charitably, and perhaps more justly, regarded them as men honourably fulfilling their duty to their country and not to be held responsible either for the breaches of faith of which their leaders were guilty or for the atrocities committed by some of their fellows.

It is an amazing fact, and one throwing an interesting sidelight on German mentality, that when German troops first occupied Guernsey their officers expected to be received socially as officers of a British garrison quartered in the Island would have been. To the overwhelming majority of the class with which they wished to associate this was not only impossible but even unthinkable. Yet before they had been a month in the Island the German Chief of Staff, Dr Maas, who to do him justice seemed anxious to treat us with all possible consideration and courtesy, sent an interpreter to Major R.G. Davies with a message to the effect that he wished to give a dinner-party followed by a dance at which he and his officers could make the acquaintance of local ladies. Major Davies had formerly held the office of ADC to the Lieutenant-Governor of Guernsey and was therefore in a position to advise Dr Maas as to which were the leading families in the Island. Dr Maas, however, wanted not only his advice but also his co-operation. He wished Major Davies tactfully to interview local ladies and ascertain which of them would accept invitations to the proposed festivity. Major Davies told the interpreter that although he had no personal animosity against any individual Germans he himself would not accept an invitation and very much doubted whether any of the Island ladies would accept it. The interpreter, saying that Dr Maas was very anxious to give the party, urged Major Davies at least to ascertain the opinion of others on the subject and Major Davies, feeling perhaps that he was not justified in taking for granted the attitude of others, reluctantly consented. He approached a lady whom he knew had many friends in Germany and who might on that account have felt inclined to accept the invitation. She refused it so emphatically and a lady who happened to be calling on her expressed such indignation at the proposal that Major Davies was able to report that his doubts as to a favourable reception of Dr Maas's overtures had been confirmed.

Dr Maas, unwilling to disappoint his officers of the promised entertainment, was now in a difficult position. He was rescued from it by a Guernsey resident, comparatively a newcomer to the Island, whose social position was based less on culture or good birth than on self assurance and the possession of a larger income than most Guernseymen enjoy. This man, apparently with the hope that he might receive benefits denied to others, such as permission to retain the use of his car and motor-yacht, had fraternised with German officers from the first, inviting them to his house and accompanying them on a rabbit-shooting picnic to Herm. He saved Dr Maas from an embarrassing situation by persuading one or two women of his own kidney and somewhat nebulous position to accept the invitation of the German Chief of Staff and by canvassing barmaids, shop assistants and domestic servants, a sufficient number of whom were prepared to sacrifice such national pride as they possessed for the excitement of dining with, and being treated as the social equals of, military officers. The dinner and dance took place but that did not give the German officers the opportunity of making the acquaintance of any ladies whom they would have regarded as *hochwohlgeboren*.

It was no doubt good policy on the part of the German authorities to attempt to induce the Guernsey people to feel amicably disposed towards those who for the time being were their conquerors, and few who came into contact with Dr Maas, however briefly and however unwillingly, can have doubted his own personal sincerity and goodwill towards us. It was a misfortune for the Island that he was transferred to other duties after being in Guernsey only for a brief period. With the hope, no doubt, of establishing friendly relations between the German rank and file and Guernsey people of a corresponding social position he asked that public subscription dances, suspended since the occupation, should be resumed, and that German soldiers should be admitted to them. The dances, however, proved a source of friction, because many Guernsey men refused to dance with girls who had danced with Germans, and after a five-weeks' trial the German authorities forbade the attendance of soldiers at them.

Some Guernsey people, especially those of the working class, were prepared to be friendly with the Germans. Not having had the leisure to read or sufficient education to understand the leading newspapers and reviews they knew little or nothing of the infamies that had marked German methods of warfare or at any rate realised that the guilt of those infamies lay on the German leaders and that the German rank and file should not be held responsible for them. Some of the latter were genuine objects of pity; bewildered home-sick youths who yearned for sympathy, sought it by exhibiting photographs of their sisters and sweethearts, and showed genuine gratitude for any kindness shown them. Animosity against such men as these – mere cannon-fodder who had had no voice in making the war – would have been unreasonable, and some of them did receive kindness and even hospitality from Islanders whose social station corresponded with their own. A sharp distinction should be drawn between those, on the one hand, who befriended Germans without seeking to gain any advantage from their friendliness and, on the other hand, those sycophants who made advances to the Germans in hopes of profiting by their servility. The latter lowered their country's dignity; the former enhanced it. It was probably with a feeling that the German rank and file could not be held responsible for their leaders' conduct that – a few weeks after the occupation began – a Guernsey football team challenged a German team to play against them and the organisers of a swimming gala invited Germans to compete. The Commandant did not allow soldiers to join in the swimming races, possibly, it was suggested, because he feared that they might be too conspicuously beaten by Islanders accustomed to swim from infancy. The football match took place but was not played very seriously; the last goal credited to the Germans was kicked by the Guernseyman who officiated as referee. After that one game the Germans played football only among themselves.

Probably because of the chilliness with which Dr Maas's overtures of friendship had been received the German authorities made only one more attempt to get into social contact with leading Islanders. The Commandant, when announcing that the Association of Berlin Artistes was to give a concert at the Regal Theatre, published a general invitation to Islanders to attend it, saying that it had been arranged mainly for their benefit, and that seats and programmes would be free. The Bailiff endeavoured to secure a good audience not only by publishing his wish that as many as could do so would attend to support him 'on this auspicious occasion' but also by canvassing among his personal friends. The music, as was to be expected, was good but in spite of the Bailiff's appeal and example only half the auditorium was filled. It is said that one of the German officials described the attitude of the Guernsey gentry towards himself and his colleagues as 'passive insolence' and few to whom British dignity is precious would have wished it to be otherwise. Perhaps he was stung by the jest of a Guernseyman who, when the order demanding the surrender of all firearms was amplified to include air-guns and air-pistols, handed the German authorities a toy pistol bought for sixpence at Woolworth's Stores. That is possible; but it is not probable; the average German has too little sense of humour to know when his leg is being pulled.

Though some suffered punishment for insolence that could scarcely be described as passive the attitude of the working classes as a whole towards the Germans was more passive than insolent. This was especially the case with people employed by them. International Law relating to the employment of people in an enemy-occupied country enacts that 'the personal services of inhabitants may be requisitioned provided that the services required do not directly concern the operations of war against their own country'.[18] None of the tasks to which women were set could help the German war effort nor could some of those such as grooming horses – to which men were set. But other tasks included digging shelter trenches, building hangars and even transporting ammunition. Refusal to work at these tasks would almost certainly have been punished with imprisonment. There was no umpire to whom a workplan who objected to the nature of his task could appeal and, rightly or wrongly, the workers believed that in any dispute the Labour Bureau would side with the Germans. Many of them had been recruited to work for the Germans by the Labour Bureau and on pay days all found in their pay envelopes a slip of paper on which was printed the following notice:-

> CONTROLLING COMMITTEE OF
> THE STATES OF GUERNSEY
> It is a condition of employment and re-employment in each States Department that the employee shall proceed from place to place and do such work as he may be required to do from time to time by the head of the department or the organiser or foreman concerned.
>
> JOHN LEALE,
> For and on behalf of the Controlling
> Committee of the States of Guernsey.
> 3rd December, 1940.

There was also the consideration, though this was known only to the Controlling Committee, that the German authorities threatened that men who refused to work for them would be deported to France. At one time there was so much discontent among workers who felt that they were being compelled to assist the enemy's war effort that some of the bolder spirits tried

18 *Manual of Military Law*. Chapter XIV. Section VIII. Paragraph 388.

to organise a strike. The proposal, however, did not receive sufficient support. There were not enough workers willing to face the risk. Moreover those who wished to organise a strike had to contend with the fact that many men who had little or no patriotism actually sought employment by the Germans because the pay was one-third above the current Island rate and in many cases a bowl of soup was given at midday -a great temptation especially during the winter months.

Such lack of militant patriotism was perhaps excusable in working men who had to consider the welfare of their families as well as their own needs but the conduct of many women of the same class aroused much resentment among decent people of all classes. Although the German officers had failed to establish friendly relations with Guernsey women of their own social standing they found no difficulty in cultivating the society of women of the empty-headed type to whom a smart uniform is an irresistible attraction, even if it is the uniform of their country's enemies, and during the first few months of the occupation, when the officers could obtain as much petrol as they liked, one might occasionally see a young Guernsey woman sitting by the side of a German officer in a luxury car and endeavouring to look like what she supposed a duchess would look like.

One girl of that type, a domestic servant, had an unfortunate experience. At about ten o'clock one evening she was walking with a German officer when bombs began to fall on the airport from a British plane and anti-aircraft guns came into action. The German officer skedaddled, either because it was his duty to save his valuable life for his Fuehrer's service or from less creditable motives and the girl was left with no one to protect her, with the result that a policeman arrested her for being out of doors during curfew hours without a permit and locked her up for the night. She appeared before the Police Magistrate in due course and – her cavalier not being present to exonerate her – was fined £1. In outlining the charge against her the inspector of police took elaborate care to frame his accusation in a way that would not offend the Germans. 'This was the night when certain gunfire occurred', he said. 'She was with someone else and when it occurred he went away and she was left.'

The German rank and file followed the example of their officers and the sight of Guernsey girls giggling and flirting with German privates furtively in secluded lanes or even openly and unashamedly in crowded streets was almost as common as it was nauseating.

Guernsey people of all classes bitterly resented the association of empty-headed Guernsey women with German soldiers, especially when it became known that some of them had become mothers of illegitimate children whose fathers were German. This bare fact, unannotated, might afford weighty material for the anti-German propagandist, giving as it does the impression that licentious German soldiers gratified their brutal lust at the cost of unwilling and defenceless women. Any such suggestion, however, would be entirely untrue. The sight of women loitering on the pavement outside houses in which Germans were quartered and persistently trying to attract the attention of those within was too common for there to be any doubt in the matter. That many of these women received gifts of food from their German paramours in no way excuses their offence. They might have obtained extra food without sacrificing anything more than precious dignity, for many Germans, until they themselves were put on short rations, good-naturedly gave away food and even tobacco to Guernsey people with whom they came in contact without asking or expecting any return. The only possible excuse for the women's conduct is the fact, recognised but not fully explained by psychologists, that the excitement generated by war tends to inflame sexual passion,[19] and the only comforting thought that can mitigate the tragedy in the minds of decent people is that the stamina of many Guernsey people has suffered from overmuch inbreeding in the past and that the influx of alien blood may have good results on

---

19 The illegitimate birth-rate in Guernsey declined in the early part of the war and then rose sharply. Thirty-four illegitimate births were registered at the Greffe in 1939, twenty-seven in 1940, thirteen in 1941, forty-eight in 1942, fifty-three in 1943, and eighty-two in 1944. For how many of these births German fathers were responsible it is impossible to say.

future generations.

No account of the relations between Guernsey people and Germans would be complete without mention of two other kinds of renegade. Some farmers, in defiance both of German regulations and of those made by the Controlling Committee, sold to individual Germans – at a large profit – milk, butter and other produce that was badly needed by their fellow Islanders. When their conduct was criticised they excused themselves by saying that if the Germans had not been allowed to buy what they wanted they would have stolen it.

But if such men as these and women who cohabited with Germans are to be despised what measure of scorn is due to Islanders who, without the incentive of passion or profit to tempt them betrayed their fellow Islanders to the German police! This was done not once only but scores of times. Although tale-telling was officially enjoined on us by proclamations, the German authorities – one liked them the better for it or at any rate disliked them the less – seemed to dislike and despise informers. When a Guernsey woman, presumably as the result of a lover's quarrel, denounced her fiancé for having retained his radio, and, to prove that he had used it, stated that she herself had listened to it every evening for a month, they sent her to prison as well as the man she had betrayed and gave her a heavier sentence on the ground that it was her duty to have reported him sooner.

The German police were curiously apathetic in enforcing some of the German orders that had from time to time been promulgated and it is possible that if they had received no help from informers no Guernseyman would have been detected in possession of a radio. But they would have been exceptionally negligent if they had not acted on information conveyed in anonymous letters giving them the names and addresses of persons alleged to have retained their wireless sets. Sometimes the letters, which the German police usually produced as their justification for searching houses, gave specific information as to the exact hiding places of the radios – under the valance of a bed, perhaps, or at the back of a cupboard or behind a stack of wood in an outhouse. Happily some of the searches proved fruitless, either because the informer had been acting merely on suspicion or had given inaccurate information or because, as was sometimes the case, the owner of the prescribed radio was more nimble-witted than the German police. But in a tragically large number of cases the search resulted in the confiscation of the radio and the imprisonment of its owner, the sentences ranging from three weeks to fourteen months.

If one seeks for the motive of these anonymous informers one can arrive at only one possible conclusion. They expected no material reward and they did not even hope to curry favour with the German authorities for they concealed their identity. Any suggestion that they did it from a sense of duty to the Germans may be ruled out of the question. Inevitably we must suppose that they did it merely for sheer hatred of their neighbours.

Though we had reason to be heartily ashamed of the conduct of some of our fellow Islanders and were justified in feeling some mild contempt for the fainthearted, the querulous and those who too docilely accepted employment of a kind that might help the German war effort, we had more reason to be proud of the behaviour of Islanders as a whole: of the labouring man who stoutly endeavoured to do a full day's work on a ration scarcely sufficient to maintain the strength of an invalid in bed; of the housewives who taxed their ingenuity to devise ways of making attractive meals out of meagre and unpalatable ingredients; of those who were more concerned to lighten the burdens of others than to ease their own; and it is difficult to over-estimate the services to the community of those who saved it from despondency, nerve-strain, and groundless fears by retaining their radios, and increased the risk of punishment for so doing by imparting the news they obtained from them to others. Of the many of these stalwarts who suffered for their public spirit one died in exile in Germany and one escaped from a French prison, joined the Maquis and was killed in action.

CHAPTER XXI

NARRATIVE, 1943-1944

Nothing of outstanding importance happened in 1943 except the persistence of the typhus epidemic and the exile to Germany of ex-officers and ex-prisoners, both of which have already been mentioned. A beginning was made in the re-naming of streets – the name *Hochstrasse* was given to the road that runs westwards through St Julian's Avenue, the Grange and the Rohais – but, like much else that the Germans began to do, this step towards Teutonizing the Island was soon abandoned. In June they raided boxes entrusted to the Banks for safe keeping and seized any gold, diamonds or bearer bonds that they found therein. It is believed they got very little.

In August four men and a woman, Messrs Corbet, Bougourd, Hubert and Le Page and Mrs Le Page escaped from the Island in a motor boat, helped by misty weather and a strong spring tide which enabled them, when clear of the land, to drift as far as the Casquets before using the boat's engines. They left at four o'clock in the afternoon, reached Start Point thirteen hours later and landed in Dartmouth where they received a cordially hospitable reception but were detained in formal custody by the police until orders came from London for Corbet to report to the War Office. For the next six weeks he stayed in London going daily to the War Office to give information about the fortifications that the Germans had constructed in Guernsey. Later he lectured on Island conditions to various branches of the Channel Islands Society.

As usually happened when anything was done that annoyed the Germans public opinion was divided. The stout-hearted rejoiced at hearing of the escape. Others condemned it, gloomily predicting reprisals such as the deportation of men of military age or even the shooting of hostages. Two German soldiers were shot for not having prevented the escape and a few Guernsey people accused of having connived at it were imprisoned for a while, but the population as a whole suffered only indirectly.

Bathing and fishing from the shore was prohibited, access to all beaches was forbidden except for those who had permission to gather seaweed for manure, and for a period of five weeks no fishing boats were allowed to go out. This affected the Island's food supply as it was the height of the mackerel and longnose (garfish) season, the only season in the year when fish are really plentiful in local waters. When resumption of fishing was allowed permits were granted only to fishermen who had no relatives in England and those who received permits were made to deposit sums of from £5 to £20 according to the size of their boats.

In October a man was sentenced to deportation to Germany for inciting people to display 'V' emblems. Owing to congestion in the local prisons he was left at liberty while awaiting transport to France. Before he was taken away he gave a farewell party at Stroobant's café at which songs offensive to German feelings, such as 'We'll hang our washing on the Siegfried line', were sung more hilariously than was prudent. The German military police raided the café and imprisoned the guests, some of whom were women, for the night, and the German Commandant seized the opportunity to prohibit all public entertainments, even whist and euchre drives, but soon afterwards made an exception in favour of dances organised by Mr Godfrey Giffard in connection with the Ozanne Hall Mission.

There were comparatively few air raids in 1943 though single reconnaissance planes flying over the Island occasionally attracted anti-aircraft fire which did little harm to the planes but a good deal to roofs and greenhouses pierced by falling shrapnel. That a Commando party landed on Sark towards the end of December we knew both from a British news-broadcast and from a German report printed in *The Star*. According to the latter the raid was costly and abortive, but the BBC told us that the raiders cut a cable and took several German prisoners. Throughout the year speculation was rife as to when the long-promised second front would be opened and a number of sweepstakes on the event were privately organised. Hope dwindled as the year drew towards its close, for those who in the previous war had experienced the depth and stickiness of Flanders mud thought it unlikely that any invasion on a large scale would be attempted during the winter. During the latter part of the year the German garrison was diluted with Italians, Poles and Soviet subjects of Georgian and Circassian nationality. Many of these, if able to speak a few words of English, declared privately that, if called upon to shoot at a British plane or a British soldier, they would take care not to hit the target. That the German Command had little confidence in their fidelity was evident from the fact that they were never armed except when manning the guns, although the German soldiers carried arms both on and off duty.

Early in 1944, one rumour and one definite event warmed our hearts. The rumour, said to have emanated from friendly Germans, was that on January 2nd tip-and-run raiders had landed somewhere on the South Coast, shot a sentry and done so much damage to a cable as would take several weeks to repair.[20] The definite event was a visit from an Allied plane on January 31st which flew across the Island, and killed nineteen German soldiers with its machine-guns.

During the next four months neither sea-raiders nor air raiders paid much attention to the Island but in the latter part of May hostilities were revived with most heartening frequency. On May 22nd four planes flew down the Little Russell channel inflicting casualties on German soldiers stationed on Brehon tower. A few days later it was rumoured that British troops had landed on the Casquets and taken prisoner seven Germans who formed the lighthouse crew.

On May 27th no less than sixteen bombers attacked Fort George and its neighbourhood. Their principal targets were three large radio-location finders in the field overlooking Le Val des Terres. One of these was wrecked, one seriously damaged,

---

[20] We had previously heard similar rumours. Being merely rumours they were more gratifying than trustworthy, but after we were liberated we read in a Ministry of Information booklet, *The Steel Hand from the Sea*, a description of a successful British crew-kidnapping raid on the Casquets that was made as early as September 2nd, 1940.

one slightly damaged and a nearby gun knocked out. The barracks also received attention. Five Guernsey people were wounded: one man lost a leg, another was blinded and three women employed at the cook-house received slight injuries. Casualties were heavy among the German troops. They were taken by surprise and, as many were playing football in the Fort Field when the attack began, they afforded an easy target for the bombers' machine-guns. According to a friendly German seventy-nine were killed, one hundred and sixty-four seriously injured and two hundred and five slightly injured. Considerable damage was done to private property in the neighbourhood of the Fort. For that reason, and because of the likelihood that the raid would be repeated, occupiers of houses in Fort Road and Havelet were compulsorily evacuated, all public entertainments and organised games were stopped and children under eight years of age were excused attendance at school.

In the days that followed the radio-location finders were attacked again and again until all were destroyed and until June 5th Allied aircraft attacked the Island nearly every day – sometimes several times in one day. We told each other that something big was going to happen soon – and we were right. On June 6th the stalwarts who still possessed wireless sets learned that the Allies had invaded Normandy. This heartening news was confirmed in *The Star* by the German Publicity Officer who published an announcement made in Berlin:-

> This morning early, 5.30am, our enemies in the West have upon orders from Moscow, started their bloody sacrifice, which they have feared for such a long time. The dictated attack, so often announced, of the Western helpers of Bolshevism has begun. We will give them a very warm welcome. Germany is conscious of the meaning of the hour. She will fight with her whole might and passionate resolution in order to protect Europe, her culture and the life of her people from barbarism.

The German Press Officer seldom deliberately tried to be funny but the matter that he published in our newspapers was often very amusing. On June 8th he published in *The Star* a paragraph which told us that the Atlantic Wall extended along the western coast of Europe for thirteen hundred miles and was defended by six thousand guns supported by more than three thousand heavy anti-tank guns. Probably the paragraph had reached him from the German Press Bureau some time before. That he published it two days after the Allies, by piercing the Atlantic Wall, had made it of no more military value than a pricked bladder seems to show that he was either very inefficient or extraordinarily careless.

An hour before the Allied landing in Normandy, which apparently they had foreseen was imminent, the Germans prepared vigorously to resist an invasion. From four o'clock in the morning onwards the whole garrison was under arms, gun-crews were at their posts, the coast was patrolled and sentries in battle-kit armed with rifles and hand-grenades were posted at the Telephone Exchange, the Post Office and other vital points.

Soon after D-Day the sounds of bombardment that drew nearer day by day made music in our ears and air-attacks on targets in the Island increased until we lost count of them. A target of special importance was afforded when a German submarine, so damaged as to be unable to submerge, sought refuge in the harbour and moored at the Southern Railway's berth. During the evening of June 13th a number of Allied planes flew southwards at a considerable height above the Little Russell Channel. While these were distracting the attention of the German anti-aircraft gunners three or more bombers approached at a very low level and at great speed. After passing over the high part of the town they swooped down, flew over the harbour and dropped bombs in the submarine's neighbourhood. The submarine was not hit but a seven-hundred-ton cargo ship moored alongside her, probably as a shield, was set on fire and so badly holed amidships that she sank[21].

---

21 At a later date the Germans made several abortive attempts to raise this vessel. In July, 1945, a British salvage crew were more successful.

The submarine was moved later to the Old Harbour, but later was moved again. On June 19th early in the morning a single plane dropped an exceptionally heavy bomb in the Old Harbour within a few yards of where she had been lying until a few hours before. That particular raid besides being unsuccessful did more damage to Island property than any other Allied raid. The explosion shattered all the windows on the sea-front besides many in streets as far from the harbour as Mill Street and the Bordage. The Town Church was so badly damaged that it could not be used for divine service until the following March. Buildings on the east side of High Street suffered a good deal. Living quarters above the shops were rendered temporarily uninhabitable and in the shops themselves showcases were warped and such few articles as they contained were blown into the street.

An independent newspaper in reporting the raid might rightly have stressed the point that the damage, though serious to the owners of the damaged property, was insignificant in comparison with what many English towns had suffered. Our newspapers, however, were not independent. The *Evening Press* gave an account of the affair under the headline Anglo-Americans convert our shops into shambles. The word 'shambles' was quite unjustified for if any bloodshed at all was caused by the explosion it was due to careless handling of the broken glass, but the tone of the article, especially a sentence that pointed out that the only damage done by the raid was to several thousands pounds' worth of Island property, so pleased the German authorities that they caused it to be reprinted in *The Star*.

After this raid two carters refused to work at the transporting of ships' cargoes on the ground that the harbour was a danger zone. The German authorities, who sometimes tried to make us believe that they were tenderly solicitous for our welfare, seized the occasion to publish a 'warning' that in its way was as amusing as anything published by their Press Officer. It declared that Germany had always considered it to be her duty to provide us with the necessities of life, that German sailors had risked their lives to protect the supply ships that brought those necessities to the Island and that therefore Guernseymen should 'make every effort to assist the German departments'. Ignoring the possibility that the carters had a primary duty to their wives and families the warning accused them of failing 'to fulfil their elementary duty towards the community and this through fear and cowardice'. It continued:-

> Both drivers knew that the bomb-proof shelters on the harbour were open to them as well as to German soldiers. They were also aware that any air raid is announced in good time by the sounding of the alarm. Their cowardice is to say the least incomprehensible. As, in spite of reiterated orders, they persistently refuse to do their duty, they have been punished. The population must know that, should such cases of neglect of duty and cowardice occur again, the supply of the civilian population through the German departments could no longer be guaranteed. The Islanders will thus have these cowards in their midst to thank for the resulting hardships.

This attempt to stir up popular indignation against the two carters was quite ineffective. If Germans 'risked their lives' to bring us food as far as the harbour why could they not bring it a few hundred yards farther under conditions, as the warning wished us to believe, of perfect safety? The reference to the air raid alarm was ridiculous. The alarm was seldom sounded until the planes that occasioned it were disappearing in the distance. Had it been reliable seventy-nine Germans would not have lost their lives on the Fort Field less than a month before. A fortnight later some harbour workers, warned that they would be required to unload ammunition from a ship due to arrive on the following day, declared that they would not handle it. The official to whom they announced their refusal attempted to reduce them to docility by shouting abuse and threats. When this failed a superior officer said that Italians and Russians could unload the ammunition and cynically added that, as the ship had to run the blockade from aircraft and naval vessels, she might not arrive at all.

In the latter part of June Allied planes scattered a large number of copies of two leaflets in German over the Island: one gave an account given by a German taken prisoner in Normandy of how his division was encouraged to hold out to the last by specific promises of help that was never sent; the other declared that any German who continued to fight would fight against Germany's future because, though the Allies were determined to stamp out Nazism, they did not wish to destroy the German nation. Again from August 30th onwards for a week or more illustrated news-sheets in German were dropped daily giving accounts of the latest Allied successes. Every morning as soon as it was light squads of soldiers searched for and destroyed these news-sheets but many were picked up and eagerly read both by Germans and Guernsey people. Some packets of cigarettes and chocolate, some small bottles of cognac and a few crystal wireless sets were also dropped. As these were more likely to fall into German hands than into ours, the reason for the distribution of these welcome gifts was problematical.

On September 29th a wave of excitement swept across the Island because of the mysterious visit of a Canadian destroyer flying a white flag that hove-to for awhile off Fermain Bay and was visited by a German officer. The theory that she had brought an invitation to the German garrison to surrender gave rise to a widely-believed rumour that the garrison had agreed to do so. Bitter disappointment followed as it was gradually realised that the rumour had been quite unfounded.

Allied successes in France led many to believe that the end of the European war was near. It was perhaps because of this belief that many women, whose intimacy with German soldiers had aroused the disgust of their neighbours, now received anonymous postcards threatening them with punishment at the hands of 'Knights in Ambush'. This underground movement was condemned in letters to the newspapers. Most decent people considered that, though in many cases the women richly deserved punishment, it should not be inflicted by self-appointed tribunals.

Although the war-news that our newspapers were compelled to publish told us of great German successes and costly Allied reverses in Normandy; although we were told that German strategy aimed to gain time for a decisive stroke and that new secret weapons of a very deadly kind were on the point of being used against the Allies; although, after the Germans had lost Cherbourg, Granville and St Malo, we were told that these ports would soon be in German hands again and the supply of foodstuffs from France resumed, it was obvious that both individual Germans and the local German authorities were uneasy as to the prospects of German victories. Individual Germans visited the Priaulx Library to read books about conditions in Australia, Canada and the South American republics with a view to emigrating to one or other of these countries after the war. (Those who offered any explanation said that Europe was over-populated.) The local German authorities showed their uneasiness by an apparent desire to conciliate us. In February, 1944, after a barber had been punished for refusing to attend to a German out of his proper turn, an order had been issued that members of the German forces were to have precedence over Guernsey people in shops and in the vegetable market. This order was cancelled in August. Its cancellation somewhat alleviated our food problem for the time being. But the relief was only temporary. To prevent discontent among the troops the German authorities had to keep them as well fed as possible. Very soon there was little to buy in the vegetable market, not because the Island's stock of vegetables was exhausted but because the German authorities requisitioned them before they reached the market. The Controlling Committee protested frequently and vigorously but as they were quite unable effectively to enforce their protests little was gained by protesting. The policy of the German authorities was more vacillating than resolute. Sometimes they yielded to the Committee's requests: sometimes they insisted on their demands being met.

On one occasion they were compelled to give way. The

Platzkommandant had demanded the resignation of Dr Symons, the Health Officer, on the ground that a letter he had written on the subject of sewage disposal was couched in offensive terms, but when he found that Dr Symons could not be replaced, he carried the matter no further, and Dr Symons remained in office.

The irresolution of the German authorities was exemplified towards the end of August. A farmer and his son caught thieves in the act of stealing their potatoes. The thieves drew their revolvers, killed the farmer, a Mr Jehan, wounded his son and escaped. Though the Guernsey coroner pronounced a verdict of 'murder or manslaughter by some persons unknown' the fact that the thieves carried revolvers was sufficient proof that they were German soldiers. The German authorities tacitly admitted this, not only by sending an officer to attend the funeral but also by confining all the troops in the neighbourhood to their quarters with the threat that they should have no food until the culprits confessed or were denounced by their comrades. The threat was quite ineffective because the sentries posted at the imprisoned men's billets allowed them to go out at night to forage for food and very soon official attempts to discover the culprits were abandoned.

In September the Controlling Committee learned that States of Guernsey £1 notes were being bought for as much as 30/- worth of German paper money. They supposed that the notes were being bought by local black market profiteers who knew that German paper money, if hoarded, would eventually have to be exchanged for local or British currency and feared that the Income Tax authorities might then learn the truth about their illicitly swollen incomes. A proposal was considered to recall all Guernsey notes to be refranked and to inform the Income Tax authorities of the amounts brought in by different people. The Committee approved the plan in principle but foresaw difficulties in adopting it. The States Supervisor suggested as an alternative that half a million pounds worth of States notes should be secretly printed to replace those in circulation during the German occupation as soon as the Island was liberated. That this was done without the knowledge of the German authorities or of the general public reflects great credit on the comparatively large number of people who had to be admitted to the secret.

Black market profiteers made colossal profits. Reports that beef was sold at the rate of £2 13s 5d a pound, wheat flour at £1 12s 0d, saccharine at £1 5s 7d per packet of 100 tablets and butter at £4 16s 1d per pound, are quite credible but not verifiable, but Police Court prosecutions proved that £3 4s 1d was paid for a stolen bar of soap, that a farmer sold whole milk at the rate of 2/1 per litre, and that sums ranging from 14/11 to £3 14s 9d were paid for packets of 20 cigarettes. Black market profiteers deserve our scorn but a measure of contempt is due, also, to men who bought cigarettes at the black market price and then denounced the seller to the police, thus obtaining a refund of the difference between the price they had paid and the controlled price.

After the capture by the Allies of Normandy ports we had to depend for food on such imported stocks as had not been consumed and such produce as could be obtained from the soil.

The Island's capacity for food-growing had deteriorated. A considerable area of arable and pasture land had been ruined by the Germans in making gun positions and roads leading to them and the fertility of the rest suffered from lack of manure. Lack of transport and German prohibition of access to beaches had hampered the gathering of seaweed and to make matters worse Allied aircraft had sunk off St Martin's Point a ship that was bringing a cargo of fertiliser to the Island. Until July the German authorities had insisted on much of the area under glass being devoted to the growing of tomatoes for export to Germany. In July when export was no longer possible they allowed the tomato plants to be pulled up and replaced with crops of greater food value but as there was no coal for the heating of the greenhouses they could not produce as much as they did under normal conditions. Because of the high food value of soya beans an attempt had been made to grow them locally but those grown in the open did not mature and it was found that growing under glass involved an unprofitable amount of labour. There was little that the Controlling Committee could do to increase the food producing capacity of the land, but it granted no more permits for tobacco-planting and ordered the ploughing up of all land under daffodil and tulip bulbs that had not been satisfactorily overcropped.

On July 3rd an outrageous German proclamation announced that any hay not cut within the next two days would be confiscated. As a result many farmers lost their hay because under curfew conditions all work out of doors had to cease before 9pm and farmers had to take their turn for the service of such horses as were available. More horses became available for farm-work in August when an agreement was made between the Controlling Committee and the German authorities under which farmers might exchange bulls, steers and aged cows that gave little milk for horses that had been imported by the Germans. The arrangement was satisfactory to both parties because the Germans wanted the cattle for food, and the farmers needed the horses for work on the land. Moreover the Committee considered that if we were compelled by the growing food shortage to eat horseflesh we should obtain more meat from the horses than the cattle that had been exchanged for them.

The behaviour of the German authorities seemed to show that they were influenced by three irreconcilable considerations. On the one hand it was advisable for them to antagonise the Island authorities as little as possible lest, in the event of an Allied victory, which each week seemed more probable, they should have to justify their conduct towards us before an Allied tribunal. On the other hand they had to obey orders from their superiors in Berlin to hold the Island till the last possible moment. To this end they must not only rob us of our food but must also conserve their own stocks by reducing the rations of the German troops. But they could not reduce the rations of the troops too much lest the troops, already disheartened and insufficiently fed, should mutiny.

Perhaps because the average German has a large appetite the German troops seemed to suffer from hunger even more than we did, although their rations were more liberal than ours. As early as August it was known that they were stealing cats and dogs and killing them for food. In November seventeen soldiers were poisoned – eleven fatally – by eating the roots of the Dropwort-Water Hemlock which in the autumn, when hedges are trimmed, is dug up and thrown aside to rot. These poisonous roots smell and taste like parsnips, which they resemble in shape and colour, and no doubt the poisoned men had found them when out on a food-stealing expedition and supposed them to be parsnips.

A man who declares that he would sooner starve than steal is either a liar or has never been acutely hungry. Amenable though the German rank and file are by training and temperament the German military authorities would have found it difficult to keep the troops under control if hunger had made them desperate. It was perhaps for this reason that they did so little to protect us from German food thieves. In November it was reported that German military police, catching soldiers in the act of stealing a grower's broccoli, had fired on them, killing one and wounding another. But the case was exceptional. If a man complained of being robbed by Germans, the German police would seldom do anything unless he could identify the thief or thieves. On one occasion a thief was most satisfactorily identified. A farmer who had complained that his cows were milked every night during curfew hours obtained permission from the German police to ask two of our police to keep watch in his cowshed. At one o'clock in the morning two soldiers entered the cowshed. One began to milk a cow while the other kept guard. When the police came out of their hiding place the man on guard drew his bayonet and would have stabbed one of them if the other policeman had not grabbed the bayonet by the blade. In the course of the fight that followed one of the Germans was knocked down and the policeman whose fingers had been painfully cut by the bayonet had the satisfaction of stamping on his face with his hob-nailed boots. Both Germans escaped but the two policeman made a report that was truthful in the main but not meticulously so. 'We said that one of them would have gravel rash marks on his face', said one of them when describing the scrimmage to a friend. 'We had to call it gravel rash or we should have been for it.' The soldier whose face was lacerated was identified; he betrayed his comrade, and both, it is believed, were sentenced to terms of imprisonment.

Besides taking steps to get the utmost possible amount of food from the soil the Controlling Committee had to make our stocks of imported food last till the latest possible date. The bread ration was reduced to four and a quarter pounds per week for all except adolescents and those engaged in exceptionally heavy manual work, who received additional allowances ranging from a quarter of a pound to a pound and half weekly. In October the quality of the bread deteriorated. It derived a musty flavour from an admixture of oatmeal that had become too stale to be profitably used in any other way.

Except for a slight addition at Christmas time the standard meat ration, when any was issued, was three ounces a head, and as we got this only once a fortnight during the first half of the year and once a month thereafter, meat was more of an occasional treat than an effective addition to our food supply. The fish supply was even less effective. Owing partly to the deterioration of fishermen's gear and shortage of petrol, but principally to German restrictions, so little came on the market that most people were unable to get any fish at all throughout the whole of 1944. What little did reach the market was principally in the form of the normally despised spider-crab from which a very little meat can be picked from a large amount of shell at the cost of a great deal of labour. Queues to obtain spider-crabs sometimes began to form five hours before they were expected to be on sale.

Shortage of clothing – except as regards footwear – was less serious than food shortage, for clothes can if necessary be worn long after they have reached a stage of shabbiness which in normal times would relegate them to the rag-bag. It was therefore footwear that caused the Clothing Controller his chief anxiety. Anyone who wished to have his boots repaired had first to convince the Clothing Controller that his need was urgent. At one time the Controller announced that though enough material for the repair of 120 pairs of boots was available no less than 888 people had applied for repair permits.

Electric current lasted throughout 1944 but was rationed and from September onwards was cut off at the main between 2.15 and 7pm, to the great annoyance of listeners to British news broadcasts who depended on it.

Gas was very strictly rationed and was ruthlessly cut off from houses in which the ration had been exceeded. A few days before Christmas Day the supply ceased altogether with the result that housewives who had hitherto depended on it for cooking and had no kitchen ranges had to cook as best they could with fuel burned in their sitting-room fireplaces.

Such fuel as was obtainable for these was scarce. As early as May, 1944, the ration – allowed only to households that had no means of cooking with gas or electricity – was 2 cwt of wood-fuel and ¼ cwt of household coal per month and the same quantity of 'pan-ash residue' which was officially – and apologetically – described by the Fuel Controller as 'a poor quality of coal containing a good deal of clinker'. In July, to allow of storing for winter use, a meagre ration of wood-fuel was allowed to all. Wood-fuel, besides being scarce was also costly. Blocks of green wood from recently-felled trees cost from 11/- to 14/- a cwt and dry wood, such as was obtained from the demolition of greenhouses, from 23/4 to 25/8 a cwt. Owners of trees might not fell them without the permission – often difficult to obtain – of both the German authorities and the States Fuel Controller. People who had means of transporting tar from the Gas Works, rationed at the rate of one gallon a month, mixed it with clay or ashes so as to be able to burn it in open fireplaces. Shortage of fuel affected us in several unexpected ways. 'Bramble-tea' became difficult to obtain, not because of any scarcity of blackberry leaves but because of the difficulty of drying them. For lack of fuel with which to reduce to syrup the juice of the so-called 'sugar-beet', the sugar-beet syrup that came on the market in 1944 was so thin that the Controlling Committee prohibited the sale of any that contained less than 66 per cent of soluble sugar solids. The intention was excellent but the result of the order was to drive this costly but eagerly sought commodity off the market altogether. Because salt could be obtained only by boiling sea water it could be made only by people who besides living near the sea were able by some means or other to obtain fuel. Several men convicted of stealing coke from the Gas Company pleaded in extenuation of their offence that they had stolen it in order to make salt. According to strictly unofficial information supplied by a member of the Guernsey Police Force most of the salt that was sold was made by people who had the good fortune to live near a certain inadequately guarded German fuel store. Such salt as was offered for sale was very moist and had consequently less than half the sapidity of salt that before the occupation could be bought for 2½d a pound, yet it found a ready sale – and was difficult to get – at from 3½ to 5 marks (7/5 to 10/8) a pound.

In a review of the occupation period that he made soon after it ceased, Mr Leale, the President of the Controlling Committee, revealed that as early as the spring of 1942 the possibility of appealing to the International Red Cross for help had been considered, but the matter was dropped for the time being because Jersey, unwilling to do anything that might embarrass the Home Government and fearing that if we obtained supplies through Red Cross agency our supplies from France might be endangered, was disinclined to join in the proposed appeal. The suggestion was revived when our bread ration was cut in May 1943, and the Controlling Committee decided to try and communicate with the International Red Cross and the Swiss Minister in Berlin. As a result the Bailiff asked that delegates from Guernsey might be allowed to go to Red Cross headquarters in Geneva and Dr Symons wrote to a doctor in Paris who was connected with the Red Cross. On this occasion nothing further happened at that time. In July 1944, a few weeks after the Allied invasion of Normandy had begun, letters were addressed to the Red Cross headquarters and to the Swiss Minister in Berlin but apparently they never reached their destination. During September the Bailiff of Jersey sent a strongly worded letter (copies of which reached Guernsey) to the German Commandant of the Channel Islands in which he drew attention to the increasing scarcity of food, exhaustion of stocks of anaesthetics and the grave effects which a prolongation of the siege must have on public health, and, boldly assuming that the Allies would eventually be victors, predicted that sooner or later the Allied Powers would 'pass judgment on the authorities on whose conceptions of honour, justice and humanity the fate of Occupied Peoples depended'.

On October 13th the German Commandant of Guernsey published a statement to the effect that the German Government was aware of our food situation and intended to take the necessary steps with the Protecting Power and that the matter was 'now, of course, beyond the control of the Occupying Authorities'.

This was challenged in a spirited letter, dated October 21st, signed by the Bailiff and the President of the Controlling Committee, who referred to the Hague Convention and said 'We hold that so long as you continue to exercise under it, the rights of an Occupying Power, you cannot escape from the responsibilities thereof. The only way that you can divest yourselves of your responsibilities is by giving up the rights, that is, by ceasing to be an Occupying Force'.

In his reply to this letter the Commandant said that our food shortage was due to the fact that the Islands were besieged by the Allied forces and that if a calamitous situation arose the Allies would be responsible for it.

At a meeting of the Guernsey States held on November 1st, Deputy C.H. Cross asked a number of questions regarding our food supplies. He was told among other things that if the existing bread ration were continued stocks of flour would be exhausted by January 13th and that we should have no gas or electricity after the end of December.

Soon afterwards it was known that a party of men, headed by Captain Noyon, an experienced pilot, had escaped from the Island taking with them a copy of the Bailiff of Jersey's letter and the information as to our position that Deputy Cross's questions had elicited. It was said that Captain Noyon could easily have escaped long before but had refused to do so lest the Germans should make reprisals on members of his family and that his only reason for going was that he felt it to be his duty to carry news of the Island's plight to the British Government.

On November 5th the Bailiff was allowed to send by German radio an urgent appeal for help from the International Red Cross Society and on November 22nd the Commandant of the Channel Islands announced that we were to receive a supply of medicaments, soap and parcels of foodstuffs, as a result of 'negotiations brought about by the Occupying Power'[22].

By this time most of us were suffering from chronic hunger that sapped our energies by day and made it difficult for us to sleep at nights. It would probably be no exaggeration to say that for the next five weeks we thought more about the promised food than we thought about the progress of the war. But a fortnight passed without any further announcement. Excitement gave way to despondency and some people believed that the promise of help was a silly German hoax. Hope rose again on December 8th when the Bailiff announced that the ship that was to bring us relief had been due to sail from Portugal on the previous day. Everyone made calculations as to how long she would take on the voyage and on December 9th he told schoolchildren gathered for the Intermediate Schools Prize-giving that she would arrive on the following day or the day after that. The following day was Sunday and many people spent a great part of it on the Mignot Plateau and other points of vantage eagerly scanning the horizon. She did not come that Sunday or Monday. On Tuesday we learned – this time from a British broadcast – that a Red Cross ship, the *Vega*, really was going to bring us relief and that she would start on her voyage 'in a few days' time'.

For more than a week we were kept on tenterhooks. Then on December 14th we learned from the BBC that the *Vega* would leave Lisbon between the 17th and 24th of the month and on December 20th the *Evening Press* announced that she was due to

---

22 'The Germans' said Mr Leale, in his review of the occupation period after it was over, 'were wearyingly persistent in patting themselves on the back and urging us to show more gratitude. They would have liked us to regard them as fairy godmothers. When Red Cross supplies were announced they were positively childish in their eagerness to get full share of the credit'.

arrive on Christmas Day. Some optimists hoped that she might be unloaded in time for food parcels to be distributed in time for us to have a festive meal appropriate to the season. But the day came and went and still there was no sign of the ship.

Even without the promised food-parcels, however, we were able to give somewhat of a festive character to our Christmas dinners. The Essential Commodities Committee – after a protracted struggle with the German authorities – had been able to give us six ounces of beef – twice as much as the usual monthly ration – and in addition six ounces of rice and a little cheese and cooking fat. An account of the meals eaten on Christmas Day by the family of three that has already been twice mentioned in the course of this book may help the reader to realise the conditions under which we lived. The fat ration made possible the frying of potatoes and onions – an unwonted luxury – for breakfast. The midday meal was even more luxurious. A Christmas present of eight large Bramley Seedling apples – two of which had been bartered for sugar – and the rice ration combined to make a pudding. No milk could be spared to boil with the rice but to have a pudding of any kind was a notable event. Since the gas on which the family normally relied for cooking had been cut off some days before, the meat had to be cooked on the sitting-room fire. It was therefore fortunate that the traditional turkey had not been obtainable. Even the beef had to be stewed but in view of its age and toughness this was the best way of cooking it. A stickler for formality might have considered that the dignity of the meal was somewhat marred by the fact that while it was in progress the fire had to be used for the airing of linen – the drying of which was a constant problem during the winter months – for acute shortage of household fuel precluded the burning of more than one fire at a time in the house. It was not possible to give a festal character to the day's remaining meals. 'Afternoon tea' consisted of a very little bread spread very thinly with real butter and bramble leaf tea substitute; and for supper nothing more attractive was available than soup made of cattle carrots, turnips and parsnips with a little dry bread.

At last in the middle of the morning of December 27th a ship came to anchor in the roads and those who still had binoculars, despite German orders for their surrender, were able to descry painted on her side a large Red Cross.

CHAPTER XXII

NARRATIVE, 1945

During the first four months of 1945 our thoughts centred almost entirely on food and on the progress of the war, and not until the end was obviously near did the progress of the war take first place. By that time we knew that our food troubles were nearly over.

We had much time for thought, especially in the latter part of February when the lack of artificial light drove us to spend all the hours of darkness in bed. It was impossible to sleep for twelve hours on end and there was nothing else to do but think. The psychological effect on our thoughts of insufficient food was interesting. While the cold weather lasted one thought lovingly of rich food such as crisp pork crackling, fat ham and Irish stew. Later when our sugar had come to an end memories of jam tarts were distinctly more pleasant, and later still when bulky foodstuffs such as potatoes and roots failed us and our stomachs seemed always empty our thoughts principally turned to stodgy food. Beef-steak pudding seemed more desirable than beef-steak pie and roly-poly to be preferred to the daintiest trifle.

Occasionally something happened to divert our thoughts for a while from our food troubles. Early in January we were thrilled by a BBC announcement that a man whom we knew to be a Guernseyman, Nicholas Carey, had been awarded the George Medal for conspicuous gallantry in a burning munition factory in England. Towards the end of the month we learned that two brothers named Le Page had escaped from the Island, taking with them a Frenchman whom the Germans had imported to work for them. The two brothers took with them all available documents relating to our food situation and the Frenchman hoped to arouse the interest of the French Government in the plight of other imported French labourers. The Germans unwittingly made the escape possible. Most Guernsey fishermen no longer deposited money in order to get permits to fish, as since the previous December these had been granted only on the condition that 80 per cent of each catch was to be surrendered for German consumption. The brothers undertook to fish exclusively for the Germans and volunteered to go to Alderney for lobsters, which they said were more plentiful there than around Guernsey. The Germans supplied them with a boat and some petrol – and that was the last they saw of them!

The German Army as a rule obtained its successes more by sheer weight of men and material rather than by dashing exploits, but in March, emulating Allied Commandos, a strong party drawn from the German garrisons of Guernsey and Jersey made a tip-and-run raid on Granville. Apparently they caught the American garrison napping. According to their own account, which filled most of the front page of the *Evening Press*, they destroyed locks, set the town and harbour on fire, sank a patrol boat, destroyed five small supply vessels, captured a steamer, which they brought away, took 28 prisoners and liberated 55 German soldiers, whom they brought back with them. According to the reports of friendly Germans the liberated Germans were not at all glad to be liberated. In their prison camp at Granville they had been well fed and had even had a ration of tobacco. Here they got very little food and no tobacco at all except at outrageous black market prices.

In February the Germans released all Guernseymen who were undergoing imprisonment for having been in possession of wireless sets, because of the difficulty of feeding them. One man who had been sentenced to a term of four months was released after he had been only four days in prison. The released men were told that they must each pay a fine of 300 marks and were given three months in which to pay it. As the Island was freed before the money was due they got off lightly.

The Germans had difficulty enough in feeding their own people. Part of the soldiers' rations consisted of sausages made from the hides of horses slaughtered for food and soup made from potatoes, green vegetables and roots that were sometimes partly decayed. Some of the men begged at back doors for such scraps as potato skins and the parings of turnips and even ransacked rubbish bins – a bitter humiliation for men who had come to our undefended Island as gallant conquerors. The theft of dogs and cats for food became so marked that *The Star* commented on it. 'It is evident that thieves have an especial yearning for household pets at the present time', it said. 'One street in Town which boasted a number of fine cats has been almost systematically robbed and cleared.'

Inevitably many of the men behaved recklessly. A soldier who had escaped from prison, where he had been under sentence of death for stealing his comrades' food, was seen in Hauteville by military police. He resisted arrest, was shot and so severely wounded that he had to be taken away in an ambulance. Popular rumour reported that several Germans were shot in a fracas with military police at St Martin's. *The Star* of February 28th published an announcement that a soldier had escaped from a German prison where he was under sentence of death, and that anyone who gave him food, shelter or any aid whatsoever would be severely punished. Another escaped soldier, also under sentence of death, was found in a barn at St Peter's. An officer arrested him and handed him over to two soldiers to be taken to the nearest lock-up. On the way there he knocked both soldiers down, took their weapons and escaped again. A few days later he was discovered hiding in the branches of a tree. Challenged to surrender he shot himself and fell to the ground dead.

The German Commandant in office at that time gave evidence of weakness of will by his vacillation in alternately resisting and yielding to the protests of the Controlling Committee. No doubt he felt that the meagreness of the soldiers' rations – the German hospitals were crammed with soldiers suffering from malnutrition; there were 250 in Vauquiedor alone – had created a situation beyond his control. He applied to Berlin for permission to increase the troops' rations. This would inevitably have reduced the period in which it would have been possible for the garrison to hold out. His request was refused and he was relieved of his command.

The new Commandant was an admiral, a determined Nazi and a violent Anglophobe. One of his first actions was to order the replacement of demolition mines that some time before had been removed from the New Jetty. He was, however, a just man according to his lights and he took more vigorous steps than his predecessor to protect Guernsey people from German robbers. It was generally believed that the former Commandant, realising that Germany had no chance of winning the war, would have surrendered the Island if he had not feared that Hitler would order his wife to be shot if he did so, but that the new Commandant had announced that he would hold the Island to the last. Naturally he was not popular among the starving troops. He trebled the guard outside his headquarters after being shot at twice in one week.

One night, early in April, one of the German military police was shot dead by a Georgian soldier whom he surprised in the act of milking a cow. The soldier escaped, after trying to cut the throats of two men who attempted to catch him, Mr J.P. de Garis and Mr B.A. Martel, wounding the former severely but not fatally. On the following day a notice in German and English, published in *The Star*, announced that a named Georgian soldier, probably the same man, had deserted 'after having committed an offence', called upon the population 'to report all observations liable to assure the arrest of the fugitive' and threatened the severest penalties on anyone who fed, sheltered or helped him. Another announcement in the same issue of the paper called upon the population to report anything that might indicate the whereabouts of another named Georgian soldier who, it was suggested, might have met with an accident.

Three days later it was announced that German guards and patrols had orders to use their firearms on any thief who resisted arrest by day and to shoot without challenging at night. But robberies, many of them carried out in daylight, became more and more frequent. It was impossible for any house, except the very few in which domestic servants were still employed, to be occupied continuously throughout the day, for, as tradesmen could not deliver parcels, housewives were sometimes obliged to go out to buy food. This circumstance gave burglars their opportunity. Some of them, without doubt, were Islanders, but the great majority were certainly Germans. Many Germans employed in such work as laying telephone wires across gardens were so ill-mannered as to enter private houses without knocking. This gave German thieves the opportunity to enter houses without creating suspicion in the minds of neighbours who might see them. A number of adjoining houses in Coronation Road were thoroughly ransacked during the absence of their legitimate occupants. One German who entered a house without permission, finding the housewife there, attempted to strangle her but was fortunately disturbed and ran away. In another house the owner was thrown over the bannister to the floor below and had his arm broken. In a third the householder was compelled to surrender food at the point of a revolver. A farmer, struggling on a ladder with a German who was climbing to the loft of his barn, was shot in the foot by the accidental discharge of the German's rifle. He fell to the ground and while he was lying there the German deliberately shot him again in the hip. Another Guernseyman, who went to the assistance of Guernsey police when they found German marines raiding a potato depot, received several bayonet wounds in the head. An elderly couple in the Ruettes Brayes were brutally murdered on the night after they had drawn their Red Cross parcels. In this case the murderers, who took all the food in the house, were almost certainly Germans as the murder was committed during curfew hours.

Robberies of foodstuffs from fields, gardens and outhouses exceeded those from houses by at least twenty to one. As early as January 27th the former Commandant had published a notice laying on farmers the onus of safeguarding their stores of roots and potatoes. He ordered them to clear such stores from all outbuildings at any distance from their dwellings, suggested that their own houses and those of their neighbours should be used for storage and threatened penalties under the Order for the Protection of Occupying Forces for neglect in complying. This amounted to a tacit admission of the inefficiency of the German police. Incidentally it served to protect thieves, as farmers might hesitate to report robberies lest they themselves might get into trouble.

Farmers and others with crops still in the ground had practically no protection at all against thieves. As a result, broccoli, the principal vegetable obtained in the spring, was cut long before it matured, lest it should be stolen. Few of the heads of broccoli that came on the market were larger than hen's eggs. The Potato Controller reported to the Controlling Committee that of the produce of 115 fields that he had bought on behalf of the community 20 per cent had been stolen and the President of the Glasshouse Utilisation Board said that there was a danger that growers might cease to grow vegetables, partly because of irritation caused by the many conflicting orders they received from the German authorities and by the German requisitioning of greenhouses but principally because theft of crops on the large scale that prevailed made growing unprofitable.

As it was no longer possible to import coal from France scarcity of fuel created almost as great a problem as scarcity of food, for without fuel to cook it our food ration was useless. With a view to ameliorating the situation the Controlling Committee began to make plans as early as August 1944, for the establishment of more communal kitchens. Managers of hotels and restaurants were asked whether they could use wood fuel in their kitchen ranges and how many gallons of stew they could supply twice daily. Their answers were not encouraging and it was realised that States-owned kitchens would have to be built. A public appeal was made for the loan of coppers and galvanised iron tanks and in November it was announced that 21 communal kitchens would be opened of which five would be in St Peter Port. Those who intended to use them were required to register their names and were warned that when the time came they would have to surrender their rations of potatoes, meat and the cereal food such as macaroni, that was occasionally issued, keeping back only their bread, milk, butter and when a ration was issued – sugar. Fewer people registered than had been expected, probably because bakers, whose ovens retained heat for some hours after the bread had been taken from them, were able three times a week to help their customers by stewing pots of roots or baking dishes of potatoes. The communal kitchens opened on Christmas Day, continued to function for nine weeks and then closed down from lack of potatoes and roots to cook.

No one who lived through the German occupation of Guernsey is likely to forget the fuel shortage. Of its last few months, even one who had no first-hand knowledge of it could form an idea of its severity from a study of our newspapers of the period. In February an advertiser offered to barter anything that it was permissible to barter for flooring boards.[23] People whose garden-gates were made of wood were warned to remove them lest they should be stolen. A man, fined 10/- for stealing a door and some planks from an unoccupied house, offered no excuse except that if he had not taken them someone else would have done so. Another man who pulled down and carried away a telephone pole did not get off so lightly. He was sentenced to pay a fine of 20/- and to fourteen days' imprisonment. By the time that liberation brought us supplies of fuel from England there was scarcely a household in the Island that had not had to sacrifice wardrobes, tables, chests of drawers, writing desks and pianos to get fuel with which to cook their daily meals. Another serious result of the fuel shortage was that it became impossible for the Emergency Hospital to launder the patients' bed linen. It was illegal for anyone to fell his own trees without the permission of both the Fuel Controller and the German authorities. At a meeting of the Controlling Committee, when Mr Jones commented on the unfairness of this restriction since the Germans felled trees indiscriminately, Mr Martel said that in his capacity as Public Prosecutor he had, in recent cases, advised the magistrates to deal leniently with such offenders.

The Germans had the advantage of us in every way. Besides taking fuel that we were not allowed to take they requisitioned a large proportion of our home-grown food – beans, potatoes, roots and green vegetables – despite protests from the Controlling Committee. They demanded so much of our milk that our ration was officially reduced to half a pint (and separated milk

---

23 It was illegal to barter rationed food or the contents of Red Cross parcels. The advertiser did not offer cash because money was a drug on the market in comparison with food and fuel.

at that) on each of five days in the week – i.e. 2½ pints in the seven days – and in actual fact we often got much less. In one week in April we got no more than half a pint in the whole seven days. Sometimes the German authorities made specious excuses for robbing us. For example, soon after our first food parcels reached us they took so much of the butter that the Controlling Committee had to reduce our butter ration (which had to serve for cooking and all purposes) to 2 oz per head per week, with an additional half an ounce every fifth week. The German excuse was that:-

> The food parcels from the International Red Cross contain in the form of butter, milk-powder and cheese a sufficient quantity of fat, which, distributed over four weeks and added to the 8.6 grammes a day guaranteed by the Occupying Power in the course of negotiations with England, represents suitable supplies of fat for the civilian population.

On the same excuse they requisitioned the whole milk previously allowed to young children.

On one occasion the Germans demanded the delivery of 20 tons of potatoes on the following morning. On this occasion the demand was obeyed as the Committee was powerless to resist it, but when they demanded 1,000 tons they were told that if the demand were obeyed the Islanders would be reduced to such a state of starvation that work, on the land and elsewhere, would become impossible. Because of the very high food value of dried beans the Controlling Committee had asked growers in the summer of 1944 to grow as many as possible under glass for use in the following winter and to ensure them against loss promised to fix the controlled price at 4/- a pound, about twelve times the normal pre-war price. In October of that year the Platzkommandant demanded that the whole bean crop should he collected and sixty tons of it handed over to the Germans. The Committee feared that if the German authorities sent German soldiers to search growers' premises for beans the more timid members of the community might suffer. They therefore issued an order to growers to send their beans to the Glasshouse Utilisation Board, making it clear that the order was issued under German compulsion. The result of the order must have made the Germans realise that it is easier to make an order than to enforce it, for the response was almost negligible. Scarcely a tithe of the amount of the beans that they knew to have been grown was surrendered. What had happened was that the majority of the growers, realising that any beans they surrendered would be eaten by Germans, had decided to keep them and sell them surreptitiously to their fellow-islanders. Some of the growers profited by the urgent need of their fellow countrymen by demanding six shillings or more a pound, prices that were readily paid, but others to their honour asked no more – and would take no more – than the four shillings a pound that the Controlling Committee had promised them. It was a black market transaction, as both buyer and seller were disobeying the law, but one that, unlike most black market transactions, was entirely honourable to both parties concerned.

The Germans were told that the garrison could hold out for a year. The statement was probably made to strengthen their morale, but we gathered the impression that the Anglophobe Admiral, who was the last Commander of Guernsey, intended to hold out while any chance remained of Germany being able to get peace on terms more favourable than unconditional surrender. The fighting power of the garrison was by this time severely reduced. Many men had to be put on such light duties as cook-house fatigue because their boots were falling to pieces, and all the men were ordered to husband their strength by remaining in their quarters daily from noon till 3pm.

We were in worse case than the soldiers. Employers of labour had long before found it useless to expect a normal amount of work from their workmen and it was found necessary drastically to reduce the hours of labour. Our food ration was less than that of the German troops and as we had suffered severely from lack of nourishment in spite of our Red Cross parcels it is no exaggeration to say that without them we should have actually starved.

The *Vega*, the ship chartered by the International Red Cross to bring us relief reached Guernsey for the first time on December 27th and the first issue of food parcels was made on the following Sunday, December 31st, by grocers throughout the Island who had all undertaken to open their shops on that day and distribute the parcels to their registered customers. The parcels were of two kinds, some such as were sent to Canadian prisoners of war, others as sent to New Zealanders. The Canadian parcels contained 6 oz of chocolate, 20 oz of biscuits, 5 oz of Canadian sardines, 20 oz of milk powder, 6 oz of prunes, 10 oz of salmon, 14 oz of corned beef, 8 oz of raisins, 8 oz of sugar, 4 oz of tea, 4 oz of cheese, 16 oz of marmalade or jam, 20 oz of ham and, in some cases, a little pepper and salt and a cake of soap – a total of 153 oz of food. The New Zealand parcels contained a little less weight – 135 oz – and variety, but in the opinion of some people were of somewhat greater food value:- 6 oz of tea, 19 oz of corned mutton, 15 oz of lamb and green peas, 8 oz of chocolate, 20 oz of butter, 15 oz of coffee and milk, 10 oz of sugar, 9 oz of dried peas, 16 oz of jam, 16 oz of condensed milk, 15 oz of cheese and 6 oz of raisins. Happily, as most of the food was already cooked, it made no great demand on our very limited supplies of fuel.

As the *Vega* was said to have brought 42,400 food parcels, enough to give two apiece to everyone, we hoped that a second distribution would be made a fortnight later but three days after we received the first parcel we were officially warned to make it last a calendar month. Excellent advice but difficult to follow! Spread over a period of twenty-eight days a Canadian parcel afforded rather less than 5½ oz of food a day and a New Zealand parcel rather more than 4¾ oz. Little enough but it made all the difference between semi-starvation and actual starvation.

One elderly man, far from trying to make his food parcel last a month, feasted so grossly as soon as he received it that later in the day he had to be operated on with a stomach pump.

The sale or purchase of the contents of the food parcels was strictly forbidden. One man, convicted of selling the tea that he had received for 40 marks (£4 5s 0d) was fined £10 and the Red Cross authorities were asked to ensure that no more food parcels should be issued to him.

Besides the 42,400 ordinary food parcels the *Vega* brought 1,500 parcels of food especially suited for invalids, a small amount of urgently needed medical supplies,[24] 23 sacks of salt, 43 cases of soap, 9 cases of tobacco and cigarettes and 2 cases of infants' clothing bought from a fund raised by Lady Campbell, wife of the British Minister in Lisbon. Smokers who had smoked nothing better than dried bean leaves during the previous year or so were rejoiced to learn that tobacco had arrived but they had to wait seven weeks before it was distributed.

The Island's most urgent needs were discussed at a conference between members of the Controlling Committee, the German authorities and representatives of the International Red Cross who had come on the *Vega*. The Red Cross representatives were told that we needed fuel, especially gas coal, almost as urgently as food, and were asked to bring us as well flour, yeast, clothing, boots, candles, matches, and flints for petrol lighters. As the *Vega*'s cargo capacity was very limited hopes were held out that another Red Cross ship might be chartered, and a hospital-ship sent to evacuate invalids who required treatment which it was impossible for them to obtain in the Island. Neither of these hopes was fulfilled, though in the case of the invalids the German authorities, to whose interest it was that food-consumers who could make no contribution to Allied war effort should be evacuated, went so far as to have invalids who wished to go medically examined by German doctors.

Towards the end of the month a disquieting rumour arose that when Red Cross parcels were next issued there would not be enough to go round, because by some mistake the *Vega* had taken away to Jersey 2,000 parcels that should have been landed here. The rumour proved to be true. There was much speculation as to who would have to go without. Parcels were distributed again on Sunday, January 28th (exactly a calendar month after

---

24   By this time wounds were dressed with paper as bandages were unprocurable.

the first issue) except to residents of Sark (which was richer than Guernsey in milk and butter), children under four years old, and one member in every family of four or more persons. Hopes were officially held out that these would be compensated as soon as a surplus of parcels had accumulated.

The next disquieting rumour that arose was that our stocks of flour were so reduced that we should have no more bread after February 10th. We found some comfort in the belief that the *Vega* due to return four weeks after her first visit, or an auxiliary ship, would bring us flour. But she did not return at the expected time and anxiety deepened. Day after day our hopes were raised by rumours that a Red Cross ship had been sighted off the south-west of the Island, but sank again when the rumours proved to be untrue. As time went on even the German authorities became uneasy. They sent out enquiries by radio as to the *Vega*'s whereabouts but received no answer, and the Bailiffs of Guernsey and Jersey were allowed by the Germans to send a wireless message to the Secretary-General of the International Red Cross stating that both Islands' need of flour was urgent. At last on February 6th, nearly six weeks after her first visit, the *Vega* returned. She brought food parcels, medical supplies and salt, but no flour, and, as feared, bread rations were issued for the last time for the time being on February 10th. To alleviate distress the Bailiff's Red Cross Supplies Committee took the risk – a very grave risk in view of the possibility of a still more serious crisis at some later date – of deciding to issue Red Cross parcels twice instead of once in the coming month, and the Essential Commodities Committee promised to try and let us have more liberal grocery rations in the week beginning February 18th.

The more liberal ration when we got it consisted of macaroni, and cheese, in the usual small quantities, a little mouldy flour (the scrapings of the baker's bins) and a double ration of butter. By the irony of circumstances when we had both an unusually generous amount of butter and a supply of Red Cross jam we had no bread to spread them on!

Our entire ration in the week beginning February 25th consisted of 1½ oz of macaroni, the same weight of mouldy oatmeal flour, 5 pounds of potatoes, the same weight of roots and 2 pints of separated milk (half a pint on one day in the week and a quarter of a pint on each of the remaining days). No butter or cooking fat, no meat and, of course, no bread! In the week beginning March 6th we had no grocery ration at all. Happily, we still had potatoes though the supply did not last much longer. Cigarettes brought by the *Vega* were issued for the first time on February 19th – 40 to each adult. Many women who had seldom or never smoked before were glad to get the cigarettes as they found that smoking alleviated the pangs of hunger.

As we had been promised another food parcel on March 3rd we could afford to be a little less parsimonious in our consumption of the former one. Nevertheless, the period from February 13th onwards was emphatically a hunger period, as is illustrated by an extract from a diary kept by a member of the already-mentioned family of three.

> March 6th. Breakfast: radishes, stewed swedes.
> Dinner: stewed swedes, the greater part of a 10 oz tin of Canadian salmon, and cocoa.
> Afternoon tea: substitute-tea, jam spread on slices of cold boiled potatoes.
> Supper: radishes, stewed swedes flavoured with a sauce made of the remainder of the salmon.

The salmon, cocoa and jam were, of course, from a Red Cross parcel. Radishes by this time were fairly plentiful. Their principal value was that to a certain extent they provided the bulk that we missed when the bread ration ceased and helped to give an illusive sense of repletion. The bright side of the dismal period was that our rations cost us so little, in one week our entire food ration cost only 1/4 per head, of this sum we paid a penny for milk and the rest for bread – no groceries, no potatoes and no roots were issued. Outside the official ration we could buy lettuces and radishes fairly easily, but spinach with some difficulty and, if we were very lucky, cabbage and immature broccoli. We paid nothing for our Red Cross parcels except what we voluntarily subscribed to Red Cross funds.[25]

From February 23rd onwards we had no more electric light and had to choose between going to bed in the dark or being in bed before eight o'clock in the evening, German time. This was not so much a hardship as a blessing in disguise. Because of the acute shortage of fuel, we were never really warm except in bed and the necessity of resting for nearly twelve hours in each twenty-four helped us to feel the effects of semi-starvation less than we should have done if we had been more active.

On March 6th the *Vega* came again. This time, to our great delight, she brought 155 tons of flour besides parcels and two days later we received a ration of 2 pounds of bread. It came just in time for in that week we ate the last of our potatoes.

Once again it was possible to spread butter and jam on something more suitable than boiled potato. The temptation to indulge imprudently was too great for one person at least. With his afternoon tea that day he ate two thick slices of bread and butter, two thick slices of bread and jam and a 'captain's biscuit' lavishly spread with butter. Such indulgence seriously depleted his stock of butter and jam and, as if Fate wished to punish him for his greed, the last meal that he ate before parcels were again distributed consisted of the tough outside leaves of broccoli, minced, stewed and enriched with so-called 'calves' foot jelly' made by boiling down hides. But the orgy was worth the cost. Normally he rose from a meal feeling that he would gladly sit down at once to another, but the lavish meal that he ate so improvidently gave him a blessed sense of repletion such as he had not had for many months.

Badly needed though it was, the quality of the flour caused a certain amount of disappointment. It was of the superfine type used in making puff-pastry and luxury cakes, but as it lacked the 'roughage' to which our coarse, wholemeal bread had made us accustomed it was less satisfying and, indeed, less wholesome.

---

25 The Island's total contribution was £46,000. Besides this the Red Cross Message Bureau collected £2,500 of which £855 went to local charities, £30 to the *Secours National* in return for a gift of biscuits sent by that society to Guernsey children, and the rest to the Red Cross.

Soon after we received it very many people suffered so severely from constipation that Dr Symons, the Health Services Officer, knowing that such remedies as Epsom salts and Seidlitz powders were practically unobtainable, published a recommendation that sufferers should eat boiled stinging nettles as a vegetable, and appealed to herbalists and others who knew of other medicinal plants obtainable from hedgerows to put their knowledge at the service of the public.

The supply of tomato purée, made when in the previous summer a glut of tomatoes was caused by the impossibility of shipping them to France, came to an end early in March. We did not feel its loss so much as we might have done. Many people valued it principally because it served to disguise the flavour of the parsnips that they disliked but were compelled by hunger to eat, but by this time we had no more parsnips so we did not need sauce to help us eat them.

From March 10th onwards, owing to lack of fuel to drive the Water Board's pumping engines, the water supply was cut off daily except for an hour and a half each morning and an hour each afternoon. As often happened, the German authorities under threat of punishment for sabotage issued orders as to the use of water drawn during these hours that they could not possibly enforce. It was forbidden to use it for washing, cleansing of premises, flushing water-closets or for any other purpose except drinking and cooking, and no more was to be drawn than was needed for these latter purposes. Shortage of water in which to wash was not felt as much of a hardship as it might have been in normal times for the necessity of rigid economy in the use of soap had induced the habit of washing less frequently than is usual in self-respecting communities. Very often a housewife would look ruefully at her soot-blackened hands and hesitate whether to wash them with soap at once or – in view of the probability that if she did so they would soon be dirty again – do the best she could with cold water and a nail brush and defer using soap until just before going to bed. When next the *Vega* visited the Island she brought two doctors whom the International Red Cross authorities had sent to report on the general health of the Islanders. Under the excuse that their credentials were not in order the German authorities did not allow them to come ashore or to have any conversation with representatives of the Islanders. The real reason probably was that the Germans did not wish them to learn anything about the insanitary conditions prevailing on the Island. After former visits of the *Vega* the Health Services Officer had protested against the Germans' refusal to allow any intercourse between Red Cross officials and Island officials except in the presence of Germans.

The *Vega* came for the fourth time on April 5th, again bringing flour besides 119 bales of clothing and 153 cases of boots as well as food parcels. As she was a comparatively small vessel she could not, on the third and fourth trip, bring as many food parcels as she had previously brought. Consequently, before parcels were again delivered the Bailiff appealed to all – such as farmers – who could forego them without undue hardship to undertake to do so for the benefit of the less fortunate. The response to his appeal was apparently unsatisfactory. A distribution of parcels had been promised for April 28th but when that day came there were only 8,436 parcels (including parcels especially suited to invalids) to be divided among about 22,700 people – approximately one-third of a parcel to each. The parcels were therefore unpacked by trustworthy volunteer workers and of their contents smaller parcels were made, great care being taken to ensure that each should have approximately the same food value.

By this time the food situation was becoming desperate. Rations of old potatoes and roots had ceased and the promise of a ration of a pound a head of new potatoes grown under glass did not materialise because the Germans took them. Apart from our meagre bread ration, reduced to 3 pounds per head per week, and the small amount of foodstuffs that we got from the International Red Cross we now had practically nothing to eat except the tough outer leaves of broccoli – and it was difficult to get even these. It may be imagined with what gratitude one household received enough young greenhouse-grown carrots to make a meal and how acute was the disaster when, owing to the difficulty of cooking on a fireplace that was not designed for the purpose, the pot in which they were cooking capsized into the fire!

But now it was obvious even to the most pessimistic that the end of our troubles was in sight. There was still the possibility, however, that our Anglophobe Commandant, even after Germany had capitulated, would refuse to surrender the Island. After the death of Hitler, he had summoned the leading officers under his command to a meeting at the Royal Hotel and had announced his intention of holding the Island so long as any food remained. This information came from friendly anti-Nazi Germans who added that as soon as the officers left the meeting they discussed the matter with each other and were determined that they would not fight. We learned when we were liberated that elaborate plans for the invasion of the Island, if necessary, had been made. If it had been invaded and if – as was very doubtful – the German garrison had resisted with any stoutness, the local people could hardly have escaped a share of the bloodshed that would have been inevitable. Happily, the Commandant did not hold to his intention. But he clung to what shreds of dignity remained to him. When on May 8th a British warship arrived off the south coast of the Island to arrange the terms of surrender the Commandant sent out a subordinate instructed to say that the surrender of Germany to the Allied Powers would not take effect until one minute after midnight and that if the warship did not withdraw out of range until then she ran the risk of being fired on. The warship accordingly withdrew for the time being. Early next morning a German major-general boarded her and signed the terms of the surrender. Later in the morning the Island, which the Germans had made one of the most impregnable fortresses in the world, which still held a garrison of thousands of soldiers and had a reserve of 16,000 tons of ammunition, was occupied by an advance party of one British officer and twenty-five men!

CHAPTER XXIII

AN ATTEMPT AT A RIGHT JUDGEMENT OF OUR ENEMIES

All wars tend to sow seeds of hate which, if left to germinate, may produce more wars. Lest the one through which we have come should leave the spawn of another, perhaps still more terrible, war it is the duty of every decent man to co-operate in laying the foundations of a lasting peace by doing his utmost to eradicate any seeds of hate which the late war may have left. To do this it would be well to try dispassionately, without rancour and without sentimentality, to examine German mentality and German conduct in their proper light. Sentimentality is to be as much avoided as rancour because it is seldom quite sincere and is liable to defeat its own object in the minds of the practical minded.

For two reasons we who were under German domination for nearly five years should be exceptionally well qualified to represent the German as he really is. In the first place because, though most of us as far as possible avoided direct contact with Germans, it was impossible to hold so completely aloof from them as not to get some first-hand knowledge of them. Secondly, because it was our lot to live comparatively remote from the war's realities. We did not have to spend night after night in air raid shelters; our homes were not shattered by flying bombs; and therefore we had no excuse for feeling the animosity that others, less fortunate than us in this respect, might naturally feel.

At first most of us were inclined to regard every German with whom we came in contact with profound dislike if not with actual hatred, and to regard him, if not as a war criminal, at least as an abettor of war criminals, in that he was in the same service as those who perpetrated acts of *schrehklichkeit*[26], such as firing on the crew of the Guernsey lifeboat. Yet it was difficult to hold quite aloof from them. Some of them were were obviously anxious to make friends with us. Of these the best educated

---

26 *schrecklichkeit* (German) meaning awfulness.

seniors seemed by their manner to show that they realised that we had good reason to despise them as abettors of Nazism but the younger ones showed no sign of embarrassment when attempting to establish friendly relations with us.

As time went on most of us were compelled to admit in our own minds that many of the Germans among us were behaving very well. Examples of acts of courtesy and kindness have been given in Chapter XIX. One instance of chivalry of a very high order has been reserved for this chapter. A party of German soldiers, among whom were some Guernseymen employed by the Germans, were at work at the airport when a British plane arrived out of the blue and sprayed them with machine-gun fire. All ran for cover, but a Guernseyman who was among them tripped and fell so heavily that for the moment he could not rise, whereupon a German private lay on top of his prostrate body shielding it with his own, saying something to the effect that the airman meant his bullets for Germans, not for his own countrymen[27].

The goodwill towards us shown by some individual Germans made it impossible to behave discourteously to those who made overtures of friendship. The younger ones among these showed great anxiety to justify their country's conduct. They said that it was through no fault of the German people that their country and ours were at war, protested that Germans liked and admired the British, and asked why Britain had shattered the friendship between the two countries by declaring war without cause. If told that Britain could not hold aloof while Germany broke one treaty after another they asked indignantly if the violation of treaties was a new thing in history. If told that Germany's attack on Poland had been wanton, they merely replied that the Poles were a truculent people. If challenged to justify Germany's invasion of Denmark and Norway they said that Germany, having been 'illegally robbed' of her colonies, must seek living-

---

[27] I should like to be able to record that gallant German's name, but I did not hear of the incident until after he had left the Island. The Guernseyman who told me of it said that he believed his name to be Karl Müller, but he was not at all sure about it.

room elsewhere. They seemed really to believe that such answers were indisputable and it seemed obvious that in making them they were repeating arguments that they had heard from others.

Heated argument had to be avoided for we rendered ourselves liable to imprisonment if we uttered anti-German propaganda. Otherwise one might have pressed the matter further and asked if it were possible to justify such barbarities as the bombing of Belgrade without warning, with the consequent slaughter of hundreds of civilians, in spite of the fact that the town was undefended and that Germany had not declared war on Yugoslavia. If they had been asked such a question and if they had sufficiently come under Nazi influence it was conceivable that they might have returned an answer which, though such an answer as few Englishmen would have given, would have been logical and defensible. They might conceivably have said 'War, in any case, is a foul thing and the use of any weapon that may tend to shorten it is justifiable. It is ridiculous to be scrupulous; to maintain that one weapon is legitimate and that another is not. If it is lawful to kill your enemy with machine-guns and high explosive shells why hesitate to use poison-gas? Since the combatant that strikes first has an immense advantage over his opponent why should he be handicapped by the convention that requires a declaration of war before striking? And as for the bombing of open towns, if you can weaken your enemy by the indiscriminate slaughter of civilians of the State with which you are at war why should you be more reluctant to kill them than to kill soldiers? Civilians have their part in creating a state of war, why should they escape the horrors of war? Honour and chivalry have no place in modern warfare. They are mere abstract ideas and any nation that allows itself to be handicapped by regard for them will never attain world dominion.' It has been demonstrated again and again that this is the Nazi view as to how war should be conducted and there can be little injustice in saying that it was accepted without question by many Germans who in their private lives may be both chivalrous and honourable.

It is a defect of many schools that children are not taught to think. It seems that German schools are still more defective in that the German child is actually taught not to think. Independent thought is for his elders; his part is to believe what he is told to believe. The average German feels proud to wear a uniform and salute a superior. He likes being drilled and it is even possible that he enjoys marching at the absurdly pompous goose-step. We should not quarrel with him on that account, but he is to be blamed in that he would rather implicitly obey an order than use his own judgement as to whether an order is lawful or unlawful. John Gunter in his book *Inside Europe* said 'Scratch a German and you will find a sheep', like most pithy sayings that is true only in part. Courage, for example, is not a quality that one associates with sheep and as a whole Germans are unquestionably courageous. But it is true that the average German feels lost without a leader and is all too ready to obey any leader who calls on him to follow. It was that characteristic that gave Adolf Hitler his opportunity. When first he sprang into prominence Germany was in a state of chaos. Its empire had broken up, its emperor had fled, the Imperial Crown under which it had risen to a dominating position on the continent of Europe was abolished, and its people were impoverished, humiliated, split into warring factions, bewildered and in a mood to follow anyone – hero, prophet or political mountebank – who seemed competent to lead them. Hitler promised to restore order, to show them a way out of their misery, to revive their self-respect and create for them a greater Empire than the one they had lost – and the majority of them followed him blindly.

That the ignorant rank and file should follow Hitler blindly was perhaps excusable, especially since many social welfare movements, such as the 'Strength through Joy' organisation, for which he was largely responsible, were excellent. But what can be said for the better educated who must have realised, after he had come into power, that lies, fraud, treachery and the ruthless persecution of helpless minorities were the principal tools of his statecraft. Had they been honourable men would they not have refused to serve under him? Are we not justified in despising them as accomplices in his war guilt? If we do despise them, we must also pity them. Their position was very difficult. Hitler's rise to power was so rapid that before any but the most far-sighted Germans realised it, he and his Nazi organisation had paralysed the whole nation in a strangle-hold grip. Many escaped into voluntary exile. Those who stayed found themselves constantly watched by the Gestapo, Hitler's secret police, and had to choose between two alternatives – on the one hand submission, on the other imprisonment in internment camp for themselves and poverty and misery for their families. It was a terribly hard choice and no-one should condemn them without first considering what he himself would have done in their place.

One of the Germans who sought to establish friendly relations with a Guernseyman was asked – more out of politeness than from curiosity – what part of Germany was his home. He replied that it was in Hamburg and went on to describe going home on leave and reaching the outskirts of the city during its first heavy bombardment. He had gone into the city as soon as possible after the raiding bombers had gone and had had difficulty not only in recognising his own house but even the street in which it stood. When he did locate his house he found it partially ruined. It had been on fire in places and some of the woodwork was still smouldering. Up to that point he had spoken with restraint but his voice broke with emotion as he told of his frantic search for any trace of his wife and children; of how the heat from the smouldering woodwork was so great that the electric torch he carried became almost too hot to hold; of his difficulty in making his way through the debris that choked the stairway leading to the cellar; of how as he did so he was tormented by the smell of burnt flesh; and of how relieved he had been to find the cellar empty and that the smell of burnt flesh came from the ashes of a hutch that had contained rabbits. Could anyone, after hearing that piteous tale – told without any sign of animosity against the airmen who had wrecked his home and made his wife and children homeless – look on that unfortunate German with hatred as on an enemy or with contempt as an accomplice of Hitler's war guilt, especially when after he had recovered his composure he described the terrible power that Hitler's secret police had obtained over the German people and when, finally, he spoke of the relief it gave to his feelings to talk more freely to one who was technically his enemy than he would dare to talk to any stranger among his own countrymen? (In December, 1941, because he could do nothing to brighten the Christmas season for his own little children in Germany, this German entrusted a Guernseyman with one hundred marks, locally worth ten pounds, thirteen shillings and fourpence, to be spent on poor children in Guernsey.) That man frankly admitted that, though he was a German and proud of being a German, he looked forward eagerly to a British victory that would free the German people from the tyranny that oppressed them. One could but feel that the Allies were waging war not only for their own safety but also for the welfare and liberty of all decent Germans. Such at any rate was the conclusion arrived at by one person at least who lived for over four years under German domination – one in whom dislike almost amounting to hatred turned gradually to a more tolerant attitude, and one who, realising that no one is able to choose the land of his birth, grew ever more grateful to Providence for granting him, through no merit of his own – unless perhaps it were merit acquired in a former existence – the blessing of birth into a free nation.

INDEX

A

Africa 144
airport 36, 37, 84, 85, 86, 94, 104, 127, 144, 156, 203, 252, 254, 262, 276, 318
air raid precautions 4, 256
Air Raid Precautions Organisation 31, 84, 246, 255
air raids 4, 34, 35, 36, 75, 83, 86, 94, 103, 104, 129, 130, 131, 132, 135, 136, 137, 155, 156, 160, 189, 213, 221, 255, 281, 282, 283, 284, 285, 286, 317
air-raid warning 34, 35, 36
alcohol 37
   beer 72, 171
   benedictine 172
   brandy 172, 260, 287
   crème de menthe 172
   'Sarnia Wine' 171
   whisky 172
   wine 72, 133, 139, 171, 172, 248, 249
Alderney 6, 12, 24, 30, 31, 69, 87, 201, 202, 203, 204, 205, 206, 207, 246, 301
   British raids on 207
   forced labour 203, 207, 208
   houses demolished 207
   liberation of 207
   looting trials 204, 205, 206
   salvage party 202, 204
aliens, restrictions on 5
Ali, Raschid 225
Allan, William 99, 100
Allez Street 146
Allied invasion of Normandy xvii, 207, 268, 283, 284, 287, 290, 295. *See also* D-Day (5 June 1944)
   visible from Alderney 207
Amherst Road 263
Amherst School 128
Angell, Mr M.N. 164
Arnold, Mr S.H. 59, 164
Association of Berlin Artistes 274
Atlantic Wall 284

B

Bailiff of Guernsey vii, xvi, xxi, 7, 9, 15, 16, 17, 18, 25, 28, 33, 36, 61, 87, 97, 108, 112, 115, 117, 121, 122, 123, 126, 148, 150, 154, 198, 199, 201, 240, 245, 274, 295, 296, 297, 311, 315. *See also* Carey, Victor (later Sir)
Bailiff's Fund 150, 154
Battle of Britain 262, 263
BBC xix, 7, 41, 84, 85, 88, 107, 123, 124, 129, 130, 135, 136, 137, 138, 142, 190, 214, 218, 268, 281, 297, 300
beaches, prohibition of access 79, 281, 290
Beaucamps 263
Beaulieu Hotel 127
Bec du Nez 78
bed linen 235, 251, 306
Bel Air Hotel, Sark 209, 211, 212
Belgium, invasion of 5
Belgrade, bombing of 319
Belgrave Bay 79, 212
Bell, Mr 112
Berthou, M. 54
Best, Mr A. 59
Bichard, Herbert 91
Bichard, Mrs 149
bicycles 46, 63, 191, 245
Billet d'Etat 115
Bird, Elise 100
Bird, Mary 98
Bird, Walter 99, 100
Bird, Wilfred 98, 100
black market 159, 162, 169, 178, 184, 195, 229, 231, 238, 289, 290, 301, 308
black-out regulations 4, 38, 256
Blanchelande 187
boats. *See* fishing boats; *See* cargo boats; *See* mail boats
Boer War xii, xiii
Bolshevists 223, 224, 225, 226, 283
books, confiscation of 259
Boots the Chemist 32, 151
Bordage 285
Bordeaux 22

323

Bordeaux Harbour 57, 88, 94
Bougourd, Mr 280
Bougourd, police constable 32
Boulogne 6, 8
Boy Scouts 24
Bragg, Mr S.J. 59
Brecqhou 3, 66, 208
Brehon tower 156, 282
Bremen 88, 107, 222
British Empire 7, 39, 221, 266
British forces 37, 93, 104, 122, 133
   airmen landing 156, 242, 247
   attacks on German forces 76, 77, 83, 85, 86, 94, 103, 104, 129, 130, 131, 136, 137, 160, 189, 203, 207, 209, 210, 211, 212, 214, 222, 233, 255, 256, 263, 266, 276, 282, 283, 284, 285, 318
   in hiding 95, 96, 97
   on leave in island 37, 83, 241
   reconnaissance 79, 104, 131
British Government 7, 8, 9, 17, 18, 25, 26, 102, 148, 149, 201, 221, 227, 267, 268, 297
Brock, Air Commodore Henry Le Marchant xxi, 2
Buckingham Palace 91, 107, 262
Burhou 3, 246
bus services 46, 63, 191
butchers 159

C

Calais, France 268
Calais, St Martin's 156
Campbell, Lady 310
Canada 216, 288
Canadian destroyer, visit 287
Candie Grounds 258
Candie Road 131, 251
Cantan, Captain 78
Carey, Nicholas 300
Carey, Victor (later Sir) vii, xvi, xxi, 15. *See also* Bailiff of Guernsey
cargo boats 5, 24, 27, 28, 29, 284
cars. *See* motor vehicles
Casquets 90, 280, 282
Castel 4, 131, 267
Castel Methodist Church 267
Castel School 267
Castle Cornet 30, 80, 83, 135, 137

Castle Emplacement 30, 59, 60
casualties
   French 137
   German. *See* German forces, casualties
   Guernseymen 131, 132, 133, 135, 136, 137, 246, 283, 303, 304
cats 28, 291, 302
   theft of 302
cattle 15, 19, 23, 50, 52, 55, 68, 69, 143, 159, 181, 202, 250, 291, 298
Chamber of Commerce 4
Channel Islands Refugee Committee 190
Channel Islands Society 280
Château des Marais 30
Cherbourg 6, 214, 288
children 6, 9, 10, 11, 12, 13, 15, 16, 17, 18, 20, 21, 23, 24, 29, 44, 45, 46, 47, 69, 73, 88, 92, 108, 119, 139, 150, 153, 160, 161, 168, 170, 172, 173, 174, 179, 180, 190, 202, 209, 233, 234, 239, 244, 277, 283, 307, 311, 313, 319, 321, 322
   news of those evacuated 29
   nourishment 239
Children's Emergency Bureau 150, 172, 270
Chouet 79
Christmas 51, 73, 108, 133, 149, 177, 181, 203, 261, 264, 293, 294, 298, 306, 322
Christ's Hospital (school) xi, xiii, xxiv
Churchill, Sir Winston 160, 194, 222, 225, 226, 268
church services 39
cigarettes 72, 132, 153, 175, 176, 203, 209, 287, 290, 310, 312
   attempts at rationing 72
   black market prices 290
cinemas 4
clothing 315
   for deportees 150, 151
   shortages 150, 151, 158, 172, 173, 293, 310
clubs and societies, ban on meetings 103
coal 6, 47, 59, 60, 61, 63, 64, 68, 164, 165, 166, 180, 184, 186, 243, 250, 269, 290, 294, 305, 310
   import from France 305
Cobo 79, 156, 259, 263
Collas, Miss 93
Collenette, Mr 62

324

INDEX

Collings Road 133, 134
Collins, Mr 81
Commercial Arcade 266
communications with England 43, 49, 60, 75, 77, 87, 97, 110, 190, 191, 201, 207, 208. *See also* Red Cross, messages
Constables 9, 13, 16, 27, 31
Controlling Committee. *See* States of Guernsey, (Emergency) Controlling Committee
Corbet, Mr 280
Corbière 130
Cornet Street 146, 261
Coronation Road 304
Courier (ship) 24, 30, 31, 34, 201, 202, 205
cows 52, 55, 69, 202, 203, 244, 253, 291, 292
crockery shortage 234
Cross, Deputy C.H. 19, 296
curfew 37, 48, 113, 115, 120, 121, 139, 145, 196, 215, 236, 252, 276, 291, 292, 304
currency 231, 232, 237, 289. *See* money
  reichskreditkassen 41, 236, 237

D

dairy. *See* States of Guernsey, Dairy
Dartmouth 280
Davies, Major R.G. 271, 272
D-Day (5 June 1944) 283, 284. *See also* Allied invasion of Normandy
Dean of Guernsey ix, 86, 148, 194, 261
defence, British Cabinet debate 7
de Garis, Mr J.P. 303
de Gaulle, General Charles 6, 91
de Guillebon, M. 125
demilitarisation 3, 8, 9, 12, 13, 18, 33, 35, 262
Denmark, invasion of 318
deportation 80, 104, 133, 135, 147, 148, 149, 150, 152, 153, 154, 155, 212, 241, 249, 280, 281
  exemptions 148
  suicide 155
de Putron, Jurat Pierre 46
de Sausmarez, Admiral Lord x
Dieppe 144, 210, 211

Dixcart Bay 211
Dixcart Hotel 211
Dobrée, Bonamy xi
Dobrée, Louisa x
Dobrée, Rev Henry Carey xiii
dogs 28, 78, 245, 292, 302
  theft of 302
domestic service 187, 229, 272, 303
Dorey, William 91
Doyle Monument 76, 77
Doyle Road 32
Drake, Jurat A. 20
dropwort-water hemlock 292
du Port, Percy 91
Duquemin, Cecil xx
Durand, Charles xi
Durand, Francis xii, xiv
Durand, Havilland xiv
Durand, Mary (née Hawtrey) ix, xi
Durand, Ralph (author) iii, ix, xx, xxi, xxii, xxiii, xxiv, 2, 163, 259, 264, 313
  death of xx, 2
Durand, Rev Daniel Francis ix
Durand, Rev François Guillaume xi
Durand, Rev Havilland ix, xi
Durand, Violet (née Picton-Warlow) x, xiii, xiv, xv, xvi

E

Edmondes, Rosemary xvi, xix
education 44, 46, 233, 273
Education Council. *See* States of Guernsey, Education Council
electricity 43, 47, 51, 60, 62, 66, 158, 165, 243, 249, 294, 296
  regulation of appliances 158
Elizabeth College 4, 99, 265
employment 12, 20, 43, 45, 87, 138, 147, 187, 191, 228, 229, 269, 274, 275, 276, 279, 308
  by Germans 274, 276
entertainment 39, 75, 87, 108, 189, 235, 272
  German bands 258
epidemic 146, 147, 280
escape attempts 57, 80, 88, 89, 90, 94, 95, 110, 112, 149, 205, 280, 296, 300
espionage 40, 95, 98, 100, 216, 257
Essential Commodities Committee 20,

325

46, 51, 54, 71, 73, 74, 139, 150, 159, 179, 298, 311. *See* States of Guernsey, Essential Commodities Committee
evacuation 7, 9, 10, 12, 13, 16, 18, 19, 20, 21, 22, 23, 25, 28, 29, 32, 38, 43, 44, 46, 87, 95, 98, 112, 118, 119, 120, 152, 190, 201, 224, 235, 236, 263
Ewenny Priory xiii, xiv
exchange rate 40, 41, 232, 233, 237, 238, 289
exports 69
 disruption to 5
 tomatoes 17, 27, 28, 29, 34, 43, 51, 69, 229, 290

F

Falla, Frank xx, xxiii
Falla, Raymond Ogier 20, 68
Ferbrache, Sergeant 80, 103
Fermain Bay 78, 156, 287
Fire Brigade 84, 85
fires, restrictions on 256
Fisher, George 133
fishermen 56, 57, 58, 78, 88, 89, 103, 149, 162, 163, 174, 205, 281, 293, 300
fishing boats 80, 88, 280
 restrictions on the use of 37, 57, 78, 89, 162, 163, 244, 281, 293, 300
Flanders 83
flower-growing 45, 49, 50, 230, 291
food supplies 17, 30, 43, 44, 48, 49, 51, 54, 55, 56, 70, 71, 73, 75, 118, 146, 150, 208, 228, 288, 290, 291, 293, 296, 300, 301, 306, 307
 appeal to Red Cross 297
 apples 47, 54, 168, 298
 beans 45, 56, 69, 167, 176, 181, 182, 183, 230, 245, 290, 306, 307, 308
 beef 290, 298
 beer 72, 171
 bread 24, 27, 49, 64, 65, 153, 160, 167, 180, 185, 186, 235, 239, 293, 295, 296, 298, 305, 311, 312, 313, 315
 broccoli 292, 305, 312, 313, 315
 butter 68, 69, 70, 73, 153, 164, 167, 170, 185, 186, 195, 238, 239, 278, 290, 298, 305, 307, 309, 311, 312, 313

 calves' foot jelly 313
 carrots 171, 181, 182, 268, 298, 315
 cauliflowers 176
 cheese 48, 56, 69, 71, 153, 168, 182, 186, 298, 307, 309, 311
 chickens 47
 chocolate 72
 'chocolate spread' 185, 186
 cocoa 70, 71, 167, 168, 170, 185, 248, 249, 312
 coffee 69, 70, 71, 73, 167, 170, 171, 185, 266, 270, 309
 coffee substitutes 73, 167, 171, 270
 cultivation 159, 244
 dandelion leaves 214
 disruption following D-Day xvii, 288, 295
 fertilisers 55, 68, 290
 fish 162, 163, 281, 293
 flour 31, 49, 50, 51, 64, 65, 68, 160, 167, 170, 176, 182, 183, 185, 195, 203, 290, 296, 310, 311, 312, 313, 315
 fruit 177
 grape-nuts 171, 185, 186
 grapes 53, 54, 69, 171, 177, 252, 253
 ham 153
 imports from France 71, 73, 159, 160, 163, 169, 179, 195, 231, 293
 jam 24, 45, 47, 48, 54, 168, 171, 176, 182, 185, 300, 309, 311, 312, 313
 lettuce 312
 limpets 58, 79, 163, 182, 214
 lobster 301
 longnose 281
 macaroni 48, 167, 170, 179, 183, 185, 305, 311
 mackerel 58, 214, 281
 maize 183, 185, 238
 mangel-wurzel 170, 171, 185, 229
 meat 48, 55, 56, 65, 68, 73, 139, 152, 159, 160, 162, 163, 164, 180, 181, 182, 183, 185, 187, 214, 291, 293, 298, 305, 312
 parsnips 73, 181, 268, 292, 298, 314
 pig-farm and sausage factory 243
 pork 238
 porpoise 163, 170
 potatoes 5, 43, 45, 49, 50, 67, 146, 161, 162, 167, 180, 181, 182, 183, 184, 185, 186, 187, 196, 198, 203, 239,

INDEX

252, 289, 298, 300, 301, 304, 305, 306, 307, 312, 313, 315
prospects of shortages 19
rabbits 65, 66
radishes 186, 312
rationing 48, 59, 65, 69, 71, 72, 160, 161, 162, 163, 167, 168, 169, 182, 183, 293, 305, 308, 311, 312, 315
Red Cross parcels 298, 304, 306, 307, 308, 309, 310, 311, 312, 315
saccharine 168, 169, 172, 184, 290
salt 48, 53, 55, 59, 60, 70, 71, 159, 164, 167, 170, 176, 184, 187, 214, 230, 295, 309, 310, 311
sausages, horsemeat 301
school meals 233
seaweed 170, 214, 268
seeds 68
shortages 17, 118, 158, 162, 164, 182, 183, 185, 186, 187, 291, 293, 296
  medical effects of 182
sorrel 214
spider-crab 185, 293
spinach 182, 312
sugar 47, 305
sugar-beet 170, 294
tea 24, 31, 45, 48, 70, 71, 73, 171, 176, 177, 178, 185, 186, 266, 268, 294, 298, 309, 312, 313
tea, bramble leaf 171, 175, 185, 186, 294, 298
tea substitutes 171, 268
theft 48, 139, 145, 206, 291, 302, 303, 304, 305
tomatoes 5, 17, 27, 28, 29, 31, 34, 43, 51, 52, 53, 54, 56, 69, 168, 177, 229, 244, 245, 290, 314
tomato purée 53, 314
trade with France 68
treats 168
turnips 182, 298, 301
vegetables 288
vitamins 53, 164, 168, 183
footwear 174, 293, 315
Ford, Major-General Minshall, Lieutenant-Governor 15
Forest Church 86
Forest Road 30
Fort Field 83, 283, 286
Fort George 93, 135, 137, 261, 282
fortifications, German 3, 129, 144, 208, 269, 280, 284, 316
Fort Road 130, 283
Fort Saumarez 143
freemasons 154
  Masonic Temple 243
French, Judge 201
Froome, Private 32
Fruit Export Company 30
fuel supplies 43, 50, 61, 62, 75, 139, 164, 166, 184, 186, 187, 208, 249, 268, 269, 294, 295, 306, 309, 310, 313, 314
  paraffin 47, 62, 63, 68, 176
  peat 61, 165
  petrol 50
  seaweed 63
  shortages 158
  wood 61, 68, 165, 166, 184, 294
Fuzzey, Mrs Owen 270

G

Gartell, Mr 213
gas 4, 10, 30, 33, 40, 43, 47, 51, 59, 62, 158, 165, 172, 176, 186, 232, 234, 249, 250, 251, 252, 255, 267, 294, 296, 298, 310, 319. *See also* fuel supplies
  restrictions to use of 158
Gas Company 62, 170, 295
Gaumont Theatre 152
Gazette Officielle 27, 123
German authorities 44, 48, 51, 56, 63, 64, 66, 68, 73, 75, 76, 77, 78, 79, 81, 82, 85, 86, 88, 89, 90, 93, 94, 98, 99, 100, 101, 102, 103, 106, 108, 110, 111, 112, 113, 114, 115, 116, 120, 121, 122, 123, 125, 126, 128, 129, 134, 138, 139, 140, 141, 143, 145, 147, 148, 149, 162, 165, 172, 173, 178, 179, 184, 198, 199, 200, 203, 204, 207, 213, 215, 226, 229, 230, 231, 236, 238, 239, 243, 246, 248, 250, 251, 252, 253, 254, 255, 256, 261, 262, 269, 272, 273, 274, 275, 278, 279, 285, 288, 289, 290, 291, 294, 298, 305, 306, 307, 310, 311, 314, 315
  interference with Royal Court 198
German Commandant 38, 39, 42, 72, 80, 83, 85, 87, 92, 104, 108, 113,

327

126, 192, 219, 243, 261, 281, 295, 296, 302
announcements 38
attendance at States meetings 198
German forces
 arrival 35, 36
 attack on White Rock 29, 30, 31, 33, 34, 213, 241, 266
 behaviour 241, 242, 245, 246, 248, 250, 251, 252, 253, 255, 256, 257, 258, 259, 260, 262, 263, 264, 265, 318, 321
 casualties 78, 85, 94, 131, 132, 136, 137, 143, 145, 207, 209, 222, 282, 283, 286, 292, 302, 303, 318
 commando raid on Granville 301
 deserters 303
 disaffection amongst 263, 264, 265, 291, 303
 fraternisation with 271, 272, 273, 276, 277
 morale 308
 suicides 264
 theft of food 292, 302, 303, 304, 305, 307, 315
 theft of pets 302
 theft of property 195, 196, 206, 236, 243, 251, 252, 253, 289, 291
 theft of Red Cross parcels 304
German orders 288
 37, 39, 44, 75, 80, 89, 103, 113, 115, 121, 189, 199
 surrender of firearms 9, 37, 274
German Press Officer 149, 209, 213, 216, 217, 220, 221, 224, 225, 226, 227, 257, 260, 267, 284, 285
German surrender 287, 308, 316
Germany 14, 18, 41, 51, 69, 70, 91, 124, 126, 133, 147, 148, 172, 181, 195, 199, 208, 212, 215, 218, 221, 222, 223, 224, 225, 226, 228, 229, 236, 237, 238, 242, 243, 244, 249, 256, 257, 262, 265, 272, 279, 280, 281, 283, 285, 287, 290, 303, 308, 316, 318, 319, 320, 321, 322
Gibson, Dr 105
Giffard, Godfrey 281
Gillingham, Joe xx
Glasshouse Utilisation Board. *See* States of Guernsey, Glasshouse Utilisation Board

Goebbels, Dr 225
Gould, Mr E.C. 56
Goupillot, Private 83
Grandes Rocques 79, 99, 254
Grand Havre 79
Grand Mufti of Jerusalem 225
Grange 29, 34, 252, 280
Grange Club 252
Grange Lodge Hotel 92
Granville 68, 123, 195, 288, 301
Great Russell 132
greenhouses 43, 45, 51, 52, 56, 66, 131, 132, 145, 166, 196, 197, 235, 244, 245, 281, 290, 294, 305
Greffe 147, 148, 198, 199, 277
Guernsey Brewery Company 171, 172
Guernsey Defence Volunteers 9
Guernsey Evening Press (newspaper) 9, 16, 84, 134, 136, 137, 150, 171, 204, 222, 243, 258, 267, 268, 285, 297, 301
Guernsey Jam Company 53, 54
Guernsey Press Company 17
Guernsey Railway Company 60, 234
Guernsey Society iii, iv, ix, xxi, xxii, xxiii, xxiv, 2, 336
Guernsey Underground News Service (GUNS) xix, xx, 1, 126, 144, 264
Guillemette, Mr L.A. 7, 25
Gunter, John 320

H

Hague Convention 9, 100, 142, 296
Hamburg 321
harbour 5, 6, 8, 22, 23, 24, 29, 30, 33, 38, 50, 57, 78, 83, 89, 91, 120, 132, 135, 136, 137, 154, 155, 166, 219, 269, 284, 285, 286, 301. *See also* White Rock
 Cambridge berth 30
 defences 5
 New Jetty 303
 Victoria Pier 16
Harbourmaster 38, 91
Harwood, Mr 23
Hauteville 146, 302
Havelet 283
Hawtrey, Montague x
Hawtrey, Rev John x
Heggs, Mrs Winifred 172

INDEX

Herd Book Council 55
Herm 37, 66, 132, 156, 201, 208, 272
Hess, Rudolf 221
Hickey, Canon 86
High Street 14, 140, 249, 270, 285
Hitler, Adolf 102, 194, 218, 221, 222, 223, 225, 253, 260, 261, 262, 264, 265, 276, 303, 316, 320, 321
  assassination attempt 262
  death of 316
Hitler Youth Movement 253, 254
H.M. Comptroller 82, 198
H.M. Greffier 199, 200
H.M. Procureur 15, 16, 17, 18, 19, 29, 36, 40, 87, 99, 118, 139, 172, 178, 191, 306
H.M.S. Charybdis 261
H.M. Sheriff 198
Hobbs, Frederick 31
Hockey, Mr Frederick 91
Holland
  invasion of 5
Home Office 7, 19
Home Secretary 17
honey 56, 182
Hore-Belisha, Mr 217
horses 47, 64, 68, 163, 197, 234
Hospital, Castel 4
Hospital, Children's 4
Hospital, Emergency 48, 105, 306
hospital supplies 235
Hospital, Town 28
Hospital, Victoria 21, 85, 105, 132
housing 44, 46, 75, 195
  German billets 195, 235, 246, 248, 249, 250, 251, 260, 264
Hubert, Mr 280
Hubert, Mr W.G. 68

I

Icart 79
income tax. *See also* States of Guernsey, Income Tax Authority
Income Tax 46, 47, 109, 235, 289
informers 278, 279
International Law 40, 102, 120, 198, 242, 243, 274
invalids 21, 28, 32, 69, 158, 161, 168, 187, 201, 212, 229, 250, 310, 315
Iran 225

Iraq 225
Isle of Sark (ship) 30
Italy 14, 58, 126, 221, 225
  entry to war 221

J

Jackson, Rev Hartley 133, 148
Le Jaonnet 97
Jerbourg 78, 130, 143, 156
Jerbourg Barracks 78
Jersey 31, 37, 38, 40, 41, 49, 94, 111, 113, 148, 153, 156, 179, 209, 257, 258, 295, 296, 301, 310, 311
Jerusalem 225
Jethou 66, 132
Jews 75, 133, 190, 198, 199, 200, 226, 243, 259
  measures against 198, 199, 200, 243
Johns, Mr R.H. 20, 45, 61
joke, practical 111
Jones, Mr 306
jurats 17, 18, 19, 20, 22, 42, 46, 59, 61, 62, 108, 117, 198, 200
justice 194, 195, 204
  German interference 81, 82

K

King George 39, 87, 91, 93, 118, 198
kitchens, communal 167, 305
Knights in Ambush 287

L

labourers, foreign 3, 48, 135, 136, 137, 144, 146, 147, 201, 202, 208, 237, 250, 255, 269, 300. *See also* Organisation Todt
  treatment of 145
Ladies' College 150, 151
Lainé, Jurat Sir Abraham 20
L'Ancresse 76, 129, 130, 263
land-mines 78, 79
  casualties from 79
land utilisation 27, 55, 79
laundries, public 64, 71, 187
leaflet drops 91, 92, 93, 94, 131, 287
Leale, Jurat the Rev John 18, 19, 20, 22, 42, 59, 61, 62, 108, 117, 118, 119, 120, 231, 275, 295, 297

329

anonymous lampoon of 119
Legg, Ernest xx
legislation 39
Le Havre 6, 8, 79, 88, 94
Le Marchant Street 243
Le Masurier, Mrs Ada 79, 80, 110, 142, 242
Le Page, Messrs 300
Le Page, Mr 280
Le Page, Mrs 280
Le Patourel, Major 40
L'Eree 133
Le Riche Ltd 81
liberation, plans for 316
Lieutenant Governor 15, 28, 39, 81, 198, 271
lifeboat 31, 34, 201, 205, 257, 269, 317
lighting, ban on use of 158
Lihou island 59
Little Russell 132, 213, 282, 284
livestock 47, 55, 201, 202, 205
Long Store 30
Lovell & Co 174
Luftwaffe 129
Lukis House 147
Luxembourg, invasion of 5

M

Maas, Dr 271, 272, 274
Machon, Charles xx
Mahy, William 91
mail boat 29, 30, 33
mailboat 33
malnutrition xx, 189, 208, 302
Mareth Line 225
Margot, Private 32, 33
Mariette, Jessie 98, 100
markets, fish 58, 162
Marquand, Mr H.E. 46, 99
Marquand, Mrs M.E. 23, 24
Martel, 2nd Lieut Philip 79, 80, 103, 242, 303, 306
Martel, Mr 306
Martel, Mr B.A. 303
McLeod, 2nd Lieut 83
Medical Officer of Health. *See* States of Guernsey, Medical Officer of Health

medical supplies 68, 168, 174, 296, 297, 310, 311
  herbal remedies 314
men of military age 9, 12, 13, 15, 16, 17, 18, 88, 280
MI5 xv, xix
Michaelhouse School, Kwa-Zulu Natal xiii
Michael, Mrs Dorothy 79, 80, 110, 142, 242
Mignot Plateau 297
milk supplies 19, 24, 29, 44, 52, 55, 68, 69, 70, 92, 144, 161, 168, 170, 171, 185, 194, 197, 202, 203, 233, 239, 250, 278, 290, 291, 292, 298, 305, 306, 307, 309, 311, 312
Mill Street 285
Model Yacht Pond 60, 164
money 69, 230, 231, 232, 236, 237. *See also* exchange rate
morale, islanders 266, 267, 268, 270
  hysteria 14, 15
Moscow 223, 283
Mosley, Sir Oswald 103
Motor House 111, 112, 113
motor vehicles 46, 63, 103, 234, 248
  fuel restrictions 38
  tyres 73
Mouat, Miss Kay 28
Mulholland, 2nd Lieut Desmond 79, 80, 103, 242
Müller, Karl 318
Mussolini, Benito 221

N

Nazi (Nationalist Socialist) Party 35, 41, 139, 198, 199, 207, 213, 216, 218, 221, 226, 228, 243, 264, 265, 302, 316, 319, 321
news, circulation after radios confiscated 106, 107, 143, 144, 269, 279. *See also* Guernsey Underground News Services (GUNS)
newspapers 27, 29, 38, 44, 48, 58, 59, 61, 62, 66, 76, 78, 82, 84, 85, 91, 92, 94, 95, 97, 105, 108, 112, 113, 115, 116, 121, 123, 124, 125, 126, 128, 131, 133, 135, 137, 138, 141, 142, 154, 173, 179, 182, 193, 194, 199, 203, 204, 206, 212, 213, 214,

INDEX

216, 217, 218, 224, 226, 227, 228, 238, 243, 244, 253, 267, 273, 284, 285, 287, 288, 306
German control of xix, 133, 135, 136, 137, 138, 193, 203, 213, 214, 215, 216, 217, 218, 221, 222, 223, 224, 225, 226, 227, 262, 283, 286, 288, 301
New Year's Eve 133
Nicolle, 2nd Lieut Hubert 97, 99, 100, 101, 142, 216
Nicolle, Elsie 99, 100, 142
Nicolle, Emile 98, 100, 102, 142
Nicolle, Frank 98, 100, 102, 142
Nicolle, Hilda 99, 100, 142
Nicolle, Private R. 32
Normandy 7, 195, 207, 283, 284, 287, 288, 290, 295
Norway, occupation of 129, 318
Noyon, Captain 296

O

oil, local fish liver 164
Old Government House Hotel 260
Oliver, Mr 85
Organisation Todt 144, 145, 147, 156, 197, 255, 264, 265, 268. *See also* labourers, foreign
ormers 57, 58
Ozanne Hall Mission 281

P

La Palice 155
Paris 126, 193, 295
Parker, Captain 93, 98
Parker, Lieutenant-Colonel 93
La Passée 263
Petit Bot 255
Petit Port 77, 80, 98, 99
Pezeries 79
Picton-Turbervill, Beatrice xiv
Picton-Turbervill, Charles xvi
Picton-Turbervill, Colonel John xiii
Picton-Turberville, Colonel John xvi
Picton-Turbervill, Edith xiii
Picton-Warlow, Arthur xiv
Picton-Warlow, Colonel John. *See* Picton-Turbervill, Colonel John
Picton-Warlow, Ivor xiv

Picton-Warlow, Rev Frank xiv
Picton-Warlow, Wilfrid xiv
Piette Saw Mills 164
pigs 52, 55, 159, 164, 196, 202, 239, 243, 252, 260
Pittard, Mrs 211, 212
Pleinmont 94, 131, 156
Poland 86, 126, 225, 256, 318
    invasion of 225, 256, 318
Police Court 81, 139, 245, 290
Police force 31, 32, 36, 37, 81, 82, 111, 116, 121, 123, 127, 139, 140, 245, 254, 276, 290, 295
    trial and imprisonment of 135, 138, 139, 140, 141, 216
Pollet 32, 263
Portinfer 104
postage stamps 110
Post Office 14, 37, 110, 202, 284
poultry 27, 28, 48, 52, 55, 65, 66, 70
press freedom. *See* newspapers, German control of
Press Office 17, 28
Priaulx Library ix, x, xvi, xxiii, xxiv, 228, 259, 288
price controls 180
Price Determination Committee. *See* States of Guernsey, Price Determination Committee
Price Restriction Ordinance 178
prison 228
    congestion 238
    postonement of sentences 228
prisoners 83, 95, 96, 105, 111, 112, 113, 121, 155, 194, 242, 246, 301
    escaped 302
    sent to France 79, 80, 93, 97, 99, 101, 125, 140, 142, 194, 281
Procureur of the Poor 172
propaganda xix, 39, 92, 93, 94, 105, 106, 128, 138, 208, 209, 210, 214, 215, 216, 220, 221, 223, 224, 225, 226, 227, 228, 238, 253, 268, 319. *See also* newspapers, German control of
Pumping station, St Martin's 33

R

radios. *See* wireless sets
Raffles, Deputy Stamford 19, 20, 22,

331

28, 45
railway 269
rape trial 241
Red Cross 24, 34, 110, 155, 168, 174, 190, 191, 193, 205, 258, 295, 297, 299, 304, 306, 307, 308, 309, 310, 311, 312, 313, 314, 315
    food parcels 298, 304, 306, 307, 308, 309, 310, 311, 312, 315
    contents 309, 310, 311, 312
    messages 190, 191, 192, 193
    steamship Vega 297, 309, 310, 311, 312, 313, 314, 315
refugees
    French 6
Regal Theatre 108, 154, 274
Rennes 155
resistance. *See also* 'V' for victory campaign; *See also* Guernsey Underground News Service (GUNS); *See also* sabotage, acts of
    futility of 19, 119
Robert, Mr 23
Robilliard, Mr P. 124
Robinson, Mr Heath 234
Rohais 280
Rommel, Erwin 225
Roosevelt 222, 223, 225, 226
Rostov, Battle of 223
Royal Air Force (RAF) 38, 41, 91, 104, 124, 130, 131, 133, 136, 137, 138, 203, 204, 255, 256, 262, 266, 267
Royal Court 7, 9, 10, 15, 16, 39, 57, 81, 115, 140, 198, 199, 200, 201, 228, 243, 254
    German interference with 198
Royal Guernsey Light Infantry xv
Royal Guernsey Militia 3, 4, 9
Royal Hotel 36, 37, 38, 77, 131, 316
Royal National Lifeboat Institution (RNLI) 34
Ruettes Brayes 304
rumours 19, 76, 77, 194, 267, 282, 311
Russia 14, 223, 225, 263
    entry to war 223

S

sabotage, acts of 95, 113, 114, 115, 116, 117, 120, 121, 122, 127, 142, 155, 247, 248, 269, 314

safety-deposit boxes, raiding of 280
Sark 6, 30, 39, 41, 201, 203, 208, 209, 210, 211, 212, 222, 256, 281, 311
    Commando raid 209, 210, 211, 212, 222, 281
    murder of German officer 209
Save-the-Children Fund 270
Savings Bank 14
schoolchildren, evacuation of 9, 10, 11
schools 10, 11, 46, 129, 174, 233, 234, 319
seaweed
    eating of 170, 214, 268
    fertiliser 281
    fuel 63
    gathering of 79, 281, 290
Secours National 270, 313
Sherbrooke, Mrs 111
Sherwill, Ambrose xxi, 15, 17, 19, 29, 43, 87, 88, 90, 94, 95, 96, 98, 99, 100, 101, 102
    radio broadcast 87
shops 32, 61, 79, 81, 82, 124, 151, 169, 173, 174, 182, 205, 229, 234, 256, 266, 270, 272
Sisters of the Sacred Heart 188
slaughter house 30, 60, 187
slaughter of livestock 30, 55, 60, 159, 187, 253, 319
slave labour 17
Smith Street 28, 29
soap 71, 152, 170, 177, 187, 251, 268, 290, 297, 309, 310, 314
La Société Guernesiaise xvi
Special Aid Society 27, 270
Spitfire 128, 156
sport
    cricket 75, 83, 99, 265
    football 6, 75, 83, 189, 273, 274, 283
    restrictions on 4
    swimming gala 274
Stalin, Joseph 192, 225, 226, 268
St Andrew's 131, 190
St Anne, Alderney 207
Start Point 91, 280
States of Guernsey xx, 8, 18, 19, 64, 231
    Accountant 233
    Agricultural Officer 50, 65, 68
    Chemical Department 164
    Committee for Agriculture and Fisheries 49

INDEX

Committee for the Preservation of Tomatoes 52, 53
Controller of Clothing and Footwear 150, 151, 173, 293
(Emergency) Controlling Committee 18, 20, 27, 28, 43, 44, 49, 50, 51, 54, 55, 56, 59, 62, 65, 66, 67, 68, 69, 70, 71, 72, 84, 87, 89, 94, 99, 102, 104, 108, 112, 115, 116, 117, 119, 122, 127, 166, 167, 169, 175, 177, 179, 191, 215, 229, 230, 231, 232, 233, 234, 235, 236, 238, 239, 245, 267, 275, 278, 288, 289, 290, 291, 293, 294, 295, 296, 302, 305, 306, 307, 308, 310
   criticism of 179
   protests 239, 240
Controlling Committee xvii, xxi
Custodian of Business and Industry 46
Custodian of Dwellings 46, 150
Dairy 69, 70, 161, 186
Economic Officer 62
Education Council 10, 45, 174, 233
Essential Commodities Committee 46, 51, 54, 71, 73, 74, 139, 159, 179, 298, 311
Farm Produce Board 55, 159
Finance Committee 231
finances 43, 45, 46, 47, 235, 236, 237, 238
Food Control Committee 69
Fuel Controller 61, 294, 306
Glasshouse Utilisation Board 55, 171, 305, 308
Income Tax Authority 46
Information Officer 22, 28, 44, 73, 119
Interpreter 82
Maintenance Engineer 269
Medical Officer of Health 53, 54, 86, 147, 148, 164, 168, 170, 171, 182, 234, 289, 314, 315
Potato Controller 305
pre-war defences 3, 4
Price Determination Committee 176, 177, 178, 232
Shoemaking Department 150
States meetings 198, 296
States Supervisor xx, 5, 46, 99, 289
Telephone Department 46
Treasury 42, 45, 46, 56, 187, 236 238
Water Board 30, 46, 63, 159, 229, 250, 314
St James Street 29
St John's Ambulance Brigade 14, 20, 21, 23, 24, 25, 31, 104, 201, 205
St Julian's Avenue 111, 280
St Malo 153, 155, 195, 288
St Martin's 127
St Martin's Point 76, 132, 290
St Nazaire 155
Stock's Hotel 211
Stonelake, the chemist 174
St Paul's Methodist Church 139
St Pierre-du-Bois 131, 302
St Pierre-du-Bois church 86
streets, re-naming of 280
Stroobant, Mr F. 152, 281
Stroobant's café 281
St Sampson's 31, 52, 78, 165
St Sampson's Harbour 31
St Stephen's church 133
submarine 76, 97, 98, 103, 284, 285
Symes, 2nd Lieut James 97, 99, 100, 101
Symes, James, 2nd Lieut 216
Symes, Louis 98, 100
Symes, Rachel 98, 100
Symons, Dr A.N. 20, 28, 54, 170, 234, 289, 295, 314

T

taxation 42, 46, 47, 109, 235, 289
Taylor, Private 32
teachers 10, 11, 12, 16, 45, 190, 233
Telephone Department. *See* States of Guernsey, Telephone Department
Telephone Exchange 5, 284
Telephone office 37
theft
   48, 75, 196, 197, 252, 253, 289, 292, 302, 304, 305
The Star (newspaper) 8, 35, 84, 133, 135, 136, 150, 170, 171, 178, 180, 192, 204, 209, 210, 217, 270, 281, 283, 284, 285, 302, 303
Thorneycroft's Mounted Infantry xiii
time, adoption of continental 39, 40, 181
tobacco. *See also* cigarettes
   growing 229, 235, 291
   rationing 175
   substitutes 175, 268, 310

333

toileteries, shortages 152. *See also* soap
tomato-growing 19, 27, 28, 34, 43, 44, 45, 51, 52, 53, 91, 229, 244, 290
tomato purée 53, 314
Toms, Miss Mary 266
Torteval 63, 130, 192
Town Church 285
Treasury. *See* States of Guernsey, Treasury
trees 61, 68, 84, 92, 165, 184, 261, 294, 306
  restrictions on felling 165, 184, 294, 306
Trinity Square 263
Tucker, George 135
Tunisia 225
typhus epidemic 147

U

unemployment 20, 43, 87, 228
United States of America (USA) 41, 91, 192, 220, 222, 223, 225, 261
  entry to war 222
'Useless Eustace' 256

V

Le Val des Terres 282
La Vallette 78
Van der Sluys, Mrs 172
La Vassallerie 30
Le Vauquiedor 302
Vazon 30, 61, 79, 92, 131, 165
Veal, Mr 23
Vega (Red Cross ship) 297, 298, 309, 310, 311, 312, 313, 314, 315
'V' for Victory campaign 123, 124, 125, 126, 128, 129, 242, 281
Village de Putron 78
La Villiaze 37, 85
vitamin deficiency 183
Volga, German retreat from 224
La Vrangue 165

W

War Cabinet 211, 216
war damage claims 235
Water Board. *See* States of Guernsey, Water Board

water supplies 51, 62, 66, 159, 229, 267, 314
Way, Joe 32
Weighbridge, St Julian's 13, 22, 30, 32, 33
Weymouth 22, 23, 24
White Rock 5, 8, 10, 13, 16, 20, 21, 23, 29, 30, 31, 32, 33, 94, 119, 132, 152, 241, 263, 269. *See also* harbour
  German attack 29, 30, 31, 33, 34, 213, 241, 266
Williams, Major-General 5
wireless sets 1, 40, 62, 86, 98, 99, 101, 102, 105, 106, 107, 108, 123, 127, 135, 140, 142, 143, 189, 218, 242, 253, 268, 278, 279, 283, 287, 301, 311
  confiscation of xix, 135, 142, 143
  hiding places 108
women, conscription for food production 229

Y

Yugoslavia 319

About the Guernsey Society

The Guernsey Society was founded in 1943 by three Guernseymen based in London in order to represent the interests of islanders to the British Government. It quickly grew to over four hundred members within six months.

Since the Liberation in 1945, the Society has pursued more sociable objectives.

Our aims are to promote, maintain and stimulate interest in all matters concerning the Bailiwick of Guernsey; its past, present and future and keeping alive the 'Spirit of Guernsey' both in the island and overseas.

Our main actitivities

We publish a magazine, *The Review*, three times a year.

We organise meetings in London with talks on aspects of Guernsey's past, present and future.

We also organise social gatherings, including the annual Boules Muratti against the Jersey Society in London.

Occasional trips further afield, such as our WW1 Battlefield Tours in France & Belgium.

If you are interested in learning more about membership, please visit our website at:
www.guernsey-society.org.uk